D1189825

TRAVELLING LADIES

TRAVELLING LADIES

by

ALEXANDRA ALLEN

Jupiter: London

First published in Great Britain in 1980 by
JUPITER BOOKS (LONDON) LIMITED
167 Hermitage Road, London N4 1L

ISBN: 0 906379 16 4

Typography by Elizabeth Allen.
Composed in 11-point Monotype Garamond, Series 156,
by Ronset Limited, Darwen, Lancashire, and
printed and bound in Great Britain.

For
my granddaughter
Catherine Merrion Allen
with much love

Acknowledgements

DAISY BATES

I should like to acknowledge the help which Elizabeth Salter's book; *Daisy Bates: 'The Great White Queen of the Never Never'* has afforded me. I am particularly indebted to her, for the major collection of Daisy Bates's papers is divided between the National Library of Australia (Canberra); the J. S. Battye Library of West Australian History (Perth); the Barr Smith Library (Adelaide); the Mitchell Library (Sydney) and other university and private libraries in Australia. I should also like to thank the Librarian of the Spiritualist Association of Great Britain, London.

ISABELLA BIRD BISHOP

Anna Stoddart's biography supplied much material, although Isabella's friendship with James Nugent was barely touched upon. Marshall Sprague's *A Gallery of Dudes* supplied much relevant data. I would like to thank Eleanor M. Gehres, Head of the Western History Department of the Denver Public Library for further material on James Nugent. Two books which were of vital use were David Macdonald's *Twenty Years in Tibet* and Pat Barr's *Deer Cry Pavilion*.

MILDRED CABLE AND EVANGELINE AND FRANCESCA FRENCH

My sincere thanks are due to Miss Edyth Banks, of the Overseas Missionary Fellowship (Editor), formerly China Inland Mission, for her help in providing dates and Miss Edith John Lindgren for her 'In Memoriam' in the *Journal of the Central Asian Society*.

ALEXANDRA DAVID-NEEL

I wish to thank the Theosophical Society, London, and the Theosophical Society, Adyar, Madras, India for their interest and co-operation. I would also like to express my thanks to the India Office Library for assistance with

Madame David-Neel's stay in India. I acknowledge a debt to Luree Miller for her book *On Top of the World*.

JANE DIGBY EL MESRAB

To Miss June McLoughlin, great-granddaughter of Kenelm Digby, I extend my sincerest thanks and appreciation for the loan of material. I should also like to thank Margaret Fox Schmidt for the help I received from her book *Passion's Child*.

KATE MARSDEN

For the early years of Kate Marsden and her family, I would like to acknowledge the great help I received from the Chief Librarian and Cultural Officer of the London Borough of Enfield and to Mr. Dalling. Also to Mr. Brian Watkin for his excellent article on the Prince of Wales Hospital.

MARIANNE NORTH

My thanks are due to the Curator of the Hastings Museum and Art Gallery for great interest and help, which was so willingly given. I am also indebted to Pauline Allen, of Hastings, for her researches into the early years of Marianne North at Hastings Lodge.

MAY FRENCH SHELDON

To Madame Jeanne Steegmans, of Brussels, I extend my sincere thanks for her very great help, and for the promptness with which she attended to our correspondence. I also wish to acknowledge the assistance of Monsieur Émile Vandewoude, Archiviste du Palais Royal.

That I succeeded in procuring adequate material is due in no small measure to the Library of the Royal Geographical Society and I wish to thank the Librarian and staff; the staff of the Map Room; and the Archivist of the Society. I am greatly indebted to the Royal Botanic Gardens, Kew, for the privilege of researching archive material. I also wish to thank Mrs Dorothy Middleton, for the loan of books.

Preface

THE AGE OF VICTORIA was the age of the lady travellers, those well brought-up, fastidious, fearless, and happy 'loners', who trod their own paths in the wilder places of the globe and left their comfortable homes in a frenzy of terrestial navigation. There were quite a few who achieved world-wide renown; Lady Hester Stanhope, Gertrude Bell, and Mary Kingsley are perhaps the better-known, but there were many other ladies who were just as indefatigable and courageous as their sister-travellers. Aimée Dubucq de Rivery; Isabelle Eberhardt; Lady Paget Walburga; Ellen Cornish; Mary Moffat; Olive Pink of Australia; Aurélie Piccard of Algeria (who, like Jane Digby el Mesrab, imported a grand piano from Europe for the use of her Arab prince); Mrs Littledale, who attempted with her husband to reach Lhasa in 1895; Alicia Bewicke Little, who claimed to be the first white woman to visit Tatsienlu; and Dr Susie Rijnhart, who recounted her adventures in a remarkable book; *With the Tibetans in Tent and Temple*, published in 1901. The eight ladies about whom I have written were British, with the exception of Daisy Bates, who was Irish; Alexandra David-Neel, who was French; and May French Sheldon, who was American. Only one was not strictly a Victorian; Jane Digby was a child of the Regency and died twenty years before Victoria came to the throne, but I have included her as her unusual way of life and her determination to pursue her Byronic course, defying all the rules which cage the human spirit, places her in the same category as those other women who travelled far and suffered much.

A middle-class background seems to have been the common denominator of the travelling ladies. With two or three exceptions, their families had both money and prestige; relatives and near-relatives, friends and acquaintances, British and foreign government officials, opened their doors to them and letters of introduction afforded them comfortable passages *en route*. In the less rough parts of the globe, land and sea conveyances were arranged without too much trouble, and when a short or long stay was needed, there were always cottages, villas, and even luxurious retreats, to be rented for a nominal sum. Isabella Bird Bishop recalled her stay at Soglio 'where we lived in an old palace of the De Salis, built in 1538, and with furniture of the sixteenth century'. Servants were in plentiful supply and could be paid off when no longer required; the thrusting social questions of the day impinged very little on the consciences of the globe-trotters and while they were extremely appreciative of the care taken of them by the lower classes, their welfare was considered to be quite safe in the hands of those elected to Parliament. Money paved the way and absent husbands sent what cash they could; May French Sheldon was a wealthy woman in her own right. The servers, such as Kate Marsden and Mildred Cable and the French sisters, trusted in God and laid down their heads in whatever humble resting place came their way. Their upbringing taught them to endure physical hardship to a degree which would seem to us almost impossible and the enduring flame of belief in their own destiny was kept alight by a constant subjugation of their own, often frail and sickly, bodies.

Nietzsche wrote;
Woman has every reason to be modest. It will be unfortunate if she unlearns her perspicacity, her arts and graces, her playfulness and aptitude for agreeable passions and beautifying life. What she abhors is – truth. Her great art is falsehood, her chief concern is appearance. A profound man can only consider woman as property, as a being predestined to domesticity . . . They are very delicate, fragile, wild, strange, sweet, ravishing, but things which have to be caged, lest they fly away.

Quite a few ladies 'flew away' and it is surprising to learn just what the Victorian lady traveller took with her on her long journeys. The better-off had no compunction about loading up with contraptions to make life in the rough as comfortable as possible; there were folding-beds, folding chairs, tin baths, expanding dining tables, and tins of goodies from Fortnum and Mason's. May French Sheldon bumped along her exquisite palanquin and an 'extensive medical kit' and Madame Alexandra David-Neel, that most ascetic of voyagers, speaks of 'luggage-laden mules' on their way to the Chinese-Tibetan border, although much of the luggage was in the form of presents for lamas *en route*. May French Sheldon remained fashion-conscious in the African bush and carted along her precious rhinestone-studded ball gown and blonde wig as an added attraction whilst visiting impressionable and unstable chiefs. Lillias Campbell Davidson published an admirable book in 1889, *Hints to Lady Travellers at Home and Abroad*, in which she stressed those points of travel for ladies which should be noted, such as etiquette at table d'hôte, tipping of porters, use of hot-water bags, ladies' maids, and Scotch tours. She is a little patronizing, though, when it comes to the reading of a railway time-table; 'there are actually few women in my personal experience who can look out a route in "Bradshaw" without a single error'.

Some of the lady travellers wrote books about their peregrinations around the globe (a good deal of which was still coloured red) and many of them penned long and informative letters to their families back home patiently awaiting the next screed. A few achieved fame by their well-presented lectures to professional bodies, lectures which were not always reported in the best spirit. Lady travellers were strange animals, and it took some time before they were officially recognized as reputable and trustworthy travellers. A witty, interesting talk, accompanied by lantern slides, was one thing, but a lecture digressing into the field of anthropology was another matter; it was considered 'indelicate' for a woman to expound upon the social and sexual behaviour of native tribes and Daisy Bates had her own private war with Radcliffe-Brown, expressing views which were later upheld.

Professional bodies were slow to admit women. The Royal Statistical Society began admitting women in 1858, when Florence Nightingale was elected as a member. The Royal Geographical Society suggested an honorary membership for Alexine Tinne in 1860, but this proved abortive. Isabella Bird Bishop lectured to the Royal Scottish Geographical Society, of which she was a member, and in 1892 the Council of the Royal Geographical Society elected twenty-two 'well-qualified ladies', although there was dissension among the members. Punch put it succinctly, if crudely;

> And still the salts are fuming, and still the ladies sit,
> Though their presence makes these tars, who women trounce, ill.
> For no woman, bless her petticoats, will ever budge a bit,
> Having once been made a Fellow by the Council.

No more ladies were admitted. 'I should be very sorry to see this ancient Society governed by ladies', said a member, and Kate Marsden, who had been one of the twenty-two 'well-qualified ladies' was refused a ticket to the Anniversary Dinner as she would be the only lady among 200 men, 'nearly all of them smoking'. George Nathaniel Curzon, fresh from his Persian travels, was bitterly opposed to the admittance of women (he later conceded victory to them as the subscriptions rolled in); 'We contest *in toto* the general capability of women to contribute scientific geographical knowledge', and at a Special General Meeting threw out the proposal to admit women by only fourteen votes. The ladies, however, had a champion in Douglas Freshfield, but it was not until 1913 that women were finally admitted. The band of lady travellers was not concerned with the general welfare of the working-classes in Britain in the context of their political evolution, but they strode shoulder to shoulder with Millicent Garrett Fawcett, Elizabeth Garrett Anderson, and Octavia Hill. It was a long haul.

Contents

Bibliography

CHAPTER ONE: MAY FRENCH SHELDON

CHAUTAUGUAN. *White Queen in Africa.* 10 vols. Meadville, Pa. 1892/96.

CRITIC. Nos. 22 (NS 19), 193. 1893.

HORE, ANNIE. *To Lake Tanganyika in a Bath-Chair.* 1886.

LADY'S GAZETTE. January, 1902.

NATION. New York, 12 January, 1893.

NEW, CHARLES. *Life, Wanderings and Labours in Eastern Africa.* London, 1873.

SHELDON, MAY FRENCH. *Herbert Severance.* London, 1889. *Sultan to Sultan.* London, 1892.

SHELDON, MAY FRENCH. (Trans. by) *Salammbo.* 1887.

SPECTATOR. 29 August, 1891.

TEMPLE MAGAZINE. September, 1901. (Article by Alice Royle.)

THOMSON, JOSEPH. *Through Masai Land.* 3rd ed. London, 1885.

WOMANHOOD. November, 1901. (Article by Alice Royle.)

CHAPTER TWO: KATE MARSDEN

CZAPLICKA, M. A. *Aboriginal Siberia: a Study in Social Anthropology.* London, 1914.

DAILY CHRONICLE. 25 November, 1892.

DE WINDT, HARRY. *Siberia as it is.* London, 1892.

JOHNSON, HENRY. *The Life of Kate Marsden.* 2nd ed. 1895.

MARSDEN, KATE. *On Sledge and Horseback to Outcast Siberian Lepers.* London, c. 1892.

My Mission to Siberia: a Vindication. London, 1921.

NINETEENTH CENTURY. December, 1889.

TIMES, THE. 19 October, 1892.

WATKIN, BRIAN. *The Prince of Wales's Hospital – a Centenary History.* London, 1967.

ABOUT, EDMOND. *King of the Mountains.* New York, 1902.

ANTIQUARY, THE. No. 36, n.s. (Unpublished letters of Sir Everard Digby.)

APPONYI, COUNT. *Vingt-cinq Ans à Paris.* London, 1935.

BALZAC, HONORÉ DE. *The Lily of the Valley.* (Trans. by Clara Bell and James Waring.) Philadelphia, 1878.

BLANCH, LESLEY. *The Wilder Shores of Love.* London, 1954.

BLIGH, E. W. *Sir Kenelm Digby and his Venetia.* London, 1932.

BLUNT, LADY ANNE. *Pilgrimage to Nejd: the Cradle of the Arab Race.* London, 1881.

BOSANQUET, ELLEN. *The Tale of Athens.* London, 1932.

BURTON, ELIZABETH. *The Georgians at Home.* London, 1967.

BURTON, ISABEL. *The Inner Life of Syria, Palestine and the Holy Land.* 2 vols. London, 1876.

Life of Captain Sir Richard F. Burton. 2 vols. London, 1893.

CHANNON, HENRY. *The Ludwigs of Bavaria.* London, 1952.

CHRISTIAN EXAMINER. No. 70. Massacre of 1860. (Damascus.)

CREEVEY, THOMAS. *The Creevey Papers.* (Ed. John Gore.) London, 1934.

DIGBY, LETTICE. *My Ancestors.* (Pub. by the author.) 1928.

DOUGHTY, CHARLES M. *My Travels in Arabia Deserta.* London, 1921.

DURRELL, LAWRENCE. *Prospero's Cell.* London, 1975.

FRENCH STUDIES. 'Balzac and Lady Ellenborough.' Herbert J. Hunt. July, 1958.

GARDINER, MARGUERITE, THE COUNTESS OF BLESSINGTON. *The Two Friends.* London, 1835.

GRANT, C. PHELPS. *The Syrian Desert.* London, 1937.

GRIBBLE, FRANCIS. *Balzac, the Man and the Lover.* New York, 1930.

HUDSON, MARIANNE. *Almack's.* 3 vols. London, 1887.

IMLAH, ALBERT H. *Lord Ellenborough.* Cambridge, Mass. 1939.

MACCREGOR, JOHN. *The Rob Roy on the Jordan.* London, 1869.

MACKINLAY, LEILA. *Unwise Wanderer.* London, 1951.

MAUROIS, ANDRÉ. *Prometheus: the Life of Balzac.* (Trans. by Norman Denny.) London, 1965.

MILLER, WILLIAM. *Greece.* London, 1928.

ODDIE, E. M. *The Odyssey of a Loving Woman.* New York, 1936.

PEARS, SIR EDWIN. *Forty Years in Constantinople.* London, 1916.

QUARTERLY REVIEW. July, 1916. (Sir Kenelm Digby).

ROBINSON, GEORGE. *Travels in Palestine and Syria. Vol. 2.* London, 1837.

SCHMIDT, MARGARET FOX. *Passion's Child.* London, 1977.

SCHWARZENBERG, ADOLF. *Prince Felix zu Schwarzenberg.* New York, 1946.
SITWELL, S. *Great Houses of Europe.* London, 1970.
SLADE, SIR ADOLPHUS. *Records of Travel in Turkey, Greece and Albania.* London, 1833.
THOUVENAL, EDOUARD. *La Grèce du Roi Otho.* Paris, 1890.
WALLACE, IRVING. *The Fabulous Originals.* London, 1956.
WILBERFORCE, EDWARD. *Social Life in Munich.* London, 1864.
WYNDHAM, HORACE. *Judicial Dramas.* London, 1927.

CHAPTER FOUR: ALEXANDRA DAVID-NEEL
BELL, SIR CHARLES. *The Religion of Tibet.* London, 1931.
DAVID-NEEL, ALEXANDRA. *My Journey to Lhasa.* London, 1927.
With Mystics and Magicians in Tibet. London, 1931.
Tibetan Journey. London, 1936.
JOURNAL OF THE WEST CHINA BORDER RESEARCH SOCIETY. Nos. 15 & 16. 1945.
MILLER, LUREE. *On Top of the World: Five Women Explorers in Tibet.* London, 1976.
NOURISSIER, FRANÇOIS. *The French.* London, 1970.
RIJNHART, SUSIE. *With the Tibetans in Tent and Temple.* Chicago, 1901.
RUDORFF, RAYMOND. *La Belle Époque.* London, 1972.
YONGDEN, LAMA AND DAVID-NEEL, ALEXANDRA. *The Secret Oral Teachings in Tibetan Buddhist Sects.* Calcutta, n.d.

CHAPTER FIVE: MARIANNE NORTH
ALLAN, MEA. *The Hookers of Kew.* London, 1967.
ALL THE YEAR ROUND. No. 67.
ARGOSY. No. 52.
ATHENAEUM. No. 17. 1890.
27 February, 1892.
17 June, 1893. (Review.)
DUBLIN REVIEW. No. 119.
HASTINGS AND ST. LEONARDS OBSERVER, THE. 6 September, 1890.
MAGAZINE OF ART. No. 5. 1882.
NORTH, MARIANNE. *Recollections of a Happy Life.* 2 vols. Ed. by Mrs J. Addington Symonds. London, 1892.

CHAPTER SIX: DAISY BATES
AUSTRALIAN ASSOCIATION FOR ADVANCEMENT OF SCIENCE, MELBOURNE. Report of meeting, 1913.

[17]

BATES, DAISY. *The Passing of the Aborigines: a Lifetime Spent Among the Natives of Australia*. London, 1938.

BATTYE, J. S. *Western Australia: a History from its Discovery to the Inauguration of the Commonwealth*. Oxford, 1924.

BORDERLAND. London, 1894–96.

DURACK, MARY. *Kings in Grass Castles*. London, 1959.

HILL, ERNESTINE. *The Territory*. Sydney, 1955.

Kabbarli. Sydney, 1973.

JACK, R. L. *Northmost Australia*. 2 vols. London, 1921.

KIRWAN, SIR JOHN. *The Empty Land*. London, 1934.

MEAD, MARGARET. *An Anthropologist at Work*. Boston, 1959.

MOOREHEAD, ALAN. *The Fatal Impact*. London, 1966.

OGLE, NATHANIEL. *The Colony of Western Australia*. London, 1839.

PALL MALL GAZETTE. London, 1885–86.

SALTER, ELIZABETH. *Daisy Bates: 'The Great White Queen of the Never Never'*. Sydney, 1972.

SCIENCE OF MAN. No. 13. n.s. 1911.

No. 14. n.s. 1913.

STEAD, ESTELLE W. *Letters from Julia*. London, 1896.

My Father. London, 1913.

TIMES, THE. London, 18 December, 1871. The seizure, at Fiji, of the 44-ton ship *Daphne*.

London, 8 April, 1904. Letter from Daisy Bates.

TURNER, VIOLET E. *Ooldea*. Melbourne, 1950.

WALKABOUT. Melbourne, February, 1971.

WATSON, E. L. GRANT. *Where Bonds are Loosed*. London, 1914.

But to what Purpose? London, 1946.

WESTERN AUSTRALIAN JOURNAL. No. 7. Jan.–June, 1903.

CHAPTER SEVEN: MILDRED CABLE AND EVANGELINE AND FRANCESCA FRENCH

BROOMHALL, MARSHALL (Ed.). *Martyred Missionaries of the China Inland Mission, with a Record of the Perils and Sufferings of Some who Escaped*. London, 1901.

BROWN, FREDERICK. *'Boxer' and other Chinese Memories*. London, 1936.

CABLE, M. and FRENCH, E. *The Gobi Desert*. London, 1942.

CABLE, M. and FRENCH, F. *Through Jade Gate and Central Asia*. London, 1927.

DISCOVERY. No. 7. 1926.

DONOVAN, J. P. *Yesterday and Today in China*. London, 1923.

FRENCH, E. and F. and CABLE, M. *A Desert Journal: Letters from Central Asia*.

London, 1934.

GEOGRAPHICAL JOURNAL. No. 85. 1935.

No. 100. Nov.–Dec., 1942.

HEDIN, SVEN. *Across the Gobi Desert*. London, 1931.

Riddles of the Gobi Desert. London, 1933.

HOLM, FRITZ. *My Nestorian Adventure in China*. New York, 1923.

JOURNAL OF THE CENTRAL ASIAN SOCIETY. No. 48. 1961.

STEIN, M. AUREL. *Ruins of Desert Cathay*. 2 vols. London, 1912.

CHAPTER EIGHT: ISABELLA BIRD BISHOP

BIRD, ISABELLA L. *The Hawaiian Archipelago: Six Months Among the Palm Groves, Coral Reefs and Volcanoes of the Sandwich Islands*. London, 1875.

A Lady's Life on the Rocky Mountains. Oklahoma, 1960. Originally published, 1879.

Unbeaten Tracks in Japan: an Account of Travels on Horseback in the Interior Including Visits to the Aborigines of Yezo and the Shrines of Nikkô and Isé. 2 vols. London, 1880.

The Golden Chersonese and the Way Thither. London, 1883.

BISHOP, ISABELLA L. BIRD. *Journeys in Persia and Kurdistan: Including a Summer in the Upper Karun Region and a Visit to the Nestorian Rayahs*. 2 vols. London, 1891.

Among the Tibetans. New York, 1894.

Korea and her Neighbours: a Narrative of Travel, with an Account of the Recent Vicissitudes and Present Position of the Country. 2 vols. London, 1898.

The Yangtze Valley and Beyond: an Account of Journeys in China, Chiefly in the Province of Sze Chuan and Among the Man-Tze of the Somo Territory. London, 1900.

THE SANDWICH ISLANDS

KUYKENDALL, RALPH S. *The Hawaiian Kingdom, Vol. II*. Honolulu, 1953.

THE ROCKY MOUNTAINS

AMERICAN HERITAGE. Vol. 18. 2 February, 1967.

CHAPIN, FREDERICK H. *Mountaineering in Colorado: the Peaks about Estes Park*. Boston, 1889.

DENVER MUNICIPAL FACTS. Nos. 12 & 18. March, April, 1929.

KINGSLEY, GEORGE. *Notes on Sport and Travel*. London, 1900.

MISCELLANEOUS MEDITATION.

PUEBLO DAILY CHIEFTAIN. 30 August, 1874.

ROCKY MOUNTAIN NEWS. 23 October, 1873.

3 February, 1959.

SPRAGUE, MARSHALL. *Newport in the Rockies*. Denver, 1961.

A Gallery of Dudes. Denver, 1966.

TRAIL. Vol. 9. 12 May, 1917.

JAPAN

BARR, PAT. *The Deer Cry Pavilion*. 1968.

BATCHELOR, REV. JOHN. *The Ainu of Japan*. 1892.

DIXON, WILLIAM G. *The Land of the Morning*. Edinburgh, 1882.

LANDOR, A. H. *Alone Among the Hairy Ainu*. 1893.

MALAYSIA

INNES, EMILY. *The Golden Chersonese with the Gilding Off*. 1885.

POPE-HENNESSY, JAMES. *Verandah*. 1964.

KASHMIR AND TIBET

BISHOP, ISABELLA L. BIRD. 'Lesser Tibet.' Paper for the London members of the Royal Scottish Geographical Society. May, 1892.

MACDONALD, DAVID. *Twenty Years in Tibet*. London, 1932.

MACGREGOR, JOHN. *Tibet: a Chronicle of Exploration*. London, 1970.

MARIANI, FOSCO. *Secret Tibet*. London, 1954.

SANDBERG, GRAHAM. *Tibet and the Tibetans*. London, 1906.

TSUNG-LIEN-SHEN and SHEN-CHI-LIU. *Tibet and the Tibetans*. London, 1953.

PERSIA AND KURDISTAN

CURZON, GEORGE N. *Persia and the Persian Question*. 1892.

GREAVES, ROSE. *Persia and the Defence of India*. 1959.

RICE, CLARA C. *Mary Bird in Persia*. London, 1916.

KOREA

GALE, REV. J. S. *Korean Sketches*. Chicago, 1898.

CHINA

BERESFORD, LORD CHARLES. *The Break-up of China*. 1899.

FLEMING, PETER. *Forbidden Journey: from Peking to Kashmir*. London, 1937.

LITTLE, A. J. *Through the Yangtze Gorges*. 1888.

MAILLART, ELLA and FLEMING, PETER. *Forbidden Journey: from Peking to Kashmir*. London, 1937.

PARKER, E. H. *Up the Yangtse*. 1895.

CHAPTER ONE

May French Sheldon

Dedicated to
Eli Lemon Sheldon
To whom I owe all I have accomplished. My inspiration,
my critic, advocate, my refuge, my anchor, my
sympathizer, my friend, my comrade, my husband.
Honourable, gifted, noble, unselfish, gentleman, beloved
by all; whose sudden demise has laid upon me a tragic
burden of sorrow during the completion of this volume.
Boston, U.S.A. August 1st – 1892

‘THIS VOLUME’ was *Sultan to Sultan*, an account of the African travels of a married American lady who undertook a journey in 1891 from Mombasa to Mount Kilimanjaro, unaccompanied by any white companion, braving hostile tribes, head hunters and cannibals on a safari of over a thousand miles, at a time when the political situation was, to say the least, an explosive one. In spite of opposition from the authorities, she organized her caravan under great difficulties and pushed on into East Africa in comfort, taking with her a palanquin made of rattan, with metal mountings of aluminium, and linings of yellow Indian silk, a 'medicine belt' and a couple of 'baby guns'. She also carried an alpenstock flying a pennant upon which the words *noli me tangere* were inscribed. After a perilous journey to the borders of Masai Land, she made a descent into a crater lake on the slopes of Kilimanjaro and circumnavigated it in a craft made of two sections of a copper pontoon, which had first been used on Lake Rudolf by the Hungarian explorer, Count Teleki, and abandoned later as impedimenta. She made several descents at various times and patriotically flew her little American flag.

Ostensibly she went to collect curios and amass ethnographical and anthropological information but another important reason was to prove that where a man could go – a woman could go, too. This was the great age of exploration in Africa. The first Europeans to explore the hinterland of East Africa were the German missionaries, Ludwig Krapf and Johannes Rebmann; the search for the source of the Nile followed, with the explorations of Speke, Burton, Grant, and Samuel Baker, who took his beautiful Hungarian wife along with him, Florence von Sass, the beloved 'Morning Star' of the Africans. Livingstone was the trail-blazer and Henry Morton Stanley the conquering hero who had gone to the relief of Emin Pasha. Africa was like a giant magnet, it pulled to its dark, savage heart all those who longed for freedom, adventure, and the chance to wear a tin star. Stanley was May French Sheldon's idol and it was Africa which had proved the testing ground of his courage and endurance. May French Sheldon also had another reason for wishing to visit the Dark Continent. She wanted to make her readers 'better acquainted with the possibilities of the natural primitives whom I am proud to call my friends and be called friend by, to demonstrate that if a woman could journey a thousand or more miles in Africa, among some hostile tribes, unattended by no others than Zanzibari mercenaries, without bloodshed, the extreme measures employed by some would-be colonizers is unnecessary, atrocious, and without the pale of humanity'. She believed that she was just as capable as any man of thrashing a way through unexplored territory and, if at the end of her life's journey, she asked herself 'was it worth while?', she would be quite sure that it had been.

She was neither a server, like Kate Marsden and Mildred Cable, nor a globe-trotter, like Isabella Bird Bishop and Marianne North; she did not aspire to become a mystic like Alexandra David-Neel nor did she search after love's fulfilment, like Jane Digby El Mesrab. She was a cultured, feminine woman who was entirely unafraid of the dark places of the earth, a refined lady who carried the decorum of Boston Society into the African bush, dressing for dinner and serving the evening meal on a 'dainty cloth', with napkins and knives, forks, and spoons. To meet the various chiefs along the way she enlivened the occasions by dressing up in a silken ball-gown, decorated with rhinestones and when one African chief showed his respect by spitting on the hem, she did not turn a hair. She was no tomboy, neither was she a weakling, for she proved that she was an accurate shot by bringing down a hovering vulture with one of her 'baby guns', thereby killing the bird and quelling an impending mutiny cooked-up by the bearers. Her contribution to geographical knowledge earned her the Fellowship of the Royal Geographical Society, an honour reserved for few women.

May French Sheldon was born in America in 1848 into a Southern family of wealth and prestige, whose money came from cotton, tobacco, and sugar, a formidable combination, and one which gave her the opportunities she so eagerly sought. Her father was Colonel Joseph French, a mathematician and her mother, Elizabeth French, was the 'celebrated Dr. French'. From her early years she developed a sophisticated view of life by an education in Italy, where she acquired fluency in French and Italian, and where she pursued her interests in art and music, with translation on the side. Returning to Rome after her education, she used her time well by researching in classical literature, and also studied geology and medicine, probably qualifying in the latter discipline, although there is no indication that she ever practised. She was, like Marianne North, very close to her father, travelling four times around the globe at the age of sixteen and later becoming a good shot in the free-for-all hunting which the Rockies afforded to those with time and money. Home life may have been a trifle dull, but it was not dull through lack of interesting and entertaining talk, for her father's social circle included people of note, and constant visitors included Henry Morton Stanley and his patron, H. S. Wellcome. With Stanley she was to find companionship and a kindred spirit; their friendship lasted over many years and in later life she sent him 'copious correspondence', clippings, enclosures, congratulations, compliments and burdened him with good wishes. Stanley replied, with a certain amount of ebullience, 'I am delighted, and charmed, and overwhelmed with your goodness.'

She married Eli Lemon Sheldon, a business man with interests in London and America. To her he was always her 'Shel', a loving, sympathetic, unselfish comrade, who attended to his wealth and his various enterprises and uttered no word of reproach when she returned from her African adventure almost on the point of death. She, too, had a flair for business and founded her own publishing firm in Bouverie Street, London, the firm of Saxon and Co., with offices also in New York. This gave her an outlet for her commercial drive and for her hankerings after authorship, which bore fruit in the novel *Herbert Severance* and the translation into blank verse of Flaubert's *Salammbo*, which she dedicated to Stanley 'the man who created the Congo Free State, which is destined some day to outrival Ancient Phenicia'. Stanley threw back the accolade by a review in *The Scotsman*, suitably laudatory. *Herbert Severance* was her mirror; in the character of Edith Longstreth one sees a hint of May herself; 'Personal independence to a capable woman is a trait no sacrifice is too severe to make to secure. We seek work for another reason – we like to create something.'

She remained on the most friendly terms with Stanley all her life; after the Emin Pasha Relief Expedition *Punch* high-lighted their friendship in eight lines of verse;

> Mrs. Sheldon is back from her travels abroad,
> Were she only a man, we should hail her as manly;
> As it is, there are some who, in wishing to laud,
> Are accustomed to call her the feminine Stanley.
> But now this adventurous, much-daring she
> Through such perils has gone, and so gallantly held on,
> In times that's to come Mr. Stanley may be
> Merely known to us all as the male Mrs. Sheldon!

The year 1891 saw her embarked on her East African adventure, leaving her home, her business, her friends, and her husband. May, however, was not at all averse to going it alone, for the prospect of being spouse-less had not daunted other Victorian lady travellers who had fluttered gently out of their comfortable homes to try their wings in lands across the foam. Malicious gossips had clacked their tongues over Isabella Bird Bishop, who had apparently expressed a wish that she would like to go to New Guinea, but said that it was 'not a place to take a husband to', and Alexandra David-Neel sought her own spiritual path among the Tibetan lamaseries while Philippe Neel lived in his loneliness so many miles away in a more prosaic environment.

Charing Cross Station was the venue for the send-off. 'London was benighted in a pea-soup fog, thick, black, damp, and chilly. I was thrilled with an ineffable delight', she wrote in *Sultan to Sultan* and it says much for her initial ardour that even her friends' remarks failed to cast any cloak of gloom upon her. There were prayers for her safe return and 'gruesome remarks' to inspire her with faith and courage. '*If* you return alive, what a story you'll have to tell!' 'Do be reasonable and abandon this mad, useless scheme.' But there were also words of encouragement; Surgeon T. H. Parke, who was to accompany her and her husband to Dover, gave her 'a host of practical advice' on the administering of her medical kit and the amelioration of suffering from 'African fever', and A. Bruce, Livingstone's son-in-law admonished her; 'Remember, nothing is accomplished without giving yourself up to the work at whatever sacrifice, and that honest failure is not defeat. We believe you will succeed.' With these words went the gift of long-range field glasses 'as if to bid me to be far-sighted'.

Amidst cheers and the pelting of flowers the train left Charing Cross with

May and Eli, Surgeon Parke and H. S. Wellcome, Stanley's patron, the only occupants of the carriage. At Dover, May and Eli parted from Henry Wellcome and Surgeon Parke, who had carefully written down precise instructions as to the use of her medical kit and the numerous tablets contained therein; there was carbolic acid, cascars, nitrate of silver for the cauterization of wounds, menthol and lanolin, besides a supply of 'Livingstone's Rousers', which were tonics and aperients. There were pellets and tooth extractors and two large-sized pigskin cases, filled, two small leather emergency cases, one French-Sheldon medicine belt and lancets, splints, toilet soap, violet water, Eno's fruit salts and a traveller's surgical and medical guide. Very little, apparently, had been forgotten. The palanquin proved difficult to convey; it was too big to fit into the luggage van and had to be left in London, to turn up later in Rome and from there to be routed speedily to Naples in time to catch the ship.

On the dockside at Naples, she bade farewell to Eli, waving him 'goodbye' with a handkerchief 'saturated in tears' and probably not a little apprehensive that his consent, given regretfully, would be withdrawn. On board the *Madura*, May's East African safari was a constant topic of conversation. The steamship line was used to carrying travellers and explorers and their tales were avidly listened to during the long, hot days of boredom and lassitude. May was different, a wonder-woman, a curiosity, a red-blooded American female of wealth and position who had engineered her misplaced zeal to put her dainty feet on to the hallowed ground of the male nineteenth-century explorer. Her determination to encroach into hostile Masai territory, even without benefit of any encouragement from the authorities, must have filled her fellow passengers with awe and not a little envy.

At Aden, Sir Francis de Winton confirmed her greatest fear – that her plans would be frowned upon and her efforts to form a caravan thoroughly suppressed. But he gave her good advice, and wondered why she did not choose the German route to the interior instead of the British one. 'Then I did not comprehend why, but it subsequently became obvious that he was cognisant of the decided opposition that awaited me on the part of a certain official in the English Company.' The 'certain official' was George S. Mackenzie, representative of the Imperial British East Africa Company, from whom she received 'a very unsatisfactory letter' when the captain's gig returned from picking up the mail at Seychelee. 'Despite the assurances I had had in London from important men in the directorship of the Imperial British East African Company that everything possible would be done for me, and even that they had taken the trouble to cable their representative to use his best endeavour to procure porters for me, this gentleman evidently was neither interested in nor in sympathy with my "novel enterprise", but, to the contrary, absolutely prejudiced against it.' May realized that Mackenzie would use his influence to quash the affair and discourage her from proceeding believing that 'her advent among the natives in the English occupation of East Africa would incur altogether too much risk upon the overburdened company'; henceforth, George S. Mackenzie was to be her 'obstacle'. One can appreciate Mackenzie's concern at May's determination to push on into Masai land, for the situation in East Africa at that time was a very unstable one.

Apart from Uganda, whose people were comparatively advanced and commercially orientated, the tribes were primitive and oppressed (the use of the wheel was unknown to them) and at the mercy of slave-traders. In addition, their numbers were constantly depleted by inter-tribal warfare. It was the time of the scramble for Africa and both Great Britain and Germany were interested in 'spheres of influence', which had been allotted to them in 1886 by an International Commission; the interior of East Africa was divided up, the British lying north of a line from the mouth of the river Umbo and the North Base of Mount Kilimanjaro to Lake Victoria. Uganda was later placed within the sphere of British influence. The Masai, powerful and ruthless, were adept at making raids into territories other than their own and were ready to revolt at the slightest provocation. It was an explosive situation and not one into which a lone white woman should precipitate herself. May summed it up for herself. It was an 'open secret' that the Germans were enforcing their colonization on the natives by reprehensible methods and strict military discipline and that the British on the other hand, were exercising, with no army and no naval back-up, a more willing fealty to the English Government. By the tone of Mackenzie's letter to her, it was apparent that she would get no help from him and that he was, indeed, her 'obstacle' and that it would be expedient to proceed without his permission, organizing her caravan with that 'latent gift' which she had discovered within herself.

In Zanzibar, she found that her world-wide reputation of being a 'mad woman' had preceded her.

In America, England, Aden, and Mombasa, and now here, I had to listen to and confront as best I could public censure. The bare idea that a woman should be foolhardy or ignorant enough to dare to enter Africa from the east coast and attempt to penetrate the interior as far as the Kilimanjaro district of the late Masai raids, at a time when great disturbances had been provoked by the Germans and a revolt was brewing, and essaying thus to do as the sole leader and commander of her own caravan – the thing was preposterous and the woman boldly denounced *as mad, mad*, principally because there was no precedent for such a venture; it was a thorough innovation of accepted proprieties. It never had been done, never even suggested, hence it must be impossible, or at least utterly impracticable, and certainly outside a woman's province.

Although she had received over two thousand applications from both men and women to accompany her into the interior, the authorities did not make her path any easier; it was the Sultan of Zanzibar who offered his help and a letter in Arabic, part of which read; 'and I command that every one who meets her, or with whom she puts up, shall receive her with absolute regard and attention, and shall restrain any one who interferes with her, for she is one of those who are much esteemed by us'. The Sultan not only supplied her with a 'passport' but invited her to his palace; there she partook of coffee and sherbets in 'dainty glasses', met the Sultan's daughter, a child of five years of age, bedecked in heavy gold anklets and a crown studded with jewels, and was disdainfully treated in the harem by the Sultana, 'who rudely threw out her hand to me' before being ushered out by two greasy eunuchs with tongues cut out, lest they betray secrets. The women of the harem followed to greet her and when May arose politely the Sultan waved her down; 'Do not trouble yourself for them. There are too many, all alike, and not worth it.'

One week after leaving Zanzibar, her caravan arrived at Mombasa. George Mackenzie 'my converted friend' had lent her his large, two-storied bungalow at Kilindini and it was there that it assembled; there were ninety-five porters, *askari* palanquin bearers, headmen and interpreters – 103 Zanzibaris. Seventy were to be armed with guns, the remainder had knives. Food was to be procured along the way by the usual method of barter, beads, wire, and cloth and the men received three months' wages in advance. In addition, thirty more porters had to be engaged to carry all the loads. Mackenzie harangued the men; if they deserted they would be condemned to serve a year in a chain gang and the use of firearms incurred a heavy penalty. On a Monday in April, 1891, the boxes were loaded, and the palanquin, May's white elephant', carried ostentatiously on black and brown shoulders, and the whole lot transported by Arab dhow and boats to Railroad Point. It was 'Ho! for East Africa!'

'Much-coveted rain, with its heralded season of benefits, propitiated is, and the entire caravan was athrill with delight', wrote May in *Sultan to Sultan*. They had arrived at Railroad Point at a late hour and May put up for the night as a guest of Mr C. Macdonnell Lemmi, who lent her his premises, 'a most tasteful dwelling', furnished cheaply but with exquisite care. He was, in May's eyes, one 'who, according to Shakespeare, makes every port a happy haven'. May was now solely in charge of the 'migratory community', going into the interior of East Africa to face unknown hazards. There had been so much to plan for and so many facets of the trip to organize; the community had to be provisioned and armed; presents had to be taken for barter and for the privilege (*hongo*) of right of way through tribal lands; sickness had to be guarded against and precautions taken against tropical heat and bitter cold at night. Valuable articles had to be kept in air-tight containers and rice, coffee, and other provisions tucked away in suitable receptacles. All the loads had to be weighed and numbered and then allotted to the various porters and re-arranged, or *tangenezed*, from time to time as the load lightened or men fell sick and were unable to carry on. The porters had no objection to carrying a white man (*mzunga*) but they objected strongly to carrying a fellow porter (*pagazi*). May, however, got over this difficulty; 'Look here, my man, to-morrow you may be ill, and if you object to carry your companion to-day, who will then be willing to carry you when you are stricken? We will leave you to your fate, the prey to the wild beasts! Come, come, fall in line!'

She learnt many things on that first march; the method of dealing out the the rice at meal-times; the great difference between the porters's wages and that of the headmen, who carried no loads but were paid much more ('I was obliged to submit to the usage of the country'); the way the Zanzibari porters carried their loads (on their heads) and the use the Wa-mawenzi made of their well-developed and very muscular shoulders; the songs of encouragement which some man near the head of the caravan sang to the others; and the walk of the Zanzibaris, with one foot directly in line of the other, making a very narrow tread. May could be amusing, as well as stern. Upon one occasion, she ate an orange and then cut a section of the skin into points in imitation of teeth and pressed them over her own; this vastly amused the natives and the childish prank so interested an old chief that he implored her to show him the trick.

It was not long before they came upon Masai. They were almost nude and armed with bows and arrows, squatting on the ground while May advanced fearlessly towards them, carrying her Masai flag of truce; it was from that moment that she became *Bebé Bwana* ('Woman Master') or, as May more delicately put it 'Lady Boss'. Bébé Bwana had one aim, the pursuit of which was to tax her courage and judgement throughout the trip; she had to know her porters, assess their characters, cope with their individual idiosyncracies and, with some of them, their ungovernable tempers, which, once roused, could lead them to mayhem and murder. Flogging was the only answer; this they understood and expected but if Bébé entertained any ideas of christian kindness and thoughtful understanding of motives, these were soon to vanish with the African sunset.

Starting out on my expedition, I fondly nursed the idea that the porters could be governed by kindness and moral suasion, and that the discipline so necessary to their own individual safety, as well as the safety of the expedition, could be consistently maintained without resorting to the usual punishment with the stick. This cherished belief was soon modified by actual experience.

Pitching camp could have proved extremely difficult, but excellent directions had been given Bébé by Captain William E. Stairs, R.E., and these she followed, although some deviation had been found necessary. His watchword; 'Discipline for yourself and for your subordinates' was never forgotten. Captain Stairs lost his life almost at the end of his expedition to Katanga, when he died from haematuria 'in its gravest form' and was buried with full military honours behind the African Lakes' Company's House.

Bébé suffered much physical discomfort along with the porters. Her feet began to blister and a daily application of carbolized grease was necessary for the long marches over stony ground; her aches and pains were massaged away by Suzani, a native woman, who patiently worked away behind the privacy of body-clothes spread all around her by the women in the camp. Sleep rarely came and only the huge bonfires roaring away around the encampment kept at bay the wild beasts. 'A sense of abject helplessness momentarily possessed me, vanquished by a courage that had only been dormant.' She appears to have endured all 'without a sequel of ill effects upon my health, although every nerve was strained to its highest tension'. Did she ever, one wonders, ponder upon the man who was her 'refuge', whom she had left so tearfully at Naples?

The way to Taveta lay through hard country across the plains of Taro and here she quelled her first, and only, revolt. The men became insubordinate and refused to continue; they laughed at her orders given to them by Josefe, the interpreter, and said that she did not know the road. It was only by threatening to shoot every man not on his feet by the time she counted 'three' that she brought them under control. If they were in any doubt of her prowess with a gun they soon learnt that she could be very good indeed for she brought down a hovering vulture with a shot from one of her two 'baby guns'. ('Then I had no fear'.) Revolt was not the only hazard she faced on the march to Taveta; they marched through a hurricane to the camping ground at the foot of Mungu, Bébé encased in a waterproof coat, and rubber boots, 'marching with ease' through a leech-infested stream, and emerging 'a bedraggled-looking object'. She lost Ferusa bin Sura when he went to fetch water, stopped to gather peppers, and lost the main party, this resulted in his death by falling into a gully where he was devoured by a lion. Bébé toiled up the mountainside, regardless of wild beasts, but she was too late. 'This was the only human creature I left dead in Africa', she wrote. Her overwhelming sense of responsiblity for her caravan and her moral obligations towards those who served her were as much a part of her life as the constant hazards and the ever-present dangers. For four-fifths of the journey she undertook the care of an attendant, whom she called in her address to the British Association for the Advancement of Science (Secton E) in Cardiff in 1891, 'an English stewardess', nursing her with personal solicitude in an ambulance of one.

The way to Taveta was an interesting one, used by caravans and Bébé displayed her way with guns for game abounded and the porters were delighted to have so much fresh meat. There were minor volcanic eruptions and a great deal of rain, including a cloud-burst; 'I concluded I should like to experience a cloud-burst, hence refused to have my tent "set" ' but the country was lush and fertile and her welcome was stupendous, the Wa-Taveta people coming a great way on the road to give tribues to the 'White Queen'. The huts and officers' quarters of the English Post were placed at her disposal and she was 'deeply touched' at the solicitude shown to her. In her book she wrote; 'Gentlemen, I publicly thank you now; you had not to do with an ingrate.' In her neat dress, peaked hat, carrying her alpenstock in her hand, and her 'baby guns' tucked in her belt, she enchanted the natives who cried; '*Jambo! Jambo! Bebe Mzungu!*' Her zeal for anthropological research was fully assuaged at Taveta; burial customs, care for children, amusements, marriage customs – all provided food for study and note-taking. The jaw-shaped armlets worn by the men upon their arms led her to believe that there was some connection with the thyrsus of old and that the figures engraved on the reverse side of the armlets represented the male and female organs of generation. Taveta she regarded as *Arcadia* and a *Paradise of Children*.

On the last day of April, 1891, she made her first visit to the crater of Lake Chala and two weeks later she circumnavigated it. The lake lay at the foot of the eastern slope of Mount Kilimanjaro, and entailed a very steep descent It was a gruelling ten or twelve miles' march from Taveta to the lake and the weather had been foul; the porters were out of condition and soaked to the skin; fuel was scarce and their encampment had been erected on stony ground close beside the rim of the lake. Wild beasts and hostile Rombos were an added anxiety.

The lake had first been seen by a European, Mr Charles New, who described his visit in *Missionary Travels* in 1871. 'We had encountered hostility from a party of eighteen men; "who are you that you should go where you please in our country?"' he wrote. He described the waters as 'blue as the sea', but they had been told that no human being had ever descended to the edge of the water, nor had any animal ever drunk of it. To Charles New, Chala was 'a charmed place' of rocks, bushes, and grassy slopes, where the water was 'sweet as the sweetest spring I ever drank of'. Joseph Thomson, on his way to Masai Land, also visited the crater lake but could find no place of descent. 'I went all around it: and although I am not deficient in enterprise or nerve, I saw no place that I dared descend, not even if I could have swung from creeper to creeper like a monkey.' Mr J. W. Wray did a little better in 1886, actually descending to the water's edge.

Now Bébé Bwana was about to descend in her own inimitable way and to circumnavigate its blue waters in a most unlikely-looking craft. She did so in company with a Mr Keith Anstruther, whom she had mentioned to the Secretary of the Royal Geographical Society in London in a letter dated 26 April 1891; she informed him of her achievement in descending to, and boating upon, Lake Chala 'in connection with Mr. Keith Anstruther, who had forced a path through all obstacles from the crest of the crater lake to its waters edge some months back, with a companion and who had determined some day to get a boat or a float upon the water and circumnavigate the lake'. The craft used was a copper pontoon in two sections which had once belonged to Count Samuel Teleki von Szek, the Hungarian explorer, who had left Zanzibar on 23 January 1887 to proceed to Taveta through the hithero unmapped area known as the Northern Frontier Province of Kenya. Teleki had discarded the pontoon and the Germans had consequently given it to Anstruther. The copper pontoon was never used on the lake; Bébé Bwana now proposed to do so by placing upon it a float.

With a force of porters carrying the pontoon all the way from Taveta, Bébé determined to defy all obstacles and reach the lake at any cost. The tired and dispirited porters protested but Bébé told them with authority that 'boats had been carried over cataracts, thro jungle and forest where masses of trees had to be cut down to make a way for [them] and great rocks broke, precipices scaled not for one mile but for many and that we would make the effort – should we fail it would be thro no lack of zeal or energy'. 'The effort' was initiated by Bébé, who went first with an advance guard of only two men (Mr Anstruther had remained at the top of the crater's rim to direct the pontoon bearers) piercing impenetrable forest, and writing it all up in her book, lucidly and clearly and yet with that touch of melodrama and archaic phraseology that makes the account of her travels so fascinating.

She stood on the rim of the crater, looking down, awed by the impossibility of descending and yet determined to penetrate through the primeval forest trees.

With bill-hooks and knives they cleared a slight opening through which I managed to squeeze, on emerging to find myself standing on a bowlder, which was balanced upon another bowlder, and every moment's tarriance seemed to imperil my equilibrium; and as I dared to venture on other uncertain surfaces which presented a footing, it required cat-like agility to crawl or slide down, sometimes landing in a bed of leaves, which must have been the accumulations of centuries, and into which I frequently sank up to my armpits, and had to be hauled out by main force by my men; and then clinging and clutching to the branches of overhanging trees, after great effort and considerable peril, succeeded in laboriously attaining some other footholds step by step advancing again and again to be opposed by gigantic trunks of trees, which, lightning-smitten, had fallen as a barricade, or through some potent eruptive force had been uprooted and turned themselves top down in solemn humiliation . . . The weirdness of the scene was intensified by the strange whirring of birds frightened unceremoniously from their hitherto undesecrated homes, and the whisking of myriads of monkeys as they leaped from branch to branch without emitting a chatter in their fright. A whistling eagle beat the air with its wings directly over my head, scattering its feathers like storm-flown flowers in its wild flight, and white-hooded owls peered out from sequestered nooks and 'twoo-hooed in solemn amazement.

Surely a scene to freeze the most courageous heart!

The advance guard whispered words of warning and extended his arm to prevent her falling headlong into the abyss, but 'all this filled me with an excitement and imparted fresh courage, and re-enforced my determination to overcome the difficulties of the uncanny spot, cost what it might, so long as I should be able to climb, or crawl, or slide, or step or simply let myself go with utter blindness, and risk the incumbent results; for the goal bewitched me in anticipation'. At last they saw the water, the 'Devil's Water' of the natives and it was 'Chala! Chala! Chala!' and an enormous effort to get the men to embark on the lake for the first excursion for the crocodiles and monkeys were considered to be not friendly at all, having seen no humans for such a number of years. '*Inshalla*, we will remain with our feet under us on shore.' But Josefe 'somewhat of a dare-devil' offered his services and the gun and photographic equipment were loaded into the pontoon, now named 'French-Sheldon' in Bébé's honour. They pushed out carefully from the shore to the shouts of the amazed porters and used their paddles to get slowly on to the water. Bébé Bwana was in a 'thralldom of wonder' and it is strange to think that Charles New, on his visit in 1871, experienced the same emotions. After seeing the lake, and drinking of its clear waters he wrote that the spell which had surrounded Chala for ages was broken; 'its mysteries, its fairies, and all its wonders had vanished into thin air'. The natives regarded Chala as the home of the lost people of a Masai village which had been tossed into the air during a volcanic eruption and the strange murmurs which could be heard were the cries of the spirits of these sorrowful souls and the soughing in the trees, the lowing of the cattle and the bleating of the sheep. Captain Sir John Willoughby, who saw the crater, gives another view – that the lake was a basin in which the great Masai Mountain God could always wash his hands.

Bébé made several descents into the lake at different times, flying her little American flag like a true patriot. She was, as she wrote, 'bewitched by Lake Chala' and the 'ineffable pleasure' which she had sought for years, of being the first to visit a place undefiled by the presence of man thrilled her brain with imagination. The most surprising thing about the lake was the way the paddles were drawn underneath the float by a mysterious suction power; 'I plunged my paddle two or three feet under the water at various points, the suction was so great it would be drawn away from me, and only with difficulty could I recover it and resume control . . . At the same time the entire lake was in agitation; it was bubbling almost like a hot spring, and yet there was no rift in the rim of the crest through which currents of wind could sweep down and cause this commotion.' A sounding with a plummet line was made to 250 feet, without success, and May assumed that the lake was the reservoir for the meltings of the snow from Mount Kilimanjaro. May did not neglect her serious research and geological interests; she took back with her specimens of rock for analysis, thereby following Charles New's reasoning that the light-coloured stones at the water's edge suggested a mineral incrustation of some kind. The copper pontoon and float remained at Chala, duly buried in a bed of leaves; May retained a key which described the hiding-place.

Having finished with Lake Chala, May turned her attention to the native peoples, who had the reputation of being hostile. The Rombos were ferocious and cunning, digging great pits for the capture of wild animals which impaled themselves on sharp spikes or giant thorns: many an unwary caravan had fallen into the traps this way. May, however, had no more fear of the Rombos than she had of the Masai, although she felt some trepidation at entering their villages 'until I could decide from their manifest attitude as to the likelihood of their looting my caravan and probably murdering me'. They did neither; with four of her headmen and an interpreter she visited one of the villages and found the natives 'most civil, and eager to do Bébé Bwana homage'. She noted their shields, their bows and arrows and their nudity and received as her due their gifts of furs and other possessions. Her presents of cloth later led to misquotation, but they 'followed the fashion , noted how her own porters were dressed and adopted a new style by trailing the cloth from their shoulders, twisting it around their heads like a turban or tying it on to their leg or arm. At no time did they attempt to hide their nudity by simulating the proverbial fig-leaf 'Truly they were clothed with *toga virilis*, a robe of manhood unfashioned by any mode of civilization, but inborn.' The superstitious natives were to bring home to her the importance of trying to comprehend the various characteristics and idiosyncracies of African tribes; one day, in order to amuse some visitors to the Rombo tribe, she took out a dozen bright feather toy birds which hopped about by means of a rubber bulb. It was all innocuous and whimsical, practically a guarantee against those dull moments which affect even native tribes. It was, however, an unwise ploy, for the warriors ran off 'like the rushing wind', yelling at the tops of their voices, terrified by the small feather birds which had inflicted black magic on them. Another day, a hand-mirror was used to interest the young warriors and girls who had gathered around one of the tents; the sun's rays formed a criss-cross pattern against the lattice-work, thereby reducing the youngsters to a state of panic, imagining that the devil himself had cast a spell in the shape of a 'tatoo'. Bébé was forced to leave the territory of the Rombos as she was now *persona non grata*; this was quite a blow as she had depended on the tribe for re-provisioning before they left the territory for Chagaland.

The land of the Chagas was interesting, for here were the *fundi*, the craftsmen in metals who forged spears, knives, agricultural implements, tools, razors, bells and jewellery. Excitedly they showed Bébé the source of inspiration for the fashioning of the Masai spears (the Masai scorned the forging of the spear; using it for killing was his particular talent) and she was 'delighted to find it was the leaf of the same species of cactus as the Spanish sword bayonet, indigenous to various tropical regions'. Bells, large and small, were much in evidence and she was fascinated to find that bells were used to teach very small children to walk. Small iron bells were placed around a toddler's ankles and each time the child moved the bells would tinkle and the child would try to peer down at the ground to see them, thereby upsetting his or her balance, in an effort to maintain which he would wriggle his body about and let fly his other foot. This was repeated constantly until a balance was maintained and the toddler could walk with equipoise across the compound. Her dresses were brought out and worn for a full reception of the Court and 'all the splendours of my jewel box and portable wardrobe' graced the occasion and provided a scene worthy of the best Bostonian Reception. The so-called Crown Prince toted his twelve soda-water bottles attached to a leather girdle, probably the accumulation of years. Bébé was in full command, 'As usual, the function was a very distinguished social success, and exalted me far above mortals of common clay in the estimation of sultan, crown prince, courtiers, and plebeians.'

Kimangelia was the next stop, the frontier to Masai Land, 4,700 feet above sea level in the mountain forests on the north-eastern slope of Kilimanjaro, but the way was not pursued with the old verve which had motivated her initial setting-out from Zanzibar. It was apparent that Bébé was now feeling the strain of the long journey and the descent to Lake Chala; everyone was on the alert for wild beasts 'not one dare say he could complacently encounter a buffalo'; her personal mishaps became more frequent (she fell into three deep holes, newly excavated by warthogs); the caravan parted and fever broke out. In addition, a situation had arisen which Bébé, lacking any political interest or motivation, found irksome for the territory through which the caravan had to pass was German and dividing lines were strictly maintained between the Germans and the British. Grazing land was often in dispute and friction with the native constituency was an ever-present danger; a white woman's caravan passing through to the borders of the Masai country was a cause for apprehension and suspicion. The temperature rose and fell sharply and the damp atmosphere did nothing to alleviate Bébé's chronic asthma. 'The supreme fear of [her] life' literally descended upon her as she slept fitfully in her palanquin; she awoke with a start to find 'a cold, clammy, moving object' above her on the top of the structure, the rattans of which were slowly cracking beneath the weight of an enormous python, about fifteen feet long with a 'great, shiny, loathsome length of body' ready to coil itself around her. It was despatched by an *askari* and a

[35]

dozen porters, but the horrific experience unnerved her and she came 'very near to collapsing'.

One would have thought that Bébé Bwana's apparently timeless taste for adventure would have been halted by the ordeals which she had been through, but she was quite ready to push on towards Masai Land, her secret goal. She was not impressed by the Masai, nor afraid of them for she considered them to be cattle stealers, freebooters and raiders who terrorized their neighbours by 'merciless onslaught'. 'They recognize no law but capture and victory. They have frequently attacked the arcadian Wa-Taveta with a fierce hatred, although the Wa-Taveta are reputed to have descended from the Masai. They will not work; they have not the pride of the Wa-Chaga in forging their own spears, but depend upon the vulcans of Chaga for their fine weapons and almost all of their metal work. Donkey breeding seems to be their only legitimate labour.' Bébé's dismissal of the Masai as merely 'donkey-breeders' was to prove once again to her that the lack of knowledge of the peculiarities of African tribes could be disastrous; it was only by the gift of a few lumps of highly-prized bluestone to some Masai warriors that her life was saved.

The Masai had their own way of forbidding passage through their territory by placing two twigs stripped of foliage over a bullet in the middle of a path likely to be traversed by a person or a caravan. There was no hesitation in killing if the person proceeded. Which is just what Bébé Bwana did – to the consternation of her Head Man who viewed with horror the uplifted spears from about thirty Masai warriors who confronted her. The gift of bluestones was accepted. Bébe, however, did not consider them to be the bogey-men of Africa and was of the opinion that 'any leader of nerve and self-possession need have no fear when they threaten an immediate attack' and went on to write;

A warrior, hideously bedecked in his war paint and war toggery, having heard that I refused to pay *hongo* (tribute) to the Masai who tried to exact it from me whilst at Kimangelia, and not in Masai land, came rushing up to me brandishing his spear violently, then uplifted it as though he aimed to cleave me in two, planted it into the ground before me, yelled in a deafening tone as he bounded high in the air, 'Wow! Wow! Wow!' Quick as a flash, I reached behind me and seized my gun, rushed forward with it, pointing the muzzle towards him, and in turn yelled, 'Wow! Wow! Wow!' discharging it into the air. Suffice to confess, I own that spear. It was never called for. It cannot be denominated as either a gift, or a find, or a capture.

The idea of penetration into Masai Land may have been tantalizing to

Bébé Bwana, especially after her encounters with the warriors, but to her Head Man, Hamidi, it was positively frightening. He would have no part of it.

'Bébé Bwana, I will not conduct you thither; the danger is too great.'

'Then, Hamidi, do you mean to say that you disobey my orders?'

He turned round and faced me, looking square into my eyes without hesitation and replied, 'Bébé Bwana, I swore to Sultan of Zanzibar and to Bwana Mackenzie to protect you as far as I could from all danger, and to give you my life rather than harm should come to you. Bébé Bwana, take these pistols,' and he drew his revolver from his belt, 'kill me, but I will not go.' There was a heroic majesty about the man; I took the proffered pistols, and whether he misinterpreted my movement I know not; he opened his *kansu* without demur, and stood stoically with his breast bared before me.

'I am ready, Bébé Bwana!'

'Hamidi, go, or I shall be tempted to do something rash. Let me think it over, and whether you go or not I go into Masai Land. You and the rest of your goats may stay behind. I go into Masai Land at sun-up tomorrow morning.'

But she did not go into Masai Land at sun-up, nor at sun-down, for 'this fine man' dissuaded her from an undertaking which could only have resulted in disaster, not only for herself but for the whole of the caravan. Instead, she turned south on a parallel route through German territory and met Sultan Mireali at the crest of a hill on the way to Marungu. 'The handsomest native man in East Africa' she called him and he certainly looked that, surrounded by two or three thousand people, dressed in vestments of bright red, all eager to meet Bébé Bwana. If Bébé was disappointed at her failure to cross into Masai Land, her elegant tea-party with Mireali more than made up for it. In her resplendent court gown and her blonde wig she dispensed afternoon tea, laying out a tablecloth and a set of little china tea cups and saucers. Mireali was an intelligent man, anxious to improve himself and adopt the ways of the *mzungu* and he was thoroughly entranced by Bébé's gown and wig. Before they parted, Bébé gave him a gift of a red sunshade ('Very beautiful') and promised to send him an English saw and a hammer.

I asked, 'What do you want these for?'

He answered, 'Ah, Bébé Bwana, I want to build an English house and live like a white man.'

I promised to send him the saw. He said doubtfully, 'Ah, yes, white men all promise, but they all forget; the *mzungu* always lies.' I interrupted sharply, 'Stop Miriami [the youngest Sultan], you must not speak to Bébé Bwana in that way. I never lie. I will send you the saw.'

Mireali had his saw.

Her next Sultan was Mandara of Moschi, an intelligent man, but 'much feared for his cleverness and duplicity'. She conceded that he was a deep student in his way but his marked deficiency in uprightness, justice, mercy, or morality was a cause for concern on the part of the German Commander at Moschi for Mandara had been very curious to see a white woman and had offered up to one hundred cows if an Arab caravan could bring one to him. As Bébé was a guest of the Commander, this apprehension for her safety was justifiable, especially as she insisted on going *solus* to visit the *boma* which lay across the ravine. Finally, she made her way there, with an escort of twelve soldiers and an interpreter from her own caravan. Baron von Witzslaben feared for her safety, but told her he had his 'cannon set' and would, if necessary, 'annihilate him and his iniquitous subjects'. The fears of the German Commander proved groundless; Mandara was lying on a couch, prostrate with paralysis, his one eye 'bright and alert' and his hand extended in welcome. 'Ah, now I have lived to see a white woman, and here I am so helpless.'

His 'helplessness' had not diminished his interest in Bébé Bwana; she permitted him to stroke her golden hair and the rule of *noli me tangere* was momentarily waived as the Sultan's wives ran the fine tresses through their fingers. He gave Bébé a bracelet and asked for her photograph to put in his collection of prints of white women. It was not possible for her to take a picture of the great Sultan, for he was no longer 'the deer of the mountain', although he was the 'greatest Sultan'. Unfortunately, he had a nasty habit of squirting ejections of saliva from between his front teeth, but Bébé Bwana received these only on the hem of her skirt as he stooped down – a mark of greeting and respect. Joseph Thomson also visited Mandara and mentioned that he had 'an eye like an eagle's, but only one – the other had lost its light for ever'. The ejections of saliva from between his front teeth were mingled with beer, so Bébé escaped the cruder performance.

Back at the caravan Bébé found her invalid much frightened by a mad woman who had attempted several times to carry off 'this fever-stricken one' into the bush. It is a pity that the reader is not told more about the invalid who was carried for so long, and who was nursed by Dr Baxter from Taveta to Moschi.

The march back to the coast was fairly uneventful; Bébé saw her elephants, and hid alone in the long grass as father, mother and baby passed close by and there was a terrifying moment as she trod a goat-path on a mountain side, where the overflow from the rains of the night before simply deluged her as she clung precariously to the scant shrubbery. 'Water seemed to be my African ordeal', she wrote in her book and her last big ordeal occurred as she lay in her palanquin within a few days march of Pangani. Her strength was now being slowly sapped; mosquitoes had tortured her body mercilessly and chronic asthma had taken away any slight enjoyment she might have had on the homeward journey. It was now necessary to use the palanquin during the day and allow herself to be carried across a bridge of tree trunks over a stream swollen by rain.

I should have walked across, however, without a thought of danger I allowed myself to be carried in my Palanquin; the bark proved to be unsound and slippery; my bearers maintained their footing with difficulty; when in the middle of the bridge, over the swollen torrent which noisily tumbled in its stony bed twenty or more feet below us, the bark peeled off from the logs, and the usually sure-footed porters were hurled with me down into the rushing waters, whereas they at their peril were dashed headlong into the dubious channel, and compelled to struggle for their lives. For a hazardous moment, only a moment, although time and space are so immeasurably elongated into eternities during like terrors, I was whirled about, protected from injury by my Palanquin, but with my head down and completely submerged in thick yellow water, in jeopardy of drowning. Several additional porters – for the bearers, poor fellows, had all they could do to save themselves – precipitously descended the bank and plunged into the seething waters and extricated me with great difficulty from the Palanquin in which I was helplessly buried beneath a confused mass of cushions, besides being under water.

She was now disabled, with serious injury to her spine – her one thought being to proceed on her journey to the coast by promises of extra pay to the porters. They carried her in a light hammock, lifting her tenderly in and out and tempting her to eat with dainty morsels. Dysentery added to her discomfort and it was soon apparent that she was very ill indeed. 'The doom of death seemed upon me', she wrote in her usual dramatic vein. At Zanzibar she embarked on the *Madura*, seeing once again her old friend, Captain Stairs, who was forming his own caravan, fortunately unaware of his impending death after his Katanga expedition. At Naples, where it all started, Eli Lemon Sheldon met his wife; the vibrant American amazon who was now, to all appearances, a dying woman, a Bébé Bwana who had traversed over a thousand miles on safari in East Africa among hostile tribes and in great physical discomfort, with only her staff, her pennant, and her 'baby guns' to support her and her glittering court gown and dainty table-ware to add lustre to the crude barbarism of savage survival.

'Does she live?' asked Eli – her own dear 'Shel'. 'Ah, yes, she did live, and felt that from henceforth protected and safe, she would surely recover, proud and happy in the thought to be at last in sheltered, loving arms; and, more than all, success was imbued with a new glamour, for he smiled and in well-measured adulation approved', Mrs Sheldon wrote in *Sultan to Sultan*. Friends were shocked at her appearance and condition and were deeply concerned for her; 'That you should have come out at all from the terrible country is wonderful', wrote Dorothy Stanley (formerly Dorothy Tennant, but now H. M. Stanley's wife) in a sincere tribute to her which was most touching as both she and her mother, Lady Tennant, had been apprehensive about meeting an American woman who was also that most formidable of ladies – a journalist! In August 1891 May French Sheldon addressed the British Association, Section E (Geography) at Cardiff and on the following Tuesday Isabella Bird Bishop mounted the rostrum to recount *her* travels. May's was the largest audience that the British Association had ever assembled and the talk was well received, though not without a good deal of under-play on the part of a journalist representing one of the more sober journals. He considered that her explorations were 'unnecessary and futile', but conceded that they 'diverted her audience'. He went on; 'The honour that is done to these "Lady-Errants" is not likely to encourage still further the feminine spirit of unrest, and the uneasy jealousy that is for ever driving the fair sex into proving itself the equal of the other.' A Miss Dowie had travelled in the Carpathian Mountains alone 'wearing knickerbockers and smoking cigarettes' and now 'another lady has been called upon to enliven the Association and has added her quota to the entertainment of its guests'. With regard to the raw-hide whip with which Bébé Bwana subdued rebellious porters, he doubted whether a frail woman could successfully whip 130 Zanzibari coolies at one time and, as for the crocodiles showing her 'the greatest kindness' (as she pointed out in her address), he could not see in what way they could do so. The President of the Geography Section, however, introduced her in warm tones and Sir Francis de Winton thanked her for her lecture and congratulated her on her achievement. In 1892 the Royal Geographical Society elected her as a Fellow, along with a chosen band of 'well-qualified ladies' and it was now evident that her contributions to geographical knowledge were serious. *Sultan to Sultan* came out in 1892 'under the crushing weight of a supreme sorrow', the death of her husband, Eli Lemon Sheldon, who had refused to have her recalled from Boston where she had gone for purposes of business. The year 1894 saw her off again on her travels, now apparently recovered and in good health. That year also saw another traveller, Isabella Bird Bishop, who embarked at the age of sixty-three on her adventures to the Far East, with the burden of a bad heart and rheumatism to contend with.

May's goal now was the Congo, to research amongst native tribes at the bequest of King Leopold of the Belgians. It was his wish 'that Mrs. French Sheldon shall be the freest and most independent person throughout our Congo domain. She shall not be denied free access to any documents, and shall be given every opportunity of investigating every branch of all work done by natives at all times by officers in command.' There appears to be little or no material left by May about her work in the Congo, but we get a glimpse of it in a letter to Scott Keltie of the Royal Geographical Society where she stressed the amount of travelling she had and the hardship she underwent 'in every district but one in the Congo Free State. I have become very well versed', she wrote, 'with the geographical, geological, and agricultural, to say nothing as to the political situation.' She seems to have accomplished a great deal as the emissary of King Leopold.

Her work in geology was serious and painstaking. 'The Kensington Museum expert', she wrote, 'has done me the credit to announce I have brought back the first specimen of the oyster bed in the district of the Kasai on the San Kru river. These formations are known on the Nile and in other sections, but not in this region of the Congo.'

She was still an ardent lecturer and in March 1897 she gave a résumé of lectures before the Tyneside Geographical Society and its branches at Durham and South Shields. The title 'England's commercial and industrial future in Central Africa' gave her ample scope for her political beliefs; it is surprising to note how forward-looking were her views and how great was her understanding of the necessity to 'rationally proceed, step by step, at a well calculated pace' in the education, industrially and agriculturally, of the African native. In 1914 she went to America to raise funds for the Belgian Red Cross and for this work, and for her work in the Congo and with refugees, she was made a *Chevalier de l'ordre de la Couronne* by King Albert of the Belgians. A letter written by King Leopold II (draughted by his secretary Edmond Carton de Wiart) to Sir Alfred Jones, General Consul of the Independent State of Congo, at Liverpool, and dated 6 March 1905, begins; 'I received with great interest Mrs. Sheldon and Lord Mountmorres . . .'

In 1936 May French Sheldon died in her London flat in Pembroke Square, surrounded by her trophies and mementoes. Her funeral took place at Golders Green, then a quiet suburb in an almost rural area, far removed from the savagery of the Black Africa with which she had come to terms. There is an aftermath in her book;

Querying was it worth while? After serious retrospection over the pros and cons, the expenditure of time, money, personal force, hazards, loss and gain, and finally facing as best I may the irrefutable sorrow which is upon me, requiring more courage to bear up under than all else which has befallen me, or can befall me, I am prepared to answer the query provisionally, without a tinge of cant.

Yes, it was worth while, if it lies in my feeble power after the quest I ventured to make to contribute something substantial towards the betterment and enlightenment of the natives, as well as to be instrumental in convincing their future rulers and teachers that more humanity and practical common-sense will be more fruitful.

CHAPTER TWO

Kate Marsden

*It is my earnest desire that all sympathy aroused may be
directed to the suffering lepers, and not to me, and all
praise to him who had enabled a feeble woman to set her
hand to a work which was waiting to be done.*

THUS WROTE Kate Marsden in the opening chapter of her book; *On Sledge
and Horseback to Outcast Siberian Lepers.*

The 'work waiting to be done' was a journey through Russia and Siberia,
undertaken in 1891, with the humanitarian purpose of bringing aid and
medical care to the 'outcast lepers'. It was a journey of such terrifying
magnitude and such self-sacrifice that only a Kate Marsden would have
stayed the course. Her cheerfulness and her resilient disposition, her faith in
God and her iron determination to overcome all obstacles, supplemented
her training as a nurse and enabled her to temper her ambition with logic
and commonsense. Nursing was her vocation; she was proud to be a nurse,
but she regarded cheerfulness as of paramount importance and this creed she
fervently believed in and practised with all her being.

She was born at Tottenham in Middlesex on 13 May, 1859. After Kate's
birth the family moved to Edmonton, where her father, Joseph Daniel
Marsden, Esq., resided at No. 10, The Parade, Silver Street and was listed
on the Electoral Register for 1874 as tenant of the house. The house cannot
now be identified with any certainty for the little row of middle-class houses
was destroyed in an air-raid in 1940. The 1861 census reveals that Joseph
Marsden was forty-seven years of age and was born in Durham. His wife,
Sophia, aged thirty-nine, was born in St Marylebone and the children were;
Joseph (12); James (11); Esther (10); William (7); Alice (5); Frank (3);
Kate (2). There were four servants in this comfortable, happy home; a cook,
a housemaid, a nurse and a nursemaid. But in 1871 the census reveals a

[43]

depleted household for Kate's mother had died in the intervening years and Joseph Marsden had re-married, his second wife being Sarah, a Londoner. Only William and Alice were at home; it would appear that perhaps Kate was away at school. Only three of the staff remained, two housemaids and a cook.

Joseph Marsden was a prosperous solicitor, practising in Cheapside and travelling 'up to town' each day on the railway in the comfortable 'first class' compartment; the working man arose earlier and paid his tuppence for his ticket each day, often cooking a late kipper on the waiting room's cosy fire. There was Victorian gentility in Joseph Marsden's household and sedate walks and young laughter carefully controlled when the children took their walks amongst the flowers of Pymmes Park and Tottenham's fields. The girls had been brought up to take their places as refined young ladies, thoroughly domesticated and aware of their position in life and their duty to their parents, to the Queen, and to their country. Marriage was a sore subject, for the family was keenly aware of the spectre of consumption, that dreaded Victorian killer, which had claimed many young lives in the Marsden family. The girls resolved never to marry.

Kate was the tomboy of the family and an original thinker and doer; sewing and needlework appealed to her not at all and fairy tales she regarded as 'stuff and nonsense'. She preferred outdoor life, looking after the birds, constructing rabbit hutches, and tending to sick and helpless animals. Perhaps at this early age, her inclinations towards nursing and her disinclination to take her place in the family circle as a thoroughly domesticated and genteel Victorian young lady began to show. Lessons, too, had little interest for her and she undoubtedly suffered for being a 'child of nature' for she was inquisitive and intensely practical, wanting to know the whys and wherefores of everything. Upon one occasion she almost suffocated as she attempted to trace the boiler-pipes in the greenhouse as far as possible. With great tenacity she became a skilled carpenter and 'positively revelled' in her finished work; hen-houses and dog-kennels were all expertly planned and executed. Animals she loved and adored and the death of an animal was, to her, a 'serious matter', necessitating a form of burial service of great sincerity and gravity. In one respect, she proved herself a true Victorian – she loved and cared for her large family of dolls, those delightful waxen and wooden extensions of the family circle; their broken limbs were mended, their torn clothes refurbished and their imaginary coughs and colds treated with the expertise of a trained nurse.

The time came for Kate to leave home and go to boarding school, that haven for exuberant bodies and gentle souls, but she made little progress and punishment became more frequent for the little girl who had been told on so many occasions that she was 'very naughty'. The death of her father necessitated her withdrawal from the school, for although he had been a prosperous and successful lawyer in the City, and had provided for his family a well-appointed and well-run home, he had died in circumstances which did not allow the children to continue living in the style to which they had become very much accustomed. They were ill-provided for and the beautiful house at Edmonton, with its spacious rooms, gardens and greenhouses, had to be broken up. Consumption had taken its toll of the children and only Kate and one son, William, remained to look after their widowed mother, now sadly reduced in circumstances. Something had to be done and Kate's practical attributes were called upon. With initiative, drive, and her inborn cheerfulness, she began to answer advertisements for nurses and applied to the Tottenham Hospital in Edmonton, the Hospital which later became the Prince of Wales General Hospital. The Hospital developed out of the Ragged School founded by Dr Michael Laseron, born in Germany in 1819 of Jewish parents. He was converted to Christianity and came to England as a young man, opening his ragged school at Dawson's Buildings, Edmonton, on 6 January, 1856. The school was expanding rapidly and moved to an old chapel in Church Street, Edmonton, where it maintained a Sunday School, Night School, and a Day School until the building was condemned, whereupon it moved once again to Union Row, Lower Tottenham, to a piece of land provided by a Mr William Booker. Now there was an innovation, for the school also became a home for orphan girls and the call for nurses to aid the sick and the poor was a necessity. Wisely, Dr Laseron believed that girls untrained in nursing would be ineffectual and deemed it wrong to send out into the field very young persons. He established a Deaconesses' Institution Training Hospital on the lines of the one at Kaiserswerth in Germany, where Florence Nightingale had been for a time.

A Deaconess came from the Bethanien Deaconess Institute and three volunteers were duly instructed. About 1867 a wealthy patient, a Mr John Morley, of Upper Clapton, gave Dr Laseron £6,000 and an old mansion, Avenue House, on Tottenham Green, became the next 'home'. Sister Libussa von Schmeling was the first lady superintendent of the Deaconesses' Institution and Training Hospital and she was succeeded by Miss E. C. Dundas (Sister Christian) a deeply religious woman who gave twenty-six years of her life and a great deal of her own money to the Hospital. It was she who gave Miss Marsden her testimonial upon her leaving, after serving less than a year.

She assisted vigorously in nursing the sick Sisters, and also did her part exceedingly well in Hospital, showing decided nursing talent and ability, and treating her patients with true interest and kindness of heart.

Michael Laseron's Institution was not a religious institution, such as those of the Anglicans and Roman Catholics. The requirements were simply that the applicant should be an evangelical Christian and should be willing to partake of the Lord's Supper along with the other Sisters. The annual report for 1869 pointed out to parents the benefits of 'practising love and self-denial' which were inculcated in their offspring; a later pamphlet described the Institution as 'a voluntary association of Christian women for the performance of works of active benevolence, such as the nursing of the sick, the training of the young, etc.' The Deaconesses could become engaged, leave in order to get married, and took no vows. They had to provide themselves with dark dresses and bonnets and were promised care and attention when sick, and freedom from exploitation when sent out to nurse families suffering from typhus, smallpox and other diseases. Twenty-five Deaconesses were in constant demand, not only from private families but from other hospitals.

On the outbreak of the Franco-Prussian War, four Sisters were sent out to tend the sick and wounded and received the Cross of Merit from the Empress of Germany for their skilful nursing of the wounded Prussian soldiers. The Sisters were now in such demand that their call to duty took them to places such as the Cork Union Hospital and to hospitals in Perth, Bournemouth, and Sunderland, but it was the sufferings of the troops and the dreadful carnage of war which set Kate Marsden's feet on the path which ultimately led her to work with the lepers. She was eighteen when the war between Russia and Turkey broke out; Dr Laseron went to Belgrade taking with him six Sisters who later received the Order of Turcova from a grateful Servian Government, and Kate herself, much to her surprise, was allowed to join a party of nurses going to Bulgaria. Henry Johnson, her biographer, tells us that 'they travelled in strong rough waggons, with straw for cushions' and we can well believe that it was during the war that she developed the high qualities of courage and sympathy for the sick and needy which had been implanted in her at the Deaconesses' Institution.

Professional nursing was in its infancy; in Britain, the Nightingale School had been established at St Thomas's Hospital in 1860 and the first trained nurses worked in a Workhouse Infirmary in Liverpool in 1865 where their founder, Agnes Jones, died after only three years of arduous and devoted care for the sick. In the Report for 1891 it was stated that; 'Efficient nursing is the best handmaid to the Gospel: not only do doors fly open but hearts also, when the people find that the Sisters have come to bring them practical comfort for body and soul.' Kate Marsden's deep religious principles and her devotion to the care of the sick was to stand her in good stead in later years.

After her return from nursing the wounded, she received the Russian Red Cross Society's decoration and undertook nursing duties at Westminister Hospital and later at the Woolton Convalescent Home in Liverpool, where she spent four and a half happy years as Sister-in-Charge, meeting people of all nationalities and admiring the qualities of the North-country folk.

When she left owing to ill-health she received several testimonials, drawing attention to her 'efficient manner' and her 'considerable administrative, as well as Nursing ability'. She also received a cheque for £100 and a tricycle which, no doubt, would have enabled her to get about in her quest for health in Australia, where it was thought she would probably go as so many sufferers from lung trouble did in those days (at least, the middle-class sufferers did, the poorer classes slid through life like wraiths, coughing their hearts out until a merciful death transported them to a better world).

She left Woolton in 1882 and in 1884 left for New Zealand, taking her mother with her to see an invalid sister now dying of the family complaint, consumption. All her love and devotion, all her practical nursing experience, and all the fortitude and courage which she had acquired at the Deaconesses' Institution at Tottenham and the Woolton Hospital failed to save her sister. The climate of 'The Garden of the World' had done nothing for her.

It did quite a lot, though, for Kate; she took a post at the Wellington Hospital and greatly impressed the miners with her efficiency and cheerfulness, for they suffered greatly from accidents in the mines and had to be carried miles with broken limbs, often in great pain. Kate was now fully occupied in New Zealand; she founded a Branch of St John's Ambulance Brigade, Lady Jervois accepting the Presidency with Kate as honorary secretary. It would have seemed that Kate had planted her feet very firmly on a soil which would have produced seeds of immense happiness for her, but she gave up her work at the Hospital and a successor was duly appointed; the Chairman of the Hospital Committee, in his letter to her of 23 December, 1885 spoke of 'your unfortunate accident' and her biographer referred to a 'severe accident' and wrote that she was 'dangerously ill'.

Whatever the cause of her leaving, she entered into a new life at Nelson and was 'charmed' with the surroundings and evidently restored by the climate and the outdoor parties and wonderful fortnights spent in tents amidst green foliage and ferns, making beds of bracken and cooking on stoves in the open. 'Going right away from everybody and everything', she observed. She worked, too, giving lectures which were well received and reported. In her nurse's garb, in her own cheerful and self-effacing way, she described her life and work in nursing and at one lecture in a Drill Hall the Mayor was greatly impressed by her 'easy conversational style of imparting information on the subject in which she is an expert'. Her health had improved and her ambition to carry on with her nursing work had returned; whatever the reason for her 'accident' at the Wellington Hospital and her subsequent mental break-down, it had now become clear to her that she must find another outlet for her energies.

In the Russo-Turkish war, amongst the sick and wounded troops, she had seen all the horrors of war; the dirt and disease, the putrefying sores, the pain and the suffering, the dysentery, the typhus – and the leprosy. No doubt but that it had made a lasting impression on her mind. Ever acutely aware of suffering in man and animals alike, the horror of the unfortunate creatures, God's creatures, must have greatly distressed her. Shklovsky in his book *In far north-eastern Siberia*, published in 1916 wrote;

Why were our hearts wrung with pain when we were thus warmly welcomed? Why were we choked with painful emotion which we strove to repress, as we looked upon these poor, kind savages? The unfortunate creatures were nothing but living corruption!

Such were the lepers whom Kate Marsden came across and now resolved to help.

The leper settlement on Molokai had been Father Damien's life's work; Kate, fired with enthusiasm and the great interest in leprosy shown at this time by the Victorian middle-classes, made enquiries of the Hawaiian Consul. Her services, however, were not required as the Government of Hawaii intended to make its own arrangements for workers in the field. India was next on the list; its 250,000 sufferers were more than enough to occupy the energy of Kate Marsden but, once again, wise friends pointed out the advisability of obtaining the right credentials from the right people. The support of Royalty would certainly assure a much-needed helping hand to Kate's plans for help for the lepers. She sought the honour of presentation to Her Majesty in 1890 and three days after the presentation the Princess of Wales commanded her presence at Marlborough House and 'showed the warmest interest and sympathy, and promised to write and solicit the approval and assistance of Her Imperial Majesty, the Empress of Russia, in accomplishing the end I had in view'. Having been invited to visit St Petersburg to receive a medal from the Russian Red Cross, Kate grasped the opportunity to present herself to the Empress. 'She showed the utmost kindness, entered heartily into my plans, and gave me an invaluable letter, requesting Russian officials to facilitate my wishes in visiting hospitals and leper settlements in the Empire.' The letter was signed by Prince Ivan Golitsyn, who expressed interest in the 'highly Christian and sincerely philanthropic significance of the journey so undertaken by the writer'. Kate Marsden's work in search of the leper colonies and the healing herb of Siberia was always influenced by a 'a spirit of union in Christian and philanthropic work, as well as the same forgetfulness of sect and creed which was shown by Our Lord in his works of love and mercy'.

It must have been a great surprise to Kate when the Empress confirmed a report that a herb existed which purported to alleviate the sufferings of lepers and that it was to be found in the Yakutsk province of Siberia. Ever since her encounters with leprosy on the Bulgarian battlefields, her main thoughts had been the wants of the lepers and the procurement of any medical remedies which could bring relief to their terrible sufferings; many countries were now caring for lepers and fine hospitals had been built, but other parts of the world had shamefully neglected them and it seemed that in some inhuman quarters the only cry was 'Shoot them – poison them – anything to put them out of their misery!' She regarded them as 'Christ's lepers' and knew that the alleviation of their miseries would be her life's work. She decided to journey to Siberia in search of the far-flung leper colonies and to visit leper settlements in other countries before she embarked upon the stupendous journey across Russia. At the age of thirty she knew her mission in life and took steps to carry out the first part of her plan.

This was to visit the leper colonies in the East; in Alexandria she was greatly impressed by the orderliness and attention in the German Hospital and in Jerusalem the Moravian Church had opened a leper hospital on the road to Bethlehem, tending with loving care the 'outcasts' committed to their care in a fine building erected in 1887. Kate stopped off in Cyprus and in Constantinople, reached the leper house and was rowed to a 'dismal-looking place' at Scutari which was, in spite of cypress trees and white stones, 'an immense burying-ground, filled with hundreds and thousands of graves, closely packed, and surrounded with cypress trees, standing a few yards apart. Turning to her [sic] guide she asked him the reason for there being such a number of this one kind of tree. "To counteract the smell from the graves, Madam", was the reply.' Her main concern now was to find the healing herb of Siberia and so alleviate in some small part the sufferings of the lepers, but enquiries as to its exact whereabouts produced no concrete results; medical specialists appeared to be totally ignorant of its existence; the inaccessibility of the plant precluded any gathering of it (provided that specimens could be found); its whereabouts, if known at all were jealously guarded. Furthermore, it was asserted on good authority that there were no lepers in Siberia, although there was abundant evidence of the existence of leper colonies elsewhere.

Kate Marsden arrived in Moscow by travelling across the Black Sea and the Caucasus, arriving in the 'Golden City' in November, 1890. Fascinated as she was by the golden domes of the churches, with their thin sheets of real gold, and stunned with the Russian winter, which her thin English clothes were 'ill-fitted to face' she presented herself in audience to the Governor of Moscow, Prince Dolgoroukow, and outlined her plans for finding the herb. In her nurse's garb, all brushed up, and wearing her bonnet with a clean pair of white strings, she hid her nervousness and told him of her plans. He was kind, questioned her about her work and presented her with a beautifully-bound book on Moscow. But there were innumerable difficulties yet to face; twice she visited St Petersburg, where the Empress again received her and later sent her a gift of a thousand roubles, and where the Countess Alexandrine Tolstoi 'also did everything in her power to further my plans'. Kate was overwhelmed and wrote; 'Let those who trust to exaggerated and unfavourable newspaper reports, and are under the delusion that little good can come out of Russia, bear in mind that there are numbers of noble men and women in the country always ready to stretch out the hand of fellowship to anyone coming in the Master's name to help His sick and suffering ones.' Friends rallied round and sent food to her hotel, nursed her in sickness, and the Princess Gagarine wrote an article about her work in the *Moscow Gazette*. She spoke no Russian and was, in some quarters, regarded as a spy.

The long weeks passed; letters of introduction were obtained from influential friends and the problem of adequate clothing was finally settled.

I had a whole outfit of Jaeger garments, which I prized more and more as the months went on; then a loose kind of body, lined with flannel, a very thickly-wadded eider-down ulster, with sleeves long enough to cover the head and face. Then a sheepskin reaching to the feet, and furnished with a collar which came over the fur one. Then over the sheep-skin I had to wear a *dacha*, which is a fur coat of reindeer skin. It was not surprising that, when accoutred, broadened and lengthened by a great many inches, I failed to recognise K.M. in the looking-glass, which a laughing girl held up before me.

Everyone was eager to suggest the kind of food to be taken. There was tinned and potted meats and fish, bottled fruits and boxes of sardines and biscuits. Necessary articles were such things as the little oil-wicks which 'were not to be had for love or money in Siberia', and precious candles. She also took a pair of gentlemen's thick hunting stockings, a pair of Russian felt boots, a large fur bag, and shawls and wraps. Finally, all was deemed ready and with a Russian-speaking friend, Miss Ada Field, she set off by train for Zlatoust, where they were to commence the journey to Siberia by sledge. 'Our experience of sledging along a road terribly broken up, owing to the immense traffic and almost endless string of sledges carrying heavy loads of goods to the annual Siberian fair, held in February, will be repeated in your case, dear reader, if you ever undertake a similar journey to Siberia at a corresponding period', she wrote in *On Sledge and Horseback to Outcast Siberian Lepers*. It was a dreadful journey; the high sledge bumped and jolted over lumps of snow and across ruts in the broken road, the driver constantly yelled, and the horses galloped wildly on. There were wolves, too, with their eyes gleaming in the darkness of the forest.

'Driver [Yemstchick]', shouts your companion, 'can't we stop a minute at one of those huts?'
'Eh, what, madam [Tchevo Barienya]?'
'Those huts where the lights are – can't we rest there?'
'Lights? They're wolves [Eto seriae poshli]!'
'Oh!'

The primitive hotels were few and far between, with sheep-skin rugs laid on the floor to act as beds, and no waiters and no 'fees'. There were 'moving specks' upon the walls and the air inside was hot and fœtid, almost causing suffocation.

The next stop on the way was at Ekaterinberg and here they found accommodation at the American Hotel 'the best hotel that I came across on this journey. The servants here are a model to their race, for they do not swarm around for fees on the traveller's departure.' They went to the fair at Irbit, as it was only a hundred miles distant, and were enchanted with the many nationalities represented and the vast assortment of merchandise on display. Kate hoped to meet a merchant from Yakutsk who might have known about the existence of the healing herb, but he 'positively refused to believe the statement in view of the almost insurmountable difficulties it entailed'. He knew of the lepers but had no information to give about the herb. From Irbit to Tjumen was a journey over a hundred miles of rough road, 'that hundred miles of shaking and bumping down holes and up holes, and over huge lumps of snow that looked like the remains of ancient buildings, so wearied and dazed us that, I believe, on arriving at Tjumen we were more dead than alive'. At Tjumen a surprise awaited them, for here they were accommodated in the house of Mr and Mrs Wardroper of the British and Foreign Bible Society, who gave them supper and a welcome night's rest, 'We tumbled on to the soft and dainty bed just as we were, and soon fell asleep.' Whilst visiting an estate they were approached by an old man who implored Kate to do the nearby villagers a service. The river was polluted by the refuse from a paper-mill; cattle would not drink it and the villagers had to walk six miles to the nearest village for water. The villagers turned out to see her, imploring her to help. Kate, with her usual practicability and cheeriness, found indeed that the water was polluted from the filthy rags thrown into it from the mill. 'I certainly had not come into Siberia to look after polluted rivers; but how could I refuse to listen to the touching appeal? She promised to see the Governor at Tobolsk and, with Mrs Wardroper seeing her off as far as the river, wondered 'whether I should ever see another English face in this vast wild Siberia'.

The journey to Tobolsk was a nightmare. The horses were at 'full gallop' and the young driver 'a rare specimen of "Young Siberia" ' seemed to get 'a little reckless' as darkness fell. Kate and her friend became 'nervous' and much concerned about the harness; sledge accidents were often caused by the harness, 'One peculiarity amongst Siberians is the obliviousness of the fact that nature makes horses of various sizes; for the harness is all of one regulation size. So you may see a horse hands high with harness fit for one of fifteen hands, and *vice versa*. The effect is often ludicrous, and sometimes painful to lovers of animals.' They arrived at Tobolsk 'about midnight' and found the usual hotel; the double windows were cemented; the two bedsteads and one mattress without sheets; the walls dirty and the room hot and airless. They pressed on, stopping at villages where the peasants, attracted by the red cross painted on the sledge, were given Christian comfort in the form of New Testaments. 'I knew I was the least worthy to do any work for the Master; but as I looked at the eager faces around me, I asked him to use me in bringing to the people I came across the glad tidings of great joy.'

[52]

On the way to Omsk, they visited a night-refuge for vagrants which thoughtful and compassionate peasants had built, and went to a prison which no Englishwoman had ever visited. The unfortunate convicts, 'some shoeless and all hungry' were given tea and sugar and Testaments. It was typical of Kate Marsden that she could say; 'I tried to reach their hearts by first attending to their bodies.'

Omsk was reached and Miss Field had to return home on account of ill-health, 'I dreaded to think of the difficulties I should have to encounter without her presence.' However, the Governor of Tomsk sent a special official to accompany Kate, one who could speak French and a little English and so all fears of future emergencies disappeared'. Travelling on her way, she met gangs of weary men and women, often trudging along in the dreaded Siberian snow-storms, their chains clanking and their groans filling the sharp air.

On meeting such a company, I usually ordered the driver to stop, and then prepared to go amongst the convicts. I never could go to them clad in furs from head to foot, with my morsels of tea and sugar, when they were only scantily clothed, and every blast of wind pierced through and through them. My furs would have burnt me had I gone to the poor creatures thus clad. So I took off some of them; then, stuffing the large pockets of my ulster with tea and sugar, and with two large bags strapped over my shoulders, and getting a soldier to carry two or three baskets, I went into the midst of the gang. To see the grateful looks of those men, as I put one of the packets of tea and sugar and a Testament into their hands, was worth all the trials I had suffered, and all that were to come.

She pushed on to Krasnoyarsk for her work was 'to get to the lepers'. But there were dangers now with the spring thaw; the Yenessei had to be crossed, and to be crossed in a *tarantass*, 'a nerve-shaking and bone-trying contrivance'. Straw was laid on the melting ice and through the kindness of an official Kate changed from the *tarantass* to a light carriage which would support the weight. An old shaky bridge came next but the crossing was made, 'I knew I was in God's hands, and felt sure no accident would happen, and that he would allow me to reach my final destination amongst the lepers.' For her journey to Irkutsk she bought a *tarantass* for thirty roubles; the *tarantass* has no springs, runs on wheels and is quite high to get into.

Now, when you are once in a tarantass, loaded in the 'hold' with all sorts of packages, upon which you lie, you have to make up your mind before starting that, during a journey of one thousand miles or so, you will be brave, patient, and resigned. At the very first move of the vehicle you will probably find yourself

[53]

thrown on to its edge, with your poor feet dashed against the front part, which consists of sharp wood. Then, after scrambling back into position, the thing lurches, and you feel as if you were trying in vain to keep up with it; but, after an hour, you give up all effort, and leave your body to do just what is required.

Your limbs ache, your muscles ache, your head aches, and, worst of all, your inside aches terribly. 'Tarantass rheumatism', internal and external, chronic, or, rather, perpetual, is the complaint from which you will have to suffer during that thousand miles.

At Irkutsk she called upon the General-Governor, who corroborated all she had heard about the lepers at Yakutsk. A Committee was formed and help offered to Kate from officials, including the Archbishops of Irkutsk and of Kirensk. 'One of the happiest days of my life, for my plans were now to receive official recognition and aid.'

There had been official correspondence regarding the lepers and leprosy since 1827 but by 1891 no hospital had been provided especially for them.

Think for a moment what these forsaken ones have to endure in their exposure to extreme cold and intense heat. Yakutsk is the coldest place in the world. For about eight months in the year the mean temperature is 45 of frost (92 Fahr. below freezing-point). The ground is frozen for thirty feet, and the immense forests are scenes of utter desolation. The heat in summer is so great that myriads of mosquitoes and flies infest the air, torturing both man and beast, and attacking especially the sores of lepers, who sometimes are too weak to keep them off. When once a man is known to be tainted with leprosy he is thrust out from his people, and driven away, as if he were some noxious animal, into a lonely spot in the forest, or on the marshes, where he is doomed to a living death.

After a stage of 235 versts Kate and her escort came to the river Lena and continued the journey to Yakutsk by barge, 'little more than a raft'. She slept among the cargo and roughed it for three weeks until they came to Yakutsk at last. Yakutsk was the chief administrative centre for the Viluisk Circuit and had a 'dreary, dead appearance' with no recreations; the people played cards and smoked 'sometimes six hours out of twelve'. Stores came in once a year from Irkutsk. Kate saw the Bishop and was impressed by 'his noble, peaceful face' and learnt that he sent missionaries up to the north among the tribes of Yakuts to preach 'God's love'. It must have seemed to Kate slightly hypocritical that the good Bishop's solicitude was confined to matters of spirit and not to the welfare of their minds and bodies. But she received his blessing and was undoubtedly grateful for his solicitude and care for her whilst in Yakutsk.

Now came the buying of stores for the 2,000 mile journey to Viluisk.

There was dried bread; tea; sugar; tobacco; tinned meats and biscuits; 'and an "en-route" basket from Drew & Sons, Piccadilly'. Her clothes she considered 'inelegant'. 'I wore a jacket, with very long sleeves, and had the badge of the red cross on my left arm. Then I had to wear full trousers to the knees. The hat was an ordinary deer-stalker, which I had bought in London. I carried a revolver, a whip, and a little travelling bag, slung over the shoulder. I was obliged to ride as a man for several reasons – first, because the Yakutsk horses were so wild that it was impossible to ride safely sideways; second, because no woman could ride on a lady's saddle for three thousand versts; third, because, in the absence of roads, the horse has a nasty propensity of stumbling amongst the roots of the trees, which in these virgin forests make a perfect network, thus precipitating the unfortunate rider on to the ground; and, fourth, because the horse frequently sinks into the mud up to the rider's feet.' Not a happy prospect for a young lady born and brought up in a middle-class Victorian household in Edmonton. On 22 June, 1891, they set out on their journey of 2,000 miles. There were fifteen men and thirty horses, with the cavalcade led by the Cossack, Jean Procopieff, who had kindly lent Kate all the horses she needed for the journey to Viluisk.

The journey was long, and made longer by the 'zig-zag' manner of travelling which they undertook in order to contact the lepers who were scattered. Kate evidently regarded her earlier travelling with the cheeriness and sense of humour which always characterized her work; never daunted for long, she had endured, wrapped in 'God's love' the most appalling horrors on the way to Yakutsk but now, 'my "experience" began'. They sank into bogs; they endured terrible bites from mosquitoes which she found impossible to drive off for 'I dared not let go of the reins, which, by the way, were very primitive of their kind and very hard – made of horses' tails – and, before long, wore out my gloves and blistered my hands. All my riding gear, including the quaint Yakut saddle, made of wood – most inconveniently wide – with a cushion fastened on to the top of it, the bridle and reins, and all my own attire I have brought home with me as a curiosity, and also many other things used both in my sledge-riding and horseback-riding, which all speak plainly of the difficulties under which our journey was accomplished.'

She slept in a graveyard, experienced her first forest thunderstorm, saw a large number of eagles, slept in a 'filthy' post-house in the full glare of the midday sun, pushed on regardless through endless forests and bogs. Bears were a constant terror, but they saw none; perhaps their 'simple devices' for scaring them were effectual. 'But, you see, we were not hunting for bears, but searching for lepers, which makes all the difference in the world.' Such a sense of humour amidst such horrors! At Viluisk, 'one of the quietest places I ever visited', Jean Procopieff, the Cossack, said good-bye. The Yakuts had marked out a track for the cavalcade along 1,500 versts, and with Father John Vinokouroff, she rode on through the endless forests, her horse often sinking into holes made by the roots of trees. Beyond a lake were two *yourtas*, homes of lepers. 'My instinct was true to me; and the peculiar thrill which passed through my whole frame meant that, at last, after all those months of travelling, I had found, thank God! the poor creatures whom I had come to help.'

The creatures whom she had come to help were pitiful in the extreme;

It was terribly sad to listen to the feeble voices of these weak lepers; to see them on their knees making the sign of the Cross with their poor maimed hands, often without fingers and without strength so that they could hardly lift up their arms; their faces frightfully disfigured by this disease; in their eyes you could read that all hope was lost. Their feet were toeless, so that some could not walk at all, and could only drag along their bodies with the help of a low stool. This picture of a dying life, without any consolation, touched us so deeply that the remembrance of it will remain with us all our days. In this place there were two yourtas about thirty yards apart; and between them seven graves, as if to take away the possibility of these poor creatures forgetting for one moment that death always follows them, and is always near.

When a leper dies, he remains in the same yourta, with the living, for three days. Will you just look into the interior of this yourta? It is so small that the inmates are obliged to sleep on the benches along the wall, without any mattress, and so near to each other that the feet of one leper touch the head of the next, whilst the others have to sleep on the bare earth, these *yourtas* having no floors. There is a frightful odour from this disease, and the cold in the winter is so terrible that when the door is opened for a minute one is almost frozen. The cows are in the same hut, and the dead bodies have to remain there on the benches, adding to the frightful strench of the lepers. When the coffin is brought a leper is obliged to go out in the terrible cold, and drag as best as he can the coffin into the hut, put the corpse into it, and, after that, put it on an old sledge and drag it for some yards to the grave. Indeed, these people have been cruelly forsaken and forgotten; but it is hoped that a brighter time is about to dawn for them, and that the greatest bitterness of their sorrow will soon be of the past. When they had the small-pox there no one visited them, neither the doctors nor any of the Yakuts; they were obliged to bear the suffering of this disease also quite alone, without any one to aid them; no beds for their suffering bodies, and almost without clothes, with the exception of the disgusting shoubas (fur cloaks), which only augmented the irritation so terrible in this disease. What they endured no one will ever know.

Although the *yourtas* were small, Kate found as many as ten people there. 'The dirt, the frightful odour from the lepers, the absence of any sanitary place, their food, chiefly consisting of fish, and often rotten fish, butter and grease that they drink, and bark of trees, and their disgusting clothes, will hardly give you an idea of the miserable conditions under which they barely exist.'

The round of visits ended and the little cavalcade started back to Yakutsk 'my catalogue of leper miseries' duly noted both in the head and in the heart. It was again a nightmare journey; they rode about seventy miles a day and struggled and floundered through dark forests, marshes and bogs, with frightened horses stumbling into holes 'as awkwardly as ever'. They were almost bitten to death by mosquitoes and frightened out of their wits by the thought of bears; the horses were driven to the point of madness as they galloped wildly through the forests 'flying like the wind' as they smelt the animals from afar off. To add to the dangers, they encountered subterranean fires as they entered an immense forest, where the horses made a 'peculiar noise' as they stumbled over the hollow ground. It was explained to Kate that this was a place where the earth was in a state of combustion.

The fire begins a long way below the surface, and burns slowly, still more slowly when there is no vent for the smoke. The burnt earth creates great hollows, and there is always danger of a horse breaking the crust and sinking into the fire. I thought little more about the matter except speculating on the causes of this alarming phenomenon in the bosom of Mother Earth.

Night came on, and all was gloom around us. By and by I thought I saw in the distance several lights; going on a little farther the lights became a glare, and then my horse became restive and almost unmanageable. We emerged from the forest and stood in an open space. What an unearthly scene met my eyes! The whole earth, not the forest, for miles around seemed full of little flickers of fire; flames of many colours – red, gold, blue, and purple – darted up on every hand, some forked and jagged, some straight as a javelin, rising here and there above the earth, and, in places, seeming to lick the dust, and then, having gained fresh energy, springing as high as the others . . . Coming, full of nervous apprehension, out of the dark forest on to such a scene, I half fancied that those flames were endowed with life. The lurid spectacle looked like a high carnival of curious creatures, let loose for a time from the prison-house, careering about in fantastic shapes. Blinding clouds of smoke every now and then swept into our eyes, and the hot stifling air almost choked us.

But Kate stuck to her saddle, although the horses were in danger of bolting, and prepared for any emergency by slipping her feet to the edge of the stirrups. They moved slowly, picking their way in and out of the flames, Kate holding on to the terrified horse with tight reins.

Complete physical exhaustion came at last. I had never been on a horse before, except once, for a short time, several years ago; and after all these weeks of riding on a hard saddle, with little sleep and food, and all the perils and alarms of the journey – well, it was time, perhaps the reader may think, that I did get exhausted. So I had to rest, and I began to feel symptoms of an internal malady, which, at first alarmed me; and I thought I might have to die there in my little tent, and leave, only just commenced, all the work I wanted to do. But the Master's presence cheered me and banished all depression. A day's rest, and then I started again, although in great pain, which, unfortunately, lasted till the end of the journey.

At Yakutsk she went straight to bed and slept for twenty-four hours, comforted by the pastoral letter she had received from the Bishop of Yakutsk and Viluisk.

By God's help you have already accomplished this journey, having visited the Viluisk district, overcoming unheard-of obstacles along the road. What with the dangers, the risks to your own health, the pain and difficulty of riding on horse-back for over 3000 versts and the frightful contagiousness of the disease, you came to them with your fellow-travellers like angels from heaven to comfort them.

A reversal of the outward journey was now made, Kate travelling on the river Lena to Irkutsk amongst a company of 150 men from the gold mines, along with their wives and crying children, changing to small post-boats when the river became shallow, exposed to 'rain, wind, and fog at both ends'.

At Irkutsk she 'begged hard for help for the lepers' and received a sum of about £150 for warm clothing. It was typical of Kate that she knew exactly in which quarters to place her pleas; she finally obtained a sum of £1,000 in contributions by stating her intention of 'laying the sad state of their existence before her Imperial Majesty the Empress'. She adds, however, that she hoped the Siberians would come forward and help their own outcast people first.

She left Irkutsk for Tomsk in October, 1891 and found that, after the Grand Duke's tour, many of the buildings had been white-washed and post-stations scrubbed and cleaned. The station-keepers, now, were anxious to please, helping out her few words of Russian by dumb-show, showing 'all sorts of little kindnesses' when they helped her out of the *tarantass* 'looking like a bundle of dirty rags'. She was obliged, once again, to pray and wait for 'God's help' as the horses ascended and descended several steep hills, flying down at 'terrific speed' on roads made glassy by ice.

Continuing her journey on a low sledge, where there was no protection against stones and mud thrown up by the horses's hind hooves, she eventually came to Tjumen, a distance of over a thousand miles from Irkutsk. She met up with her friends, the Wardropers and 'my dear friend' Miss Field but decided to proceed towards St Petersburg, in spite of remonstrances in view of her exhausted condition. Once again, in 25 degrees of frost, in company with dirty fellow-travellers and the ubiquitous vermin, she journeyed on to the rail-head at Zlatoust.

When we approached Zlatoust, and I saw the steam from engines and the station in the distance, a curious fit of emotion took hold of me. I was almost like a child, full of glee and excitement at seeing for the first time a railway-engine. My feelings can be well understood. Sledge-jolting, tarantass-bumping, horse-riding, and voyaging in cargo-boats had now all come to an end, and the luxury of a railway-train was to be experienced once more.

She arrived in Moscow in December, almost eleven months after setting out on her long journey to the lepers of Siberia. She had not found the herb of healing, but she had accomplished much in her mission and had undertaken the most rigorous and appalling tasks in a spirit of cheerfulness, patience, and acceptance. Her article entitled 'The Journey of an English Sister of Mercy into the Yakutsk Government to help the Lepers' helped the Leper Fund; 40,000 copies were reprinted and distributed throughout Russia and sold with the proceeds going to the Fund. Visits to the leper colonies in the Baltic followed and newspapers took up the cause. The Princess Shachovskoy and a community of Sisters of Mercy in Moscow begged to be allowed to go and 'nurse the poor creatures'. His Highness, the Grand Duke Cezarevitch remitted the sum of 5,000 roubles to help the unfortunate lepers of the Viluisk Government. England and America also helped and Kate hoped that she would be able to carry out her plans for the lepers from the proceeds of her books and from her lecture tours in America. A Hospital was opened at Viluisk in 1897 with ten separate houses for the lepers; two hospitals ('one for each sex'); a doctor's house; a laboratory; a church and a library. Each house was provided with a garden and two cows, and with a 'proper stable'.

It was unfortunate that Kate's efforts were not so well received in all quarters. In 1893 she published her book *On Sledge and Horseback to the Outcast Siberian lepers*, but not all reviewers were kind.

'Difficult to see what useful purpose the volume can possibly fulfil.'
'About the plant she says little, and about the lepers she does not say much more.'

'Quite as many lepers in London as there are in the whole of Siberia.'
'Steps already decided on to build a Hospital for 60 lepers.'
'Her account of her journey is not even interesting. She saw nothing new, and, beyond discovering the fact that bears feed on human beings, contributes nothing to existing knowledge of those parts.'

One reviewer regarded Kate Marsden as an 'adventurous philanthropist' and wrote;

It must be admitted that a madder scheme never entered into the mind of a human being than that which seemed to enter like a maggot into Miss Marsden's brain, defying all attempts to assuage it.

The Countess A. Tolstoi's letter was a vindication;

The work Miss Marsden has undertaken in our country is so important, so full of humanitarian charity, that we cannot fail to see in Miss Marsden an instrument chosen by the Lord himself to alleviate the miserable condition, moral as well as physical, of the poor lepers.

An address delivered by the Vice-President of the Moscow Venerological and Dermatological Society on 22 April, 1892 begins; 'Much-respected Miss', and Princess Marie Schubatasky, *Demoiselle d'honneur de Sa Majesté Imperatrice de Russie*, wrote; 'I never believed and will not believe until evident proofs of the contrary, that Miss Marsden undertook her self-denying travel in Siberia in other interest than in her philanthropic views.'

Kate was acutely aware at the time that many regarded her mission as a 'wild-goose chase' but 'if you have a plain straight-forward motive, although others may think it fanatical and foolish yet one's very earnestness and straight-forwardness is almost bound in the long run to gain the day, and so it was in Russia.'

She had hopes of having a Leper Work Exhibit as part of the Chicago World's Fair Exhibition held in 1893, but little interest was shown; the space allotted to her was only nine feet and, although a few friends supported her, the project was not the success she had hoped and worked for. After four months of very hard work, she returned to England. It was evident that before her proposed visit to the lepers of Kamschatka, that she would have to deal with the unfair and slightly cruel campaign of vilification that had arisen over her Siberian journey. Her testimony was supported by letters from prominent clergy and scientists and the President of the Moscow Venerological and Dermatological Society, A. Pospeloff, in his vote of thanks after the address delivered by the Vice-President of the Society at the meeting on 22 April, 1892 said; 'Thanks to energetic, self-denying, and tender-hearted Miss Marsden, the question of caring for the lepers of Yakutsk province has now received an immense impetus towards its accomplishment. At the present time the Government has already given directions about the organisation of a colony in accordance with contemporary medical opinion, similar to the colony built near Riga. Miss Marsden has already collected over 25,000 roubles, which she has remitted into due hands, and we cannot but feel exceedingly grateful to Miss Marsden for such a beginning.' It would appear, however, that in Kate's eyes, there was the desire for expiation in her searching out of the Siberian lepers and that she was 'Living her repentance and sorrow' for those lapses when she 'took many backward steps and turned away from Christ – a memory ever fraught with the keenest regret'. In 1892 she became one of the ladies elected to Fellowship of the Royal Geographical Society and proudly placed the F.R.G.S. after her name on her private stationery when she lived at Bexhill-on-Sea. Queen Victoria gave her a gold brooch which she donated to the Society in 1916. The brooch represented the Angel of Victory standing upon the world and in her letter to the President of the Society she wrote that; 'I value it beyond words, indeed, only next to my 24 years of fellowship of this Society.' She continued lecturing and gave well-reported lectures in many cities and had the honour of being invited by the Queen to give an account of her travels. Princess Christian also bestowed upon her the special badge of the Royal British Nurses' Association and the Grand Duke Serge, brother of the Czar, testified in an interview to the high estimation in which she was held in Russia. Eventually, however, the idea of going to Kamschatka had to be abandoned for she was now in failing health. To the President of the Royal Geographical Society she wrote on 2 October, 1919; 'I am so ill and poor and helpless but I *do* want people who have never failed me . . . to know that all I said I did, I did, and gave my whole life and risked taking the disease to help those poor lepers, who through my help now have their own colony, which Mr. Harry de Windt saw when he was last at Viluisk.'

Kate Marsden's travels had come to an end. She died at Hilling in Middlesex in 1931, worn out from years of work and ill-health.

CHAPTER THREE

Jane Digby el Mesrab

Thus though righteous Heaven above
Forbids this rebel heart to love
To love is still its fate!

JANE DIGBY, age nineteen

IN AUGUST 1881 the funeral took place of Jane Digby, Lady Ellenborough, also known as 'the Honourable Mrs Digby el Mesrab'. She was a Christian married to a Bedouin, Sheik Abdul Medjuel el Mesrab, and she was given a Christian burial in the self-styled 'oldest city in the world' – Damascus. There were few mourners at the funeral of this seventy-four-year-old English lady. The life of the bazaars went on as usual and the clergyman officiated at the graveside in the Protestant section of the Jewish Cemetery with the customary decorum and gravity. Sheik Abdul Medjuel el Mesrab, a devout Muslim, suffered the closed black carriage and strange Christian rites until he could do so no longer then, with a heart full of grief, he left the stuffy contraption and fled in the opposite direction. Minutes later, galloping furiously along on his wife's black mare, he caught up with the cortège and stared into the open grave, surprising the little group of shocked and silent mourners. Then he was gone, as quickly as he had come. On her gravestone a single cross was carved; her name in Arabic was placed there on a stone at the foot by Medjuel in honour of the love of his life. Those few pregnant and silent moments encompassed a lifetime of happiness and sorrow, a web finely spun by a tempestuous fate to entrap many souls and to exalt and crucify those she had especially selected.

Jane Digby el Mesrab was one of the most flamboyant, romantic, sensual, and tantalizingly enigmatic women who ever left England's shores for adventure and love in countries far removed from the stuffy, conventional atmosphere of the Victorian drawing-room. She was also one of the kindest, one of the most cultured, one of the most generous, and one of the sincerest women who ever bestowed the warmth of their affection on their friends and saved quite a modicum for their enemies, too.

There were legal loves in her life, and there were illegal loves, and Jane Digby coped with them all; she became Lady Ellenborough; Baroness Venningen; Countess Theotoky and, finally 'the Honourable Mrs Digby el Mesrab', wife of a Bedouin Sheik who loved her passionately. On the long trail of her manifest destiny she charmed other men; a librarian from the British Museum whom she met in the very springtime of her life, and Honoré de Balzac who called her his 'Desert Swallow' and 'this creature who glows with a strange phosphorescence'. The glittering prizes fell into her hands like baubles from a Christmas tree for among her devotees she numbered other Bedouin sheiks and an Albanian brigand. She was the epitome of romantic love in an age of Byronic elegance; what she did, she did for love and never brought that love down to a mercenary level for she spent large sums of money on her lovers until the steady flame of passion burned itself out, fanned by circumstances into a thousand dancing sparks which left her, like Niobe, weeping. She did not, however, weep for long. There were geographical frontiers to cross, leading her ever eastwards until she found the love of her life in the desert with Medjuel el Mesrab, while they rode like the wind in a freedom hardly dreamt of in the minds of her prim sisters atrophied in their conventional Victorian lives.

Jane Digby was born on 3 April, 1807 to Lady Andover and her husband, Captain Henry Digby, a hero of Trafalgar, at Holkham in Norfolk; her maternal grandfather was the famous Coke of Norfolk, a Whig, devoted to George Washington, an agriculturist and landowner, heir to an enormous estate, much of it marshy and unworkable. He reclaimed it, built parks and gardens and began the building of Holkham in 1734. William Kent, nearly fifty years of age at the time, designed Holkham, which was described by Mrs Lybbe Powys as 'a stone building esteemed the most elegant of its kind in England'. However, the house was not built of stone but of yellow brick. It was said that this colour was used because yellow brick was found in antiquities brought from Rome and the brick could be made in Norfolk. The whole effect was one of length and was the biggest private house that Kent designed.

The Digbys traced their ancestry back to Aelmar; in the reigns of Edward the Confessor and William the Conqueror they helds lands in Leicestershire, their descendants sometimes called Diggeby de Tilton or just plain Tilton. Sir Everard Digby was a conspirator, born in 1578. He was converted to

Catholicism in 1599, joined the Gunpowder Plot against James I, was tried in Westminster Hall and executed on 30 June, 1606. 'Twas his ill fate to suffer in the Powder-plott. When his heart was pluct out by the Executioner (who, *secundum formam* cryed, "Here is the heart of a Traytor!") it is credibly reported, he replied, "Thou liest!" ' (Aubrey's *Brief lives*).

Sir Kenelm Digby, born in 1603, 'the ornament of England' was probably the ancestor closest to Jane; Kenelme (then spelt with an 'e') had his estates restored to him by James I and went to Oxford at the age of fourteen. He was held to be 'the most accomplished cavalier of his time' and was a 'goodly handsome person, gigantique and of great voice'. He was also a scholar, in constant touch with Sir Luke Holstein who had been appointed as Librarian to the Vatican in 1636. In his unpublished letters there are requests for the loan of erudite Greek and Latin books, with pledges that he would see them safely and expeditiously returned. In order to collect money for the royal cause, he went personally to Rome in 1645. He fell madly in love with the beautiful Venetia Stanley, but the course of true love did not run smooth for Kenelme went to a masked ball in Paris, where the Queen-mother, Marie de Medici, became enamoured of him, thus forcing him to flee the Court. He and Venetia married secretly in 1625 and his description of her could be the prototype for Jane Digby; 'She had a most lovely and sweeet turn'd face, delicate darke-browne hair. She had a perfect healthy constitution; strong; good skin; well-proportioned; much enclining to a *Bona Roba* (near altogether) . . . The colour of her cheekes was just that of the Damaske rose, which is neither too hott nor too pale. She was of a just stature, not very tall.' Aubrey has quite a lot to say about Venetia; 'I have now forgott who first brought her to Towne, but I have heard my uncle Danvers say (who was her contemporary) that she was so commonly courted, and that by Grandees, that 'twas written over her lodging one night *in literati uncialibus*: PRAY COME NOT NEER FOR DAME VENETIA STANLEY LODGETH HERE.' She died suddenly in her bed, some suspecting that she had been poisoned and that Digby had killed her 'by insisting on her drinking Viper-wine to preserve her beauty'.

In the descendants there was a preponderance of Johns, Simons, Georges, Edwards, Williams; an Essex and a Charlotte, all tremendously 'busy' at Court and all intensely loyal and gloriously impetuous.

Jane as a young girl at Holkham was encompassed and coddled by Regency England; the Prince Regent had set the pattern for exotic living, his Royal Pavilion at Brighton and his London residence at Carlton House being magnificent specimens of opulence in an age where the poor were huddled together in hovels with fowls, pigs, and horses, and the stink of the streets always in their nostrils while they froze and starved in their death-wish to escape from it all.

Jane's days were full; there were pastoral pursuits in spring and summer; house-parties; battue days during the hunting season; the excitement of catering for large parties of visitors who were conducted round the great house to see the treasures and, at Christmas, many weird and wonderful delights. Jane's adventurous exploits manifested themselves at an early age for she once ran off to be with the gipsies, which culminated in the building of a fence round Holkham Park, a distance of just under nine miles. It may well have been that she was inspired by the exploits of her cousin, Henry Anson who journeyed to Mecca in disguise, was discovered and languished in prison. After his release he caught the plague and was buried in Aleppo, never having seen the Kaaba.

About Jane's tenth birthday, a governess was found for her, an excellent lady 'with a range of vision as narrow as a needle'. Margaret Steele ('Steely') soon found that the tomboy child was more than a match for her, but there were compensations for she accompanied her young charge on the Grand Tour of Europe in all the panoply and trappings of aristocratic comfort. Jane drove everyone to distraction but Steely could always be counted on to overlook misdemeanours with that sweet-talk which was to enchant so many men in later life. She wrote to Lady Andover;

Dearest Mama,
   I am very sorry for what I have done. I will try if you will forgive me not to do it again. I won't contradict you no more. [She added as an afterthought] *I will eat my bread at dinner always.*

There were many dinner-tables at which Jane was to eat more than her bread. Lady Andover had begun to feel that it was high time Jane 'got out of the stables' and made a good marriage for herself, and for the socially-conscious Digbys. The London Season and a good tying-down marriage were just the thing for Jane; there had been rumours of Jane's elopement with a groom to Gretna Green and so the pastoral delights of Norfolk were exchanged for the London scene; Jane was presented at Court and took her place in the long queue to St James's Palace. From gipsies and grooms at Holkham to ageing and amorous matrons at the best houses in town, Jane trod her happy pathway, naïve and wide-eyed at the goings-on of the ladies to whom she was presented. Lady Conyngham, known as the 'Vice-Queen'; the Princess Esterhazy, whose lovers slipped in and out of the Austrian

Embassy; the Countess of Oxford, whose children were known as the 'Harleian Miscellany'.

A husband was found for her in thirty-four year-old Edward Law, Earl of Ellenborough, who was later to serve two years as Governor-General of India. Two years at Eton, St John's College ('a Tory College in a Whig University') and two years at Cambridge (where he obtained his M.A. as a 'nobleman' by virtue of privilege as the son of a peer) led to the usual 'Grand Tour' of Europe. He was tall and well built, with an abundance of hair, and arched eyebrows, but his acid tongue and blasé manners made him unpopular in certain circles. Harriette Wilson was not entranced with him, for she wrote in her diary;

Young Law, Lord Ellenborough's son, was a very smart, fine young gentleman, and his impatience of temper passed, I dare say, occasionally for quickness. His wig was never on straight on his head. I rather fancy he liked to show his own good head of hair under it.

In 1813 he obtained his seat in the Commons for the pocket borough of St Michael's in Cornwall and attracted the favourable attention of Lord Castlereagh, whose half-sister, Octavia Stewart, he married in December, 1815. In spite of parental opposition (Lord Londonderry, as Octavia's father, later acquiesced) there did not appear to be any visible regrets; Lady Londonderry called Ellenborough 'my youngest and most favourite son' and the couple seemed genuinely fond of each other. However, Octavia's health suffered from the effects of a severe cold and she died in 1819 from tuberculosis. Edward Law rebuilt a monastic chapel at Southam and transferred her remains there. His love went with her, for she was the one person who really understood him. Five years later, he married for a second time, encouraged by his mother-in-law, Lady Londonderry; 'You must marry', she wrote, 'a young and beautiful companion for an improved *noblesse*. You must again be happy in married life, for no other can make you so.' He found a 'young and beautiful companion' in Jane Digby, daughter of Rear-Admiral Digby and Viscountess Andover, who had made her début at the tender age of sixteen and whose charms were irresistible and whose affection for her cousin caused a relative, John Spencer Stanhope, to write that 'Jane is not true'. Count Walewski though her the 'most divinely beautiful creature he ever beheld', according to Creevey.

They were married in September, 1824 and spent their honeymoon at Brighton, described by a nineteenth-century traveller as filled with 'genteel lazzaroni'. It was not a love-match; Ellenborough was almost twice her age, extremely proud of his ravishing eighteen-year old wife, but not a man to inspire connubial bliss. Lady Anson, Jane's aunt, and her mother, Viscountess Andover (she insisted upon retaining the title of her first husband) were well pleased with the match; Jane's future was assumed to be safe with Edward Law. In London, Jane was left more and more to herself; the wealthy aristocrats spent a great deal of time in the City, plunged in work, while their bored wives disported themselves at Almacks' in King Street, St James's, the *salon* which had supplanted Carlton House, as Carlton House had itself been supplanted Buckingham Palace. 'Aurora', as Jane was called at this time, learnt quickly, so quickly indeed that Creevey described one of the parties she attended as composed of the 'most notorious and profligate women in London', and wrote of her conduct as 'impudent' and 'bare-faced'. Ellenborough allowed her much liberty, liberty which shocked Count Apponyi who visited London in July 1828, for he failed to find the great English decorum about which he had heard.

Left alone, she found pleasure in visits and on such a visit to her grandfather at Holkham, she met young Frederick Madden, a quiet, modest Librarian from Oxford and the British Museum who had come to Holkham to catalogue the Greek poets in the Long Gallery. He did his work in the daytime, played cards with the family in the long evenings, and spent much time thinking of his fiancée, Mary. He also thought about Jane, for he wrote in his diary that she was 'one of the most lovely women I ever saw' and in the spring of 1827 he recorded that 'she pretended to be very angry as to what passed last night'. Whatever passed between them, the affair petered out; the diary was later bequeathed to the Bodleian, where it was unsealed in 1920 according to Frederick Madden's instructions.

Jane returned to London and the whirl of the London season. There were Vauxhall Gardens, with their groves and pavilions, (where one could spend a moment or two in dalliance) temples, grottoes and lawns, all brilliantly illuminated with lamps, resplendent with the figures of the Hon. Horatio Walpole; Lord March; Lord Granby; and that 'she-meteor', Lady Wortley Montague; the vulgar were allowed to gape at them to a late hour. There was Ranelagh up the river, of which Walpole said; 'You can't set your foot without treading on a Prince or Duke of Cumberland.' There were the new Marylebone Gardens, noted for the firework displays, for George II loved fireworks. At Ranelagh there was an olive-green ceiling painted with a rainbow, and an organ inside an arched structure which poured forth music to aid the amateur theatricals and play-readings which supplemented the professional theatre of Garrick and Sarah Siddons. The British Museum could not hope to rival these. On 15 February, 1828, Jane was delivered of a child, who was christened Arthur Dudley Law; he appears to have contributed to the conjugal estrangement between Jane and Ellenborough for they moved into separate suites; Edward Law had achieved his ambitions for he had an heir and had received the post as Lord Privy Seal in the Duke of Wellington's Ministry. As usual with Jane, there had been gossip. Her cousin, George Anson, had always been close to her and since her return to London had escorted her around the London scene with many a malicious glance from the matrons. But Edward Law, happy with his heir, went about his political business. The day after the birth he wrote in his diary;

Janet has brought me a boy. I put this down as a political occurrence because I shall make him if he lives and I live a Political character. I shall ask the Duke of Wellington and Dudley to be his Godfathers, Princess Esterhazy is to be his Godmother. A good diplomatic introduction to the world.

In April 1828, Jane visited Almacks in King Street, St James. The orchestra played and the place was ablaze with light. Almack's was founded by one Almack, a Scotsman, for the edification of ladies and gentlemen of London, the 'new Babylon'. It was opened on 12 February, 1765 and was honoured by the presence of the Duke of Cumberland. The ballroom was one hundred feet in length and forty feet in width and five hundred wax lights in five cut-glass lustres blazed down on the mangificently-gowned scions of the nobility and their sycophants. The building was used for assemblies, concerts, musical evenings, and balls and the great actors gave readings and performances; Charles Kemble graced it with his august presence, reading from Shakespeare.

It was extremely difficult to gain admittance; five lady patronesses vetted the applications and the acceptance of any lady or gentleman depended on a personal visit of one of the patronesses. Almack's was the 'in' place in which to be seen and at one time 1,700 members danced in the elegant ballroom until early morning. Almack (the name was an anagram) left the building to his niece, Mrs Willis, and in 1890 the rooms known as 'Willis's Rooms' became a restaurant. Almack's ceased in 1863.

The beauties of London took themselves off to Almack's in St James, to see and to be seen, to bewitch and to tantalize, with all the arts they possessed, those young men upon whom their eyes chanced to alight. This was the Romantic Age, the age of powder and paint and artificial aids used, not to enhance, but to cover up. The skin was whitened with mercury water and ceruse containing white-lead, and spots (these were common owing to the prevalence of small-pox) were hidden by patches. The white lead and mercury left devastation in their wake for hair could fall out and gastric ulcers kill. Complexion cleaners were eagerly sought after and an 'English rose', such as Jane Digby, was something of a rarity. She was the delicate nymph, the unstudied character who could lead men into that first innocent blossoming, which could so easily turn into a passion of frightening proportions.

The fashionable sought every sort of distraction and the wealthy found amusement in various, and devious ,ways. There were spas all over England and in London there flourished such pleasure resorts as Vauxhall Gardens, Ranelagh and Spring Gardens, Kensington Gardens, Apollo Gardens, and St George's Fields. The Bayswater tea-gardens provided a degree of decorous refinement and day-time amusements succoured the appetites of the idle middle and upper classes for mild and innocuous games and fringe dalliance. The 'Temple of Flora', and the White Conduit House of Islington catered amirably for them. But, for the evenings of mystery and imagination, there was Almack's.

Jane had recovered well after the birth of her son, and Ellenborough's heir; she and Ellenborough had appeared together at a dinner and it was apparent that life would be interesting once more, especially as Ellenborough was so pleased with himself at having gained a Cabinet Post under Wellington that she would be free to live her own life. On one of the Wednesday night Balls in April 1828, Ellenborough brought Jane to the entrance of Almack's and then left to attend to his own quiet amusement in the sphere of Parliamentary politics. Jane was gorgeously clad and entrancingly captivating. Just twenty-one years of age, she soon found a partner, far more interesting and exciting than the scholarly librarian, Frederick Madden and far, far more of a passionate Byronic figure than the Edward Law she had married. Introduced by Princess Esterhazy, Felix Schwartzenberg, newly-appointed attaché at the Austrian Embassy, was the embodiment of all Jane's romantic dreams and secret longings. He was the dark, dashing, and gallant foreign aristocrat, the Ruritanian Prince to Jane's Cinderella, who swept her off her feet in that first dance at Almack's as he clasped her close to his hussar jacket. Soon they were lovers and all London society knew that Jane, Lady Ellenborough, had succumbed to this twenty-seven year-old sophisticated intellectual, this diplomat who had travelled the world as far away as Rio de Janeiro, leaving a trail of broken hearts. Count Apponyi, a frequent visitor at Almack's, noted in his diary; 'Among all these people one lady especially attracted my attention. It was Lady Ellenborough, one of the

[69]

most beautiful women I have ever seen, blond hair, magnificent complexion, big blue eyes, young, with the figure of a nymph; in fact, she is everything desirable. . . . The expression of her face is as soft as the sound of her voice, and her whole personality has something of modesty and innocence which enchanted me.' Schwarzenberg's family was one of the oldest in Europe, their history being linked with that of the Holy Roman Empire and the monarchy. They had estates in Europe (the 'Schwarzenberg Kingdom') and were blue-blooded aristocrats through and through. Felix Schwarzenberg was a scholar, had a fine singing voice, and could speak several languages. To Lady Ellenborough, the bright-eyed child of country innocence, he was the Prince of Light who had taken her hand and led her patiently through the intricacies of the quadrille in a dream sequence that was to prove devastating in its effects.

They met at his house in Harley Street and in the Norfolk Hotel in Brighton; they were spied on with relish by the servants, laughed at by the grooms, and the local folk and ostracized by those peeresses who were discreet enough to keep their own bedroom farces safely tucked away. They were seen together at parties on the river, at picnics in the Surrey Woods, at masked balls, and at musical evenings. Vauxhall, Ranelagh, Rotten Row were the venues for the two lovers and the receptions in Mayfair with upwards of 1,500 guests provided opportunities of close contact in public places; private contact was maintained in Schwartzenberg's rooms in Harley Street where Jane's green phaeton, accompanied by her groom, William Carpenter, could be seen almost daily. The gossip increased and became a scandal. Lord Ellenborough was timorously appraised of it at Roehampton by a hesitant Steely, and the Bishop of Bath and Wells himself took his nephew to task. A new name had been coined – 'cad'; it derived from a horse 'Cadland' which had won the Derby, beating the favourite, 'The Colonel'. This was a sly reference to George Anson, Jane's cousin.

There was a subsequent petition for divorce and, in the meantime, there were the usual meetings, with a rendezvous at the Norfolk Hotel in Brighton in February 1829 where a perceptive waiter, one Robert Hepple, listened intently outside the bedroom door. Thomas Creevey took a dim view of the guests;

There were Mrs. F–L– and Lord Chesterfield, who came together and sat together all night, Lady E– and the Pole or Prussian or Austrian or whatever he is they call Cadland, because he beat the Colonel. Anything as impudent as she or as barefaced as the whole affair I never beheld.

The young Arthur Dudley Ellenborough had also been brought along by his nursemaids for a change of air, but the 'good, political introduction' which Lord Ellenborough had envisaged never matured, for the baby died about a year afterwards.

A shattering event now took place – the recall of Schwarzenberg and the removal of Jane to Ilfracombe by her family in the protective custody of Steely, who must have noticed, as they walked in the country, the advancing embonpoint underneath the informal pastoral clothing of Jane. It was all too much and Jane fled, throwing away at one fell swoop the embroidery, the formal tea-drinking, and the observances of the not-too-natural habits of the fauna round about, to say nothing of the early nights and the long, hours in a cold, passionless bed. 'My situation will soon become visible', she told Steely, 'God knows what will become of me! The child is not Lord Ellenborough's but Prince Schwartzenberg's!' a fact which Steely, prim governess though she were, was not unaware of.

Felix Schwartzenberg was not oblivious of his duties to Jane and his unborn child, but marriage was not possible at this stage; his family were strict Catholics and his sister, Mathilde, had advised him to end the costly liaison with Lady Ellenborough. There remained the question of the child. Several places in Europe were suggested where Jane could be quietly confined (after all, privacy at times like these was almost routine amongst the aristocracy) and finally Basle was chosen and Jane set out on the last day of August from Ramsgate, a tortured woman, fleeing without thought to a lover whose ambitions had never included her and whose strict Catholic upbringing would, in any case, have precluded marriage with a divorcee. Ellenborough had made very generous arrangements for her, pending divorce proceedings, in order that she would not be without 'those comforts and conveniences to which her rank in life entitled her'; Jane was grateful.

On a day in August 1829 Jane left the shores of England for foreign parts. She was never, except for short intervals of time, never to return. Steely was there to help, with a sad heart bundling Jane and the maid she had found for her in Brussels into a hired coach and returning home. 'Madame Einberg', as Jane wished to be known on the journey, settled herself down with relief and expectancy, anticipating that glorious re-union with Felix which would heall all wounds. Felix did not arrive in Basle until nearly two months after Jane had set her foot on Swiss soil and her thoughts of a passionate re-union were doomed to disappointment. Felix, now older and far more prosaic, saw with diplomatic shrewdness that his ambitions did not lie in the direction of marriage and children and soon after the birth of a daughter, named 'Didi' by Felix, he left for Paris. Felix had been with her for only two weeks.

Felix was Metternich's protégé and in a city beset with political intrigue and revolutionary ideas he had ambitions to fufil. They lived in the Rue de Grenelle and the Place du Palais de Députés and Jane entered once again into the world she had always enjoyed, the world of masked balls and the endless parties. There were plenty of 'Almacks' in Paris, although the best society was closed to her.

There were other diversions, though, for Paris at this time was full of artists, writers and musicians and the Left Bank was not far from the Place du Palais. If Felix was busy in diplomatic circles, Jane could be equally concerned with those cultural and intellectual circles which best suited her temperament. She was highly intelligent, a woman of brilliance of mind, a searcher after knowledge and a person of breeding and utter refinement and unaffected charm. The literary giants were wholly immersed in the arts, for the literary side was also pictorial; Lamartine, Hugo, de Musset, Sand, were all accomplished sketchers; Gautier was a painter as well as a writer. In 1830, Chateaubriand, already in his sixties, was the acknowledged father of Romanticism and Saint Beuve, Alfred de Vigny and Prosper Merimée were soon to be well known in the thirties. Artists came from all over the world to study in Paris and discuss for hours the nature of art in the cafés of Montmartre.

Felix finally left her, pressurized no doubt by his family and by his own desire to escape the tender trap of marriage; he removed his quarters from the house in the Place du Palais and spent less and less time with Jane. She met her mother, Lady Andover, at Dover, taking Didi with her but there does not appear to have been any attempt at a reconciliation, although Steely must have ardently desired it. London and Paris were no longer the places in which a divorcée could live and expect to be received into the best society, especially if there had been gossip and scandal! Even in that pre-Victorian age there were limits to which impropriety could be stretched. The British Ambassador at the Court of Bavaria was an old friend of the Digby family and it may well have been he who suggested Munich as a place of residence for Jane and the child; after all, Munich in the first half of the nineteenth century was a lively city, with exciting new buildings, theatres, and a University. Under Ludwig I it had entered into a golden age.

King Ludwig of Bavaria was a godchild of Marie Antoinette and a protégé of Napoleon, ruling from 1825 to 1848. With enormous enthusiasm he plunged into the rebuilding of Munich; he copied Greek and Roman architecture, employing architects who shared his exuberance to the full, laying foundation stones for classical arches and building for him his new Bavarian *Griechenland,* imposing on the city a fantasia of Romanesque, Renaissance and Athenian architectural styles. The family art treasures were housed in the new *Pinakothek,* and the *Walhalla,* or Teuton Hall of Fame, was an almost exact replica of the Parthenon. The rulers of Bavaria lived in the *Residenz,* a beautiful rococo building, restored by Ludwig in the nineteenth century. The Cuvilliés Theatre added grace and lustre to the ageing edifice.

Ludwig was enthusiastic, stubborn, intellectual, and charming. He could be a wild spender on the city he loved, spending his own money on improving methods of agriculture, but in the Royal Household he was parsimonious to a fanatical degree, cutting down the kitchen budgets and refusing to order new textbooks in his University.

The King with the slight impediment in his speech, the wavy fair hair and the cleft chin had other interests, too; there were nymphs of delight, very well suited to his Athenian architecture and for love of one of them he was to lose his throne.

Lola Montez was born in Limerick in 1818 and baptized as Marie Dolores Eliza Rosanna Gilbert. She went to England as a servant girl, married an ensign in the Army, obtained a divorce, and then toddled off to Spain to become a dancer. As a 'Spanish' ballerina she popped up again in London and then went over to the Continent, where, no doubt, exhausted by flamenco whirls and twirls, she came to rest in the arms of the old King of Bavaria; the Treasury paid her and the King made her into a Countess. She was banished from Bavaria in 1848 (The Year of Revolutions) and died in America in 1861. She had great power over Ludwig, his Cabinet being known as the *Lolaministerium,* but the proposal to naturalize her came to nothing. On 20 March 1848 the King abdicated.

In the summer of 1831 Ludwig met Jane. She had decided upon Munich as the next place of residence; it was as lively as Paris and far, far less inhibited than England, where there was no escape from the results of situations which had caused so much scandal in elevated circles and where her indiscretions were never to be forgiven or forgotten; the family turned her picture to the wall in sorrow and in a growing sensitivity which touched off the encroaching tide of Victorian prudery. Jane was never soured by events, never bitter or cynical or unkind. She toiled through her years and her loves weaving the many passionate threads into a rich canvas of sensual delights and then 'all passion spent' accepted, with almost Eastern submission, the unkind fate that lay in store for her.

Jane had been in Munich only a few days when she met Ludwig. It was probably at one of his 'walk-abouts' in the grounds of the *Residenz*, as he stopped to talk to someone in the curious crowd of people who followed his every movement, or it may have been at Tambosi's, the fashionable coffee-house at the entrance to the *Hofgarten*. Wherever it was, it is certain that the English beauty with the shining hair and unmarked skin attracted his attention and engaged him in conversation, acquainting him of her position with her usual disarming frankness. Ludwig's obsession with beautiful women was no secret; he had thirty-six of them, including Jane and Lola Montez, and their portraits, painted by Stieler, gazed down from the walls of the *Nymphenburg,* the summer palace of the Wittelsbachs, with a haughty acceptance of their order in the Kingly hierarchy. Jane and Ludwig lived an almost idyllic life and met almost every day, exchanging letters and little gifts. Her interest in classical architecture delighted him and soon they were 'Ianthe' (the Greek form of Jane) and 'Basilli' (the Greek version of his name). The Queen, Theresa of Saxe-Hildburghausen had moved to separate quarters in the *Residenz* and preferred to remain aloof from any scandal; in any case, there had been a succession of ladies taking up quarters in the King's suite. This was just the romantic interlude that Jane needed, a meeting with a kindred spirit who was also a friend and an adviser. Although everyone accepted the fact that they were lovers, it may well have been that the friendship was platonic for in many letters she addressed him as 'my best and dearest friend'. She sat for her portrait to Stieler; embroidered Ludwig a cap; and asked him to advise her about her personal affairs.

Advice was badly needed at this juncture for her little stage was fast becoming crowded. Whilst out riding in the *Hofgarten* in September, she had met Karl Venningen and, for him, it was love at first sight. The Baron Karl Theodore von Venningen Üllner was a tall, handsome man from a noble family owning estates in Baden and Upper Austria. He took her to masked balls and to the opera and offered her the most glittering prize of all – marriage. Jane was now in a situation strangely comic and yet desperately tragic and wholly complicated. She was in touch with Ludwig, who had left Munich for Italy in the spring of 1832, writing to him of the opera and the music of Bellini which she described as 'magnificent'. She had expected to meet Felix Schwartzenberg in Italy but the anticipated encounter did not take place for he was pressed for time and Jane had to make do with his sister, the Princess Schwarzenberg, who suggested that the Schwartzenbergs keep Didi with them for all time. On 27 January, 1833 Filippo Antonio Herberro (Heribert in German) was born; Jane did not tell Ludwig about the child until three years later and, in fact, he spent his infancy in Marseilles. So now here she was, enmeshed in the old, familiar *scena* – Karl Venningen returning to his duties; little Heribert in Palermo; Didi with the Princess Schwartzenberg and Jane herself in Paris for a short meeting with her mother, which proved abortive.

The Digby family was only too anxious that Jane should be married and that she should finally break with Schwartzenberg as it was evident to all concerned that her passion for him was not returned. 'May Heaven efface his image from my remembrance and help me to keep my resolution of making Karl a good and faithful wife and showing my gratitude at last for all he has done', she wrote to Ludwig. On 16 November, 1833 Jane became the wife of Karl Venningen and, with a civil ceremony in Darmstadt and the title of Baroness Venningen, she was accepted by society at the Munich Court.

Jane, now Baroness Venningen, was anxious that Ludwig should act as godfather to Berthe, the little girl born after the Venningen's return from their two years in Palermo. But the child was not mentally whole and had to be confined in a mental home before she attained the age of twenty years. (Unkind persons said that it was the Wittelsbach strain of insanity, but there was no proof that Ludwig was the father.) In 1834, the Baron and his wife came to Weinheim, a pretty little town, but very unlike Munich; the new Baroness, recently elevated to Court life and royal functions by a marriage which made her 'respectable', grew bored and was ready for any small excitement which might come her way. It came in the spring of 1835 in the shape of Honoré de Balzac, 'a very ugly young man', with decaying teeth, greased hair, untied shoelaces, short legs, and subject to awkwardness. His father had intended him for the law and he duly served his apprenticeship in the offices of a notary, but later he revolted and the 'starving garret' period lasted from 1820 to 1822. Later, he set up as a printer and publisher at No. 17, Rue Visconti in Paris. He was flamboyant, untidy, and sensual, with a rich imagination. His mistresses were many; there was the Marquise de Berny (forty-five years of age and the mother of nine children); La Duchesse d'Abrantès; Madame Garraud; Madame de Castries, and Madame de Hanska, whom he married in 1850. At one time, there were two mistresses, one in Paris and one in the Ukraine. It was probably Laure de Berny who determined the type of woman with whom he was to fall in love; she was wise enough to realize that he needed women who made no claims upon his time and that he would be happiest with 'mature women disappointed in life and love'. With perception, he wrote; 'the woman of forty will do anything for you – the woman of twenty nothing'. To Zulma Carraud he requested that 'if she should happen to come across a woman with a couple of hundred thousand francs, or even a mere hundred thousand' to let him know. His manners were atrocious and his 'tempestuous deluge of eloquence' at the dinner table of his friends infuriated Madame de Hanska.

Honoré, impecunious as usual, was on his way to Vienna to meet Eve Hanska. In a hired carriage, with a manservant, Auguste, he called at Schloss Weinheim, near Heidelberg, where his travelling companion, Prince Alfred von Schönburg, introduced him to Lady Ellenborough. There were no doubt many anecdotes to relate about the famous and the infamous Lady Ellenborough and Balzac, busy with his novel *Le Lys dans la vallée* was intrigued and fascinated. This beautiful Englishwoman (whom he was later to call his 'desert swallow') with a quiver-full of discarded lovers and an enormous capacity for loving, probably gave him the inspiration for the character of Lady Arabella Dudley whom he believed was a faithful picture of an Englishwoman in love; 'I have described the woman of that country admirably in very few words.'

This beautiful English lady, so slender, so fragile, this peaches and cream woman, so soft, so mild-mannered, with her refined brow crowned by shining chestnut hair; this creature who glows with a strange phosphorescence, has a constitution of iron.

Whether the 'peaches and cream woman' was modelled on Jane, Lady Ellenborough, Baroness von Venningen, we have no exact means of knowing. Balzac was impecunious and in debt to Baron James de Rothschild who had lent him money to visit Vienna and meet Madame Hanska; in his frantic effort to finish *Le Lys dans la vallée* he avidly tapped the 'inexhaustible mine of reality' and was undoubtedly relieved to find that the character of Lady Arabella Dudley had come alive for him at Weinheim, although another Englishwoman, the Contessa Guidoboni Visconti, may have contributed to the composite picture. Jane's scandalous behaviour in Paris, where she lived with Prince Schwarzenberg from 1829 to 1831 must have been known to Balzac at the time and his wait of two hours in the park while Prince Alfred von Schönburg visited Jane ('But this miserable prince, as genuine as a counterfeit coin, invited me to go to Weinheim and left me in the garden for five hours, which he spent with his mistress', he wrote to Eve Hanska) afforded him time to mull over his fictional character of Lady Aarbella and placate Eve who was always suspicious of his out-of-town activities. There is no evidence that either Balzac or von Schönberg were Jane's lovers.

Balzac, however, with his deep and almost psychic insight, clearly grasped her fundamental qualities and it is intriguing to note that he described her passions as 'African' and her desires as 'tornadoes' in a burning desert. With what peculiar extra-sensory perception did he assess her future life with a Bedouin Sheik – a life yet to come at the end of a span of thirty years? If Jane felt any chagrin at all over her imagined portrait in *Le Lys dans la vallée*, she easily recovered. After all, Lady Blessington had pushed her ignominiously into the pages of her book *The Two Friends* as Lady Walmer, much to the delight of the sisterhood at Almack's; late joys, like late scandals, could give untold pleasure long after the sun had set.

In the summer of 1835, the Venningens returned to Munich; Karl's brother was ill. A coolness had developed between Jane and Ludwig, although he still wrote to her in affectionate terms. 'Munich is the place of all others I love best', she wrote to him and, considering that this was the time of the *Oktoberfest*, with all its attendant gaiety, it was not surprising. She was not, however, to lose her identity as a German *Hausfrau* in any easy manner, for Karl whisked her away from Munich, no doubt apprehensive that a new affair might develop with the appearance on the scene of a Greek Count Spiridion Theotoky. For centuries Greece had been under the Ottoman yoke and it was not until 1829, when Russia gained a victory over the Turks at Adrianople, that the independence of Greece was guaranteed. Grudgingly, Greece was granted a 'place in the sun' but much was left out of the brave new world of the Hellenes. The Cyclades were received into the new Greece but the Ionian Islands were not and Crete, 'the worse governed province' of the Turkish Empire, was refused autonomy. Greece sought a ruler who would bring stability and order to the country; they found him in Otto, a son of Ludwig I of Bavaria, and enthroned him in 1832 as 'The King of Greece'. He landed at Nauplia on a bleak February day to claim his kingdom, delighting Ludwig who was anxious to revive the lost glories of ancient classical Greece. The new monarchy, however, was a tender blossom, for there was, according to an observer who visited Greece in 1835, 'a want of understanding between the Bavarians and the Greeks'. Many of the Greek youth, reared in the revolutionary tradition, felt that they had exchanged the yoke of Turkey for that of another foreign power. Ludwig poured money into Greece, introducing artists and sculptors and architects, laying the foundations of a new capital and welcoming Greeks to Bavaria, dashing, dark-eyed, handsome young men afire for romance with the Bavarian maidens; he was delighted with the idea of resuscitating the classical tradition.

Spiridion Theotoky, descendant of one of the most noble families in Corfu, was young, dashing, poor, and romantic. He probably met Jane at one of the Carnival Balls in Munich, impressing her with his Byronic charm which embodied the very essence of Greek romanticism. Whatever reason Karl Venningen gave his young wife, he whisked her away to Weinheim in November; Theotoky followed, visiting Heidelberg eleven miles away. It was a wonderful place for lovers, full of classical temples and alcoves just made for discreet meetings, and in the Palace of Schwetzingen the velvet darkness of night covered them with a protective mantle. It was not long before rumours of his wife's indiscretion reached Venningen; Weinheim was a small place, its citizens fully alive to the scandalous past of the Baroness and quite prepared to sympathize with the Baron, a pillar of solid Bavarian society. It is not known what happened at this juncture; there was a ball at the Schwetzingen Palace where Karl may have confronted Jane with the gossip of her love affair with Theotoky (servants at the Palace must have been aware of the goings-on; the late autumn rides in the forest, the not-so-discreet lovers' caresses in the chilly corridors). Whatever ensued, Theotoky importuned Jane to flee with him and the thought of Greek sunshine and golden isles 'where burning Sappho loved and sung' must have appealed to her strongly in the circumstances. A post-chaise was ordered and they fled, Karl in hot pursuit as they galloped madly on the road out of Weinheim. The scene which followed, though harrowing in the extreme, was reminiscent of a third-rate romantic novelette; there was a duel with pistols, the postilions acting as seconds and Jane in anguish as she bent over the wounded Theotoky, evidently breathing his last to the consternation of poor Karl Venningen.

Spiridion survived, however, and with care at Schloss Venningen he recovered his health. Jane took up the threads of her life with a forgiving Karl, no doubt seeking to entice her back into the folds of respectability by visits to Paris and Marseilles, 'to fetch Heribert', the son who would inherit Karl's estates and titles. There were letters to Ludwig at this period and a visit to England in 1837 with Karl and her two children – all quite 'Bavarian' and respectable. Her grandfather, Tom Coke, had been given the title of Earl of Leicester and her two brothers were happily married, giving sixteen children to the nation between them. Nevertheless, Jane's visit to her family must have awakened memories, 'England has too many painful associations for me to be sorry to quit it', and she returned to the 'horrid, little town' of Weinheim, correspondence between her and Ludwig evidently ceasing after 1838. In the spring of 1839 she left for Paris to live with Theotoky – her husband, friends, and children abandoned; the cloak of Bavarian respectability falling lightly from her young shoulders; the road to Elysium open. She was now 'Ianthe' in mind and spirit. Karl Venningen never once uttered a rebuke to the butterfly who loved to alight on whichever flower that took her fancy; he never censured or blamed her.

There were carefree years in Paris before Theotoky took her to the ancestral home on Corfu. In Paris they had lived as man and wife, taking up residence at 83, Place Bourbon and on 21 March 1840 Jane was delivered of a child, Jean Henry, Comte Theotoky – Leonidas to his parents. Karl Venningen had written Jane a heart-rending letter, apparently not knowing that she had borne a child in Paris; 'in cold and sad Germany a warm and faithful heart is beating for you, a heart which will *never* forget the happiness and the heavenly bliss you gave him during several years': the 'heavenly bliss' was now given to another. Jane asked for a divorce, which was granted, with the whole question of the legitimacy of the young Jean Henry being dragged through the Courts in a legal tangle which established the paternity of the child Jane loved above all her children; Count Theotoky was the father.

Karl Venningen never re-married and remained Jane's sincere friend, anxious as to her welfare, and informing her of the progress of their children. In July 1874, humiliated, disappointed, and ever faithful to Jane, he was killed in a riding accident in Munich.

Of Jane's children, Arthur Dudley Law died at the age of two; Didi, Schwartzenberg, was brought up by the Schwartzenberg family and remained loyal to them for the rest of her life; Heribert, the son of Karl Venningen, born before they married, was brought up elsewhere than the family home as a young child; Berthe, his sister, was placed in an institution before the age of twenty, not mentally capable of dealing with life. Children came and went in those days with surprising rapidity, for infant mortality was high; if a child survived its first year it often died in early infancy and strange and fearsome instruments were used to facilitate a difficult birth. Children of the upper classes were looked after by nurses and governesses, seldom seeing their parents except for presentation before guests, where they bobbed and curtseyed prettily before being whisked off back to the nursery hinterlands. The children of the working-classes were world's apart; they were fodder for the fields and the machines, working up to fifteen hours a day and often dying by their looms.

Jane enjoyed her residence in Corfu, settling down to domestic bliss after her conversion to the Greek Orthodox faith and spending a great deal of time laying out gardens and planting trees. She imported treasures to furnish the Corfu home at Dukades and gathered books to form an English library. She learnt Greek and entertained in the grand manner with balls and levées which astounded the local upper-crust, while the long hot summers were passed on horseback exploring the sun-warmed countryside. It all ended in the summer of 1844, for Spiridion Theotoky was called to serve in Athens as aide-de-camp to Otto, the Bavarian 'King of Greece', Ludwig's son.

There were many male children with the name of Spiridion in Corcyra (Corfu). They were named after St Spiridion, who lies in a richly carved sarcophagus in the Church of St Spiridion, his little mummified body looking quite at ease and his little feet, encased in embroidered slippers, peeping out of an aperture at the bottom. He did good works and performed miracles and when he died, some years over ninety, his relics were removed to Constantinople, and brought back to Greece with those of another saint, Theodora Augusta; the two of them were tucked cosily away in two sacks strapped to an unsuspecting mule as it ambled into Greece. In 1456 they were brought to Corcyra and finally laid to rest in the chapel of Michael the Archangel. St Spiridion is brought flowers and candles and four times a year he sees something of the town as his casket is borne in procession.

Since independence had been granted to Greece, there had been much discontent, fostered by many reasons, chief of which was the granting of positions to Bavarians, instead of to Greeks who had fought to oust the hated Turks. Otto's Bavarian autocracy had not been entirely a wise one for he had immersed himself in petty details instead of applying himself to the major issues of policy and, as his own Prime Minister, he learnt and digested every decree submitted to him and 'took ten days to decide who was to be a schoolmaster in Syra'. The bloodless coup of 15 September, 1843 brought about the replacement of Bavarians by Greeks and the king was forced to grant a constitution. The result for the Theotokys was a call to Athens and the end of the pastoral interlude for Jane. It was also the beginning of a new love, more romantic and more passionate than she had ever known before, a love almost savage in its intensity.

Athens was at that date little more than a collection of fishermen's quarters down by the Piraeus; there was a Turkish quarter, with ramshackle 'shanty town' huts full to overflowing with children and chickens and a new *Neopolis* with residential houses built of marble plastered over, whose inhabitants considered themselves the cream of Athenian society, affecting a mode of dress they considered fashionable and speaking the French language. Lord Byron remarked of Greece at that time; "'Tis Greece, but *living* Greece no more.' Ruined by Turkish oppression and misrule, the cultivation of the soil and the spirit of industry was stifled by successive rulers and the Greeks, who had regarded Otto as the saviour of their country, tore their country apart by rival political intrigues, at variance in a ruined and devastated land. There were 6,000 to 8,000 troops in Greece, paid for by Greek money 'marching in hot dusty weather in the neighbourhood of Athens to the sound of fife and drum, elevating their arms and legs in the air at the word of command, and moving with conceited strut in long files'. A traveller of the time, Charles G. Addison, thought that the labour and exertions of troops marching and countermarching across the Greek plains resulted in nothing and that the money for their keep would have been better spent in fostering Greek industry and constructing canals and plantations. The countryside died and the forests shrank as the trees were felled and not replaced and goats ate up the young seedlings intended for the fields. Ludwig found Otto a bride in the young Princess Maria Frederica Amalia but the marriage was not a success and the pretty young German lady had little inclination towards responsibility. She proved to be domineering, jealous, and extravagant and, in the absence of Otto, who was painstaking to a degree, scampered through the paper-work as though she were playing at royalty.

> Lavenders Blue, Diddle diddle,
> Lavenders Green,
> When I am King Diddle-Diddle,
> You shall be Queen.

Edmond About paints us a picture of the royal pair;

The King appears older than he is. He is tall, thin, feeble and worn out with fever; his face is pale and worn, his eyes dim: his appearance is sad and suffering, and his look anxious. The use of sulphate quinine has made him deaf . . . His mind, according to all those who have worked with him, is timid, hesitating and minute. His last word in every business is always 'We will see'.

Amalia seems to have been a veritable amazon, full of a restless energy which one suspects must have contributed in no small measure to Otto's decline. About writes;

The Queen is a woman who will not grow for a long time; her *embonpoint* will preserve her . . . In the summer she gets up at three in the morning to bathe in the sea at Faliron, where she swims for an hour without rest.

About also noticed Ianthe;

I have often met Ianthe, who used to leap the ditches on a splendid white horse. She was the best rider in town; when she went out, followed by a large company of friends, she made such a grand appearance that the little boys always ran to salute her as she passed; they thought she must be the Queen. The Queen will never forget those mistakes.

The Queen did not forget, or forgive, 'those mistakes'. Jane had met Otto and had evidently captivated him, although his morals were of the strictest and he was a perfect husband, Amalia was jealous of Ianthe's popularity. She herself was spoken of as 'one of the most beautiful princesses in Europe', wearing the National (Albanian) costume with grace and galloping and riding about the kingdom oblivious of the countryside through which she passed, treeless and poor. The great grievance to her was that she was childless and no amount of sliding down the Hill of the Nymphs or drinking the orange-flower water would result in a birth.

Jane and the dashing Count were now drifting apart; according to Eugènie (Jane's maid), Spiridion had indulged in several extra-marital activities and only their mutual love for their little son, Leonidas, held them together. In the heat of the summer, Athenian 'society' left Greece for spas and bathing resorts in slightly cooler climes and the Theotoky's also left the blistering, dusty heat of Athens to spend the summer at Bagna di Lucca, a Tuscan village at the base of the Appenines, a beautiful place of trees and cool courtyards and a flourishing colony of English writers and ex-patriots who rented luxurious villas such as that of Mrs Stisted, 'the Queen of the Baths'. The house which they rented was tall, with balconies running round three sides and shutters of dark green. It proved to be a tragic house for Jane, for little Leonidas, anxious to see the guests at one of his mother's receptions, peered over a top balcony, lost his balance and fell on to the cold marble floor far below. It was a shattering blow for Jane for she had now lost the one child she really loved and had cut herself off by her misdeeds from her family in England (only one of her brothers, who had taken Holy Orders, ever wrote to her) although she did see Lady Andover from time to time.

In 1849 Jane was once again in Athens, striking up a friendship with Sophie, the Duchess of Plaisance, whose husband had been one of Napoleon's generals and whose daughter Louise had died whilst Sophie was travelling around Europe, endeavouring to find her a suitable husband. Jane and Sophie were of similar disposition; the duchess was witty and intelligent, though slightly eccentric and the fact that they had each lost children must have drawn them together. Jane, separated from Spiridion Theotoky, found

Sophie good company and her peculiar views on religion (she thought that God was personally interested in her) were, no doubt, amusing enough, but the life at the villa in Athens was no substitute for the love that loved 'too well'. Long ago, whilst in Paris with Felix Schwartzenberg, a fortune-teller had predicted that Jane would know many lovers. Edmond About recalls the incident where Jane told him about the prophesy;

IANTHE: 'A long time ago I consulted Mlle. LeNormand; she predicted that I would turn many heads ...'
ABOUT: 'One would not have to be a fortune teller to know that.'
IANTHE: '– and amongst others, three crowned heads. Although I've been searching, I can find only two.'
ABOUT: 'That's because the third one is in the future.'

The 'Third One' may have been a certain Cristos Hadji-Petros, wearing the red cap of the Greeks, or it may have been Otto, King of Greece.

Cristos Hadji-Petros had risen from a brigand-in-chief in the mountains of Albania to the position of aide-de-camp to King Otto of Greece. Literature had romanticized the brigands and public opinion had been inclined to look upon them as charming rascals and rollicking ruffians, using their lawlessness to protect the down-trodden peasantry and extort what ransom money and bribes they could from the wealthy and the powerful in the comic-opera age of Greek royalty and Greek politics. There was a darker side of the picture; well-authenticated stories, submitted to the government, told of torture and the use of boiling oil and thumb screws and no traveller cared to plan an expedition without first ascertaining which parts were free from brigands. After 1870, all this changed; the government troops came to grips with them and the last of the brigands was caught and hanged.

There remained the Palikars, the chieftains who had fought for Greek independence from Turkish rule and who now regarded themselves as conquerors and saviours of Greece; those who had harried the Turks for years left their mountain fastnesses and entered into a more enlightened age, striding about in their short gold-embroidered jackets and white kilts, with their hair swinging about their shoulders in long ringlets. They were foot-loose and without employment; for the most part petted by the aristocracy who were only too anxious to keep in well with these wild men of the mountains – the Palikars, whose portraits hang in the Museum of the Historical and Ethnological Society and whose name is a Greek corruption of 'Chevalier', from the days of the Frankish Dukes of Athens. They were not admitted to Athenian society but once a year they graced the Court Ball on New Year's Eve, living it up in style on money from blackmail and extortion and from sources which it was wiser not to question. The Minister for Foreign Affairs found it advisable to placate his unruly neighbours, for his beautiful house at Tatoi was vulnerable.

Cristos Hadji-Petros was a Palikar who came to Athens at sixty years of age; with his moustache and white hair and all the fire of the craggy mountains in his ageing blood, he was truly Edmond About's 'King of the Mountains', fascinating the English rose as he took his ease, surrounded by his loyal group of Palikars, in the house opposite Jane's in Athens. The pattern emerged once more as Jane's kindness to his small son, Eirini, brought them into contact and soon it was the familiar story of kindling passion and self-abnegation to a powerful lover who could still gallop with her over the wildest country and live with her the free life she desired. There were no rivals for Jane; for the most part the Palikar women were stodgy and uncomplaining, living their uneventful lives in bleak mountain retreats, servants and footstools for their lords and masters.

Her life with Cristos (he had tacked on the 'Hadji' as he had been on a pilgrimage to Mecca) began in 1852 in Athens, but before long he was assigned to the garrison at Lamia – it was a change of which Jane thoroughly approved. Now there was excitement of Homeric proportions, with Jane throwing caution to the winds, dressing as a Palikar woman, eating the Palikar food, and sleeping rough in the pure air of the hills, giving no thought to the morrow or the loves of yesteryear. There was only Cristos.

But it was not to last – nothing lasted with Jane. Amalia had her ear to the ground and all that she missed the society gossips supplied in full measure, providing a grand opportunity for vengeance upon the English beauty who had invaded Athens and about whom Edmond About had written;

She has great blue eyes, as deep as the sea; beautiful chestnut hair, highlighted here and there by golden tones; as for her teeth, she belongs to that élite of the English nation who have pearls in their mouths instead of piano keys.

Cristos Hadji-Petros was abruptly dismissed from his post at the Lamia garrison and the two lovers returned from the mountains to Athens to face a situation which, to Jane at least, must have seemed very familiar. Cristos petitioned the Queen in writing, explaining, with cap in hand, his motives for the liaison; 'if I am the lover of this woman, it is not for love but for profit', and explained in humble terms that he had children to bring up and that Jane's money would come in useful. The letter was published and soon all Athens knew of the affair but Jane continued loving her brigand who had such sycophantic tendencies; time passed and the situations which remained unresolved added one more year to the constant cycle of disenchantment.

Money was never any problem; her £3,000 a year was more than enough to pay her way in Greece and jewels could always fetch more. It was just as well that money was in plentiful supply, for life with Cristos had been one long outpouring of hospitality; Turks and brigands from the wild mountains, cut-throats, pillagers, and dastardly murderers who killed for ransom money – all enjoyed Cristos' lavish welcome in the mansion Jane had provided. Jane intended to marry Cristos and sought freedom from her marriage to Theotoky who was still living on his wife's income, happily going his own way and not in the least concerned about brigands and Palikars.

The marriage was duly annulled and all Athens waited for the grand finale which would unite in holy Greek matrimony the two reckless lovers, of whom one was well over sixty and the other now forty-six. The marriage did not take place, although Jane had already put in hand the building of a mansion which would be magnificent, but there were obstacles. Eugènie, the French maid who had served her well, was now growing older and had become very tired with all the hours of devoted work she had so willingly contributed to Madame's well-being and comfort and the excitement of life with Jane, settling in to fresh homes, whirling about in coaches from one residence to another as the seasons passed, grappling with Jane's moods as each new affair loomed on the horizon and spending hours in tears and sympathy as sorrow struck, was taking its toll. Now there was another small problem to be settled. Cristos Hadji-Petros was making advances to her and, loyally, she told Jane. It may have been a lie for her own self-preservation in order that she could remain with Jane on the same footing without the benefit of rubbing shoulders with the Palikars, in what could only be described as a brigands's nest. The bodyguard of Palikars were everywhere about the house, lounging and smoking in the doorways and on the stairs, thrusting their great bodies into rooms of elegance and refinement and extending the Palikars welcome to visiting friends with little observance of decorum and behaviour except that of the mountains and the wild, uncluttered hills.

Whatever the reason, Jane believed her and the result was a total cleavage with Cristos. She had been interested for some time in the purchase of Arab bloodstock from Syria and with this as an excuse she and Eugènie slipped away from Athens with Cristos unaware of the decampment. The humiliation must have cut deeply; the fact that her wild, independent Palikar lover had turned out to be a fawning sycophant, writing an abject letter of apology to the Queen, was bad enough, but to have enjoyed her money and the prestige which association with a lady of nobility brought to him and his friends and then make covert amorous advances to a *femme de chambre* was beyond belief!

The excuse of the purchase of Arab horses presented Jane with a valid excuse for departure and gave her a much-needed breathing space; she now had an escape route, not back to Western Europe, but to unknown territory further East. In the burning vastness of the deserts she could find peace and mend a broken heart; time, no longer on her side, could be halted a little and the tempestuous past placed on one side, hostage to the 'unforgiving minute'.

Little did she know that the last adventure of her life was just beginning and that the love she had searched for in ducal mansions and on goat-skin rugs in the sunless bosom of inhospitable mountains was to be found in the black tents of the Bedouin. When she sailed from Piraeus she was forty-six years of age.

She landed in Syria, planning to visit Jerusalem, Baalbeck and Palmyra. It was the age of expansion and travel; the European 'Grand Tour' was becoming routine and the Near East beckoned to those with time and money and a strong stomach who were fascinated by songs of Araby and love under desert stars. The romantic side, spawned by writers and poets, had its enthusiastic adherents but serious exploration was also taking place. Carsten Niebuhr's expedition in 1761–64 to the Yemen fostered interest in the whole of Arabia. Joseph Halévy travelled widely in south-west Arabia, making important discoveries of Sabaean inscriptions a few years after Jane landed at Beirut. J. L. Burckhardt had already won a reputation as the discoverer of Petra and Richard Burton travelled in the Hejaz as an Afghan pilgrim and reached Medina and Mecca in disguise. There were many others who travelled in the Middle East, often in great danger and discomfort. Palgrave had an intimate knowledge of Syria and the Arabic language, though his descriptions were later challenged as being geographically incorrect. Charles Doughty described desert life in great detail, discovering the famous inscribed stone at Taima which found its way to the Louvre and Wilfrid and Lady Anne Blunt travelled on a Persian pilgrim caravan in 1878, taking with them horses which were to form the Crabbet Park stud. There were many Jane did not know, but Richard and Isabel Burton she was to know intimately in a future as yet unborn.

Burckhardt's Petra, the old capital of the Nabateans, was known to Jane for she must have been conversant with the works of Strabo and Pliny from the well-stocked library at Holkham and it is almost certain that her interest in Palmyra was aroused when she first saw the architectural sketches in *The Ruins of Palmyra*, published in 1751. Jane was a woman of culture, with a lively imagination and a thorough grasp of whatever subject she happened to be studying; in spite of all her tempestuous love-affairs she had found time to read the books which came regularly in boxes from Paris and London.

Beirut was a good setting-off place, a spring board for the whole of Syria and Jane lost no time in visiting a bank and arranging for horses.

The horses were ready and no doubt Eugènie viewed the future with rather less apprehension now that the Palikars' episode appeared to be over and done with. The identification of Jane with the Arab world and the Arab mind was about to begin; the wild life of the desert was to take the place of the unfettered life with Cristos and his brigands; Oriental splendour was to supplant Albanian crudity – and the ways of the Koran were to graft themselves on to the Christian ethic.

Once again, a new passion arose in the shape of Saleh, a young Bedouin whom she met whilst bargaining for a horse. In his book *Le Grèce Contemporaine* Edmond About wrote; 'Ianthe found in an Arab tribe the thoroughbred horse she was looking for. The animal belonged to a sheik, who was young and strikingly handsome.' The sheik had three wives but About wrote; 'The sheikh found her more exciting than his three wives put together.'

The sheik appears to have been lusty and impetuous; he swept Jane off her feet and into the black tents of his tribe. Gone were the days of the 'horrid little town' of Heimein and fast fading the colourful dream of a sedate old age with a Palikar man of over sixty in an Athenian mansion full of brigands. Jane desired marriage and forgot the difference in their ages, and the parting came, as it inevitably did, with Saleh remaining with his tribe and Jane pushing on to Damascus to start the great journey to Palmyra, fast becoming a place of great historical interest to western travellers.

Jane loved Damascus. It was cool, green, and fertile, watered by the Barada river and sheltered from the fierce winds from the Syrian desert. She was magnetized by the historical associations of which she had read and fascinated by the ancient walls, the city gates, the bazaars, and the Great Mosque. There were private houses, too, away from the inner city, with great contrasts between the outside and the inside; the entrances were by means of doors leading into narrow, winding passages while mud walls and rickety, projecting chambers hid the Outer Courts with their marble pavements. Inside there were halls and chambers, with inner courts leading to the *harim*, the doors of which were guarded by eunuchs.

Jane's attempts to get to Palmyra met with opposition and she soon found that an escort for the ten days' journey on horseback was not possible. The British Consul, Richard Wood, thought it a most foolhardy idea and disclaimed all responsibility. With voluminous luggage and a reputation for dangerous, and often bizarre modes of travel, Jane's hopes of an exciting and safe trek were doomed to disappointment. She was advised to contact the Mesrab Arabs who controlled the desert in the Palmyra area. There was brigandage amongst the various tribes as there was amongst the Greek mountain-men and wealthy travellers were fair game for ultimate ransom, their release being a pre-arranged affair, one band of Arabs scaring the life out of the weary travellers with their shouts and wild cries, the other most solemnly effecting their release.

It was all, of course, a put-up job; thanks to Allah, money and valuables could be shared. Thus a journey across the desert could be very hazardous indeed, with marauding Arabs and internecine warfare between the tribes, especially if the wells along the route were not known in advance.

The Mesrabs were a desert tribe of the Anazeh Bedouins and their Sheik, Mohammed was a descendant of one of the noblest of the tribe of Saba. His younger brother, Medjuel, was educated; he could read and write and spoke several languages. He was no longer young, for he had sons and so was hardly the man to supplant the lusty Saleh. Lady Anne Blunt met Medjuel some years later and described him;

A very well bred and agreeable man . . . In appearance he shews all the characteristics of good Bedouin blood. He is short and slight in stature, with exceedingly small hands and feet, a dark olive complexion, beard originally black, but now turning grey, and dark eyes and eyebrows.

Isabel Burton, whom Jane was to meet later in Damascus and with whom she was to become friendly, had her own interpretation of Medjuel whom she also knew; 'the contact with that black skin I could *not* understand. His skin is dark – darker than a Persian – much darker than an Arab generally is. All the same, he was a very intelligent charming man in any light but that of a husband. That made me shudder.'

It evidently did not make Jane shudder, for she married him and he became her fourth husband.

But that the future held; the present was enough for Jane. The two met to

[88]

discuss terms for the journey; the well-bred, intellectual Arab and the much-travelled, much-loved English lady who had trailed her affairs and her enormous amount of luggage across Europe and into Syria. The fine linen and the exquisite silver were loaded and Jane, admired by the Arabs for her steady mounting of the camel, set out with a delighted heart across the desert, under the protection of the great Saba tribe and with the mental picture of the passionate Saleh ever before her eyes. It was a delightful escapade for Jane, her past frustrations and embarrassments shut away in a time-lock for which she had no key. The mornings began with a sparse breakfast and hot tea, with Jane taking the creases from her riding dress, and in the evenings the black goat-hair tents were erected and the insides spread with oriental rugs. During the day there was hunting, and, for Jane, sketching in the desert. The evenings were the best of all, with Medjuel explaining to Jane the life and legends of his people.

The caravan pressed on to Palmyra, Jane filled with thoughts of Saleh and Medjuel teetering on the brink of declaring his love. The name Palmyra is supposed to have been given by the Greeks, but the Arabs called it Tadmor and Josephus Thadamoura. Palmyra had arisen to meet the desert-borne trade, like Jerash and Petra, and the cultures of Babylonia, Assyria, and Syria were blended in her. With prosperity came the development of the trans-desert routes; patrolled at first by Palmyrene forces and later by Roman soldiers. Wells and fortified posts were thirty miles apart and the principal road under the Roman occupation connected Palmyra with Hit, with a branch to the Euphrates. After the capture of Zenobia and the sack of the town, it was restored by the Byzantine Emperors and under the Saracens from the seventh to the fifteenth century it once again became commercially important. First visited by an Englishman in the late seventeenth century, archaeologists discovered its historical importance in 1918.

When Lady Hester Stanhope visited the antique city she claimed that the Bedouins had crowned her queen – just like another Zenobia! Monsieur de Lamartine, on his travels in Syria, interviewed this extraordinary lady and gave his personal interpretation and the *Quarterly Review* of 1835 presented its own view;

We are rather inclined to M. de Lamartine's view of the character of this singular woman. She has so long been acting a part, at first probably assumed for the purpose of obtaining interest over wild and superstitious clans among whom she has settled in her mountain palace-citadel of Lebanon, that she has begun to act it in earnest.

Jane never acted a part; she was intensely interested in all she saw and recorded meticulously every detail of the desert scenes she loved to observe and to paint.

For Jane, Palmyra was the jewel in the lotus. She had long been conversant with the story of Zenobia, the tragic queen who monopolized all the caravan trade of the Syrian desert until she attempted to establish her autonomy and flaunted her independence from the Roman Emperor, Aurelian. It was a mistake, and Zenobia threw away her kingdom for the sake of ambition and lived to see the walls and aqueducts of her city dismembered by the Roman legions. To Jane, accustomed to German forests and Greek mountains, the sight of the ruined city must have been wonderful indeed. The great caravan road which crossed the city could be conjectured and of the original 375 fluted columns of rose-red limestone 150 still stood with their bases in the wind-blown sand. There were tombs and inscriptions and votive altars and statues erected to the honour of the *synodiarchs*, or caravan leaders, who were responsible for the trade of the city in far-away ports. Gods were honoured by altars erected to Arsu and Azizu, the patron gods of caravaners and the fiscal laws of the city were made known to the inhabitants by inscriptions upon a tablet bearing the date AD 137. The great avenue led to a triumphal arch flanked by two smaller ones, leading to the Temple of the Sun. Many travellers had seen these wonders through the ages, Saracens and Seljuk Turks and Ottoman Turks, and some had written of the great city they had seen.

Some years after Jane's death, Dr William Wright gave an account of Palmyra in his book *An Account of Palmyra and Zenobia* and described the ruins in great detail. He was not impressed by the Temple 'in its present state' and the broken walls with columns standing like a 'huge lumber-yard of columns'.

Within we find the whole area of the temple filled with clay-daubed huts, so that we can only get an idea of the place by climbing over them. We pass on straight to the Holy of Holies, which we explore with our handkerchiefs held to our noses, for the inmost shrine is the cesspool of the community. We hurry out to the fresh air; but it is not fresh, for all the offal and filth of the houses are flung out into the narrow lanes, and lie rotting in the sun. Wherever we go among these human dens there reek filth and squalor, and the hot pestiferous atmosphere of an ill-kept stye. Such is now the state of that gorgeous temple which the proud Tadmorenes raised to their gods, which were no gods, and where they glorified one another in monuments of perishable stone.

The tombs were the most interesting part of Palmyra. Sir Richard Burton, when Consul in Damascus, had visited the ruins and advised Dr Wright to take ladders and ropes and grappling irons for the ascent of the towers 'which he had been unable to examine for lack of such appliances'. The tomb-towers were more than a hundred feet high, housing grim relics of bones and skulls.

To Jane at that time it was all harmonious, different – but harmonious; the all-embracing desert by day and the soft sounds of the Bedouin camp by night. Jane was now more determined than ever to marry Saleh and settle down in Syria to a life of domestic bliss, a dutiful wife carrying out her humble duties to her Arab overlord in compliance with Koranic law. The status of women in Arabia did not interest her but she would have been fascinated, no doubt, by Doughty's account;

The woman's lot is here unequal concubinage, and in this necessitous life a weary servitude. The possession in her of parents and tutors has been yielded at some price (in contempt and constraint of her weaker sex,) to an husband, by whom she may be dismissed in what day he shall have no more pleasure in her . . . And his heart is not hers alone; but, if not divided already, she must look to divide her marriage in a time to come with others. And certainly as she withers, which is not long to come, or having no adventure to bear male children, she will as thing unprofitable be cast off; meanwhile all the house-labour is hers, and with his love will be lost. Love is a dovelike confidence, and thereto consents not the woman's heart that is wronged.

The 'dove-like confidence' was already beginning to blossom between Jane and Medjuel, and Medjuel was to prove his strength to protect her. Between Damascus and Palmyra the caravan fell into the hands of brigands the Arab raiders coming at them with pointed lancers, but the story goes that Medjuel subdued them and the caravan went on its way without further incident. It was all highly dramatic and raised Medjuel in Jane's esteem to the stature of a desert hero. The story also goes that Medjuel asked her to marry him, offering to give up his wife. In the Palmyrene ruins, lit by intense moonlight, it was just possible. But there were matters to see to which needed her attention; there was the house in Athens to sell and her affairs to wind up. Only then could she make Syria her home and live forever with Saleh.

The caravan returned to Damascus in great splendour; the camels raced to their home base, Medjuel changing to a magnificent Arab horse, and the crowd applauding and shouting words of welcome. It was a heart-warming scene, with the green background of the city and the cool courtyards inviting Jane to stay, but it was imperative that she return to Greece and settle her affairs. So the house was duly sold and her jewels put into a safe place. Sophie, the Duchess of Plaisance, evidently did not approve of the stories Jane told her; she had been willing to lend an aristocratic ear to her amusing tales of illicit love, but an Arab was quite another thing. She probably felt that Jane had, this time, gone a little too far. The friendship cooled, and Sophie died the following year.

Cristos Hadji-Petros continued to press his suit (no doubt thinking of the advantages of a regular income) but Jane had finished with Greek brigands. She longed for Saleh and returned to Syria, hot-footing it across the desert to find a young beauty installed, a dark-eyed girl named Sabla. Jane, hostage to fortune, returned to Damascus to lick her wounds once more. Now there was nothing. Europe was finished and the *salons* closed to her, but she had attained the Eden to which each country had been a stumbling step and the prospect of buying a small house in Damascus and living out her life with the faithful Eugènie was totally inviting.

Jane loved Damascus. George Robinson, an English visitor in 1837, gives us a description of the city which, in the intervening years before Jane was resident, could not have changed much.

The Hebrew name of the city was Damasek or Demesk, by which it is still known and from which is formed the Damascus of the Greeks and Latins. Damascus does not altogether answer the expectations held out by its exterior appearance.

He found the streets narrow and irregular and 'a sort of mysterious silence prevails throughout'. The bazaars redeemed the unfavourable impression for he found the shopkeepers well-dressed 'and extremely civil to strangers'.

The bazaars were closed at night with iron gates and the streets were headed off with wooden barriers; there being no lights it was extremely difficult and dangerous to visit friends. The mosques were numerous and were formerly Christian churches; the principal one was in the centre of the city and it was unwise for a Christian to enter into the courtyard. The coffee houses were 'numerous and elegant', with climbing plants, where the ear could be soothed by running streams. The gardens surrounding the city were a mass of verdure; the damascene plum or damson shed its blossom like a carpet. There were Christian associations, too, in the heaps of gravel and earth about a mile from the city which indicated the tombs of devout Christians and the spot in the wall where Paul is said to have been let down in a basket. A low wall enclosed the town and the citadel in the centre housed the residence of the Governor. Such was the Damascus into which Jane entered with Medjuel and in which she was to die.

The country of Syria was still to be explored and there was plenty of time to settle down. There were wonderful sights to see and sketch and many ancient ruins to roam over, in spite of an aching heart. Jane was never the one to spend 'many pleasant years unknown to fame' and the prospect of visiting other desert countries was exciting.

There were many hazards along the routes; caravan leaders chose those along which wells were known to exist, but often in the summer months the wadis would be dry and the water below only to be reached by back-aching digging; tolls had to be paid and gifts made, not only to cross the Euphrates, but when a stream was forded; each city exacted a transit tax and every caravanserai had a head-tax on both man and beast. The Euphrates in flood was apt to make the lowland parts of the desert slippery with mud and the laden camels could slip and upset their loads, causing a complete breakdown. Last, but not least, there was the bitter cold at night and the scourge of the winds; in September the north-east wind; in April and May the 'glass furnace' and in summer the dreaded Shamel, the 'poison wind'. There could be snow in winter and downpours of rain, when tents became soaked and bedding saturated with water.

It was a challenge Jane loved and only one thing was missing – another Saleh or Medjuel. Fate provided one in the shape of Sheik el Barrak, Jane's escort on the caravan; in the loneliness of the desert and the comfort and warmth of the evening camp-fire the perfect atmosphere for romance was produced. Jane, at forty-six years of age, still felt that passionate, and refined love was her due and with Sheik el Barrak it would seem that she had found another soul-mate. Love blossomed on the road to Aleppo but by the time the caravan had crossed the Euphrates Jane had become dis-illusioned, for el Barrak did not measure up to either Saleh or Medjuel. There were quarrels about his lack of consideration for the camels (Jane was always an animal-lover) and over his denigration of her painting talent. For el Barrak, it was just adventure, something to while away the time. He took his revenge on Jane by assigning some women of the tribe to her tent; this was a shocking invasion of her privacy and would never have been countenanced by Bedouins. It had all been a disaster, another love affair to rend her heart. 'But what folly!' she wrote in her diary.

On the way back to Damascus, Medjuel rode out to meet her, bringing a beautiful Arab mare as a gift. The caravan was now in Mesrab country and el Barrak wisely decided to forego any further dalliance with Jane. Medjuel was the same, serious man whom Jane had known. True to his word he had divorced his wife by returning to her the dowry which she had brought him and had sent her back to her people. He was now a free man, ready to marry Jane. The only serious obstacle was his family, who were hostile to her and not at all in favour of their son, a member of a proud and noble Arab family of wealth and honour, entering into a marriage with a foreign lady who was not a Muslim. Jane accepted Medjuel's proposal of marriage with all the thrill and passion of a first romance and the 'dear desert that I am so fond of' was to become her last home and her final resting place. It was not, however, all plain sailing. Richard Wood, the British Consul in Damascus, thought it all the height of folly and wondered if she were not losing her mind. Gently he pointed out the position of women in Arab society and the fact that up to four wives were allowed by Islamic law. Instructions were awaited from England which might conceivably alter Jane's mind; in the meantime the marriage took place at Homs in a ceremony according to Islamic law, which must have seemed very different from those she had experienced in the Anglican, Catholic, and Greek Orthodox churches. Medjuel made a pact with Jane; he agreed that he would live in the western fashion, taking only one woman to be his lawful wife but if he so desired in the future, he would be free to take a Bedouin woman and keep the fact of so doing from Jane so that she would have no knowledge of any more youthful rival and so remain happy and content. Isabel Burton met Jane sixteen years later; 'Gossip said that he had other wives, but she assured me that he had not, and that both her brother Lord Digby and the British Consul required a legal and official statement to that effect before they were married.'

At first they set up house in Homs and by degrees Medjuel's family came to like and respect Jane; they called her Jane Digby el Mesrab and, as a token of admiration, Umn-el-Laban, Mother of Milk, as her skin was so fair. She adopted Arab ways, wearing the traditional blue robe and yashmak and her beautiful eyes were accentuated by the use of Kohl. The Arabs were greatly impressed by her horsemanship and she obviously enjoyed the hunting days with Medjuel in the desert; the dromedaries were not the easiest of beasts to ride but Jane Digby el Mesrab rode them, quite nonplussed by their erratic pitching and tossing. 'Dear, useful animals', she called them. She began to speak the Arabic she had learnt, but with a gutteral accent, unlike the classical Arabic spoken by Medjuel. Her life was now a part of the desert; the vast, silent spaces of heat and cold and thirst held no terrors for her and the struggle against the elements was sufficient to blot out any desire to savour the artificial life of the western city. When Medjuel went off into the desert for weeks at a time, she was heart-broken, fearful that fate would take him from her and thus punish her for her marriage to a non-believer.

Her family were shattered by this final blow of marriage to an Arab and life in a Bedouin tent; Steely, who had become companion to Lady Andover, must have been mortally stricken by Jane's plunge into the world of what she would have considered the 'Victorian novelette' and addressed a letter to her as 'Madame Theotoky', refusing to recognize the black Bedouin and the black Bedouin tents.

In the autumn of 1856 Jane embarked at Beirut for a visit to England. She had received a letter from her sister-in-law with news of the death of Lord Digby; he had died childless and Jane's brother Edward was now heir to the family fortune. There were matters to settle which concerned Jane and so, she sailed once more for England. The Greek ship touched at the port of Piraeus, the port of so many memories; Hadje-Petros was there on the dockside, emotionally disturbed and tearfully reproachful, unhappy and distraught as he told her of the illness of his young son, Eirini, whom Jane had loved as her own child. Oddie, in her book *The Odyssey of a Loving Woman* tells of the reunion;

Cristodoulos struck a heroic attitude at once. Forget her? How could he forget her? Betray her love by making overtures to a common graceless creature like Eugènie? How could Jane believe such things of him? There was not a word of truth in the story. It was an infamous fabrication of Eugènie's own. Could any man who had loved Ianthe – who had been privileged to enjoy Ianthe's love and tenderness give anyone like Eugènie a thought? He went on weeping as he assured her that she had broken his heart, ruined his life, at seventy, wrecked his career.

Jane was unmoved. Greece no longer appealed to her; after the Crimean War Piraeus had been occupied by England and France and the Palikars had begun to lose the romantic image of brigands wild and free in the mountains. Besides, it all seemed a long time ago.

On 19 December she stepped ashore at Folkestone and journeyed to Tunbridge Wells in company with Jane Steele, sister of Steely, to meet Lady Andover. Lady Andover and Steely had both grown older – perhaps the wrinkles on Steely's face were due to prolonged worry over Jane's *amours*. As the days went by, there was much family talk and a thaw in the atmosphere, but Medjuel and Syria were never mentioned in kindness or affection;

Regency latitude had given way to Victorian formality and strict middle-class morality and society was now profoundly shocked. Only Jane's brother Kenelm, who had taken Holy Orders, took a lenient view and she still remained to him his dear sister. It was a harrowing time for Jane; melancholy of the deepest kind enveloped her; there was no letter from Medjuel; Karl Venningen wrote to tell her that Berthe, who suffered from mental disturbance, was growing worse; Cristos Hadji-Petros sent a tearful message that little Eirini was dead. Surely a setting worthy of a Victorian melodrama!

Jane's fiftieth birthday, 'triste and melancholy anniversary', came but she was still youthful in mind and body; her hair was still the colour Balzac had admired and her eyes, made lustrous and magnetic by the use of eastern kohl, entranced and fascinated all who met her. 6 April saw her embarked for Calais, for the damp English weather chilled and depressed her still further; she took a great amount of luggage, stopped off in Paris to purchase a piano for Medjuel, bolts of fabric and sketching materials, and set sail for Beirut with an armoury of guns for her Bedouins. To her mother, Lady Andover, she wrote; 'I would gladly be as you are, but I cannot change my nature. I am different. How different I hardly realized.'

As the days of the journey passed, the sun began to warm her, dispelling the gloom and depression of the parting from Medjuel and by the time the ship had reached Beirut she was more than ready for the longed-for meeting with him. Beirut was a stopping place *en route* for there was business to be done and arrangements to be made for the journey to Damascus. 'With beating heart I arrived at Damascus', she wrote and promptly set about making a home with the 'dear, the adored one'. The house was half-English, half-Arabic, with three wings enclosing a courtyard on the ground floor and furnished in the Arab style with a large courtyard and a *liwan* with divans and cushions. There were traditional wooden screens against the windows and two bedrooms over the centre wing. Jane had her own inimitable English style represented in the English garden and the drawing room, filled with her books, her writing desk and her easel. Isabel Burton recalls Jane's home as she saw it in 1890;

The house is made noticeable by its projecting balcony-like windows and coloured glass. We come to a large wooden gateway, and are received by twenty or thirty Bedawin of the tribe of Mesrab, lounging in the archway, and a large Kurdish dog, which knows his friends and will let me pass . . . On the other side is the reception-house for any of the tribe who happen to come into town; also the bath-house, the conservatory, and the house and play-ground for the fowls, amongst which

May French Sheldon

May French Sheldon,
Bebe Bwana

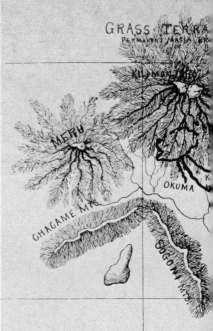

May French Sheldon's
map of the country bet-
ween Kilimanjaro and
the sea

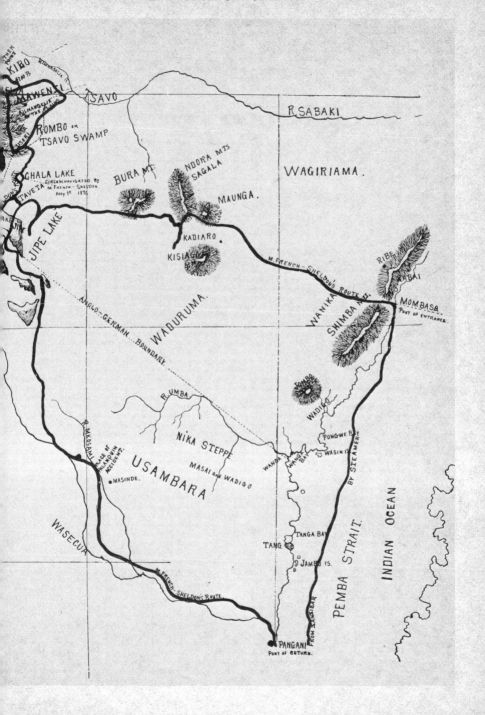

May French Sheldon in her palaquin

May French Sheldon in her ball gown

May French Sheldon on the float on
Lake Chala

Sultan Miriame and Kilme natives

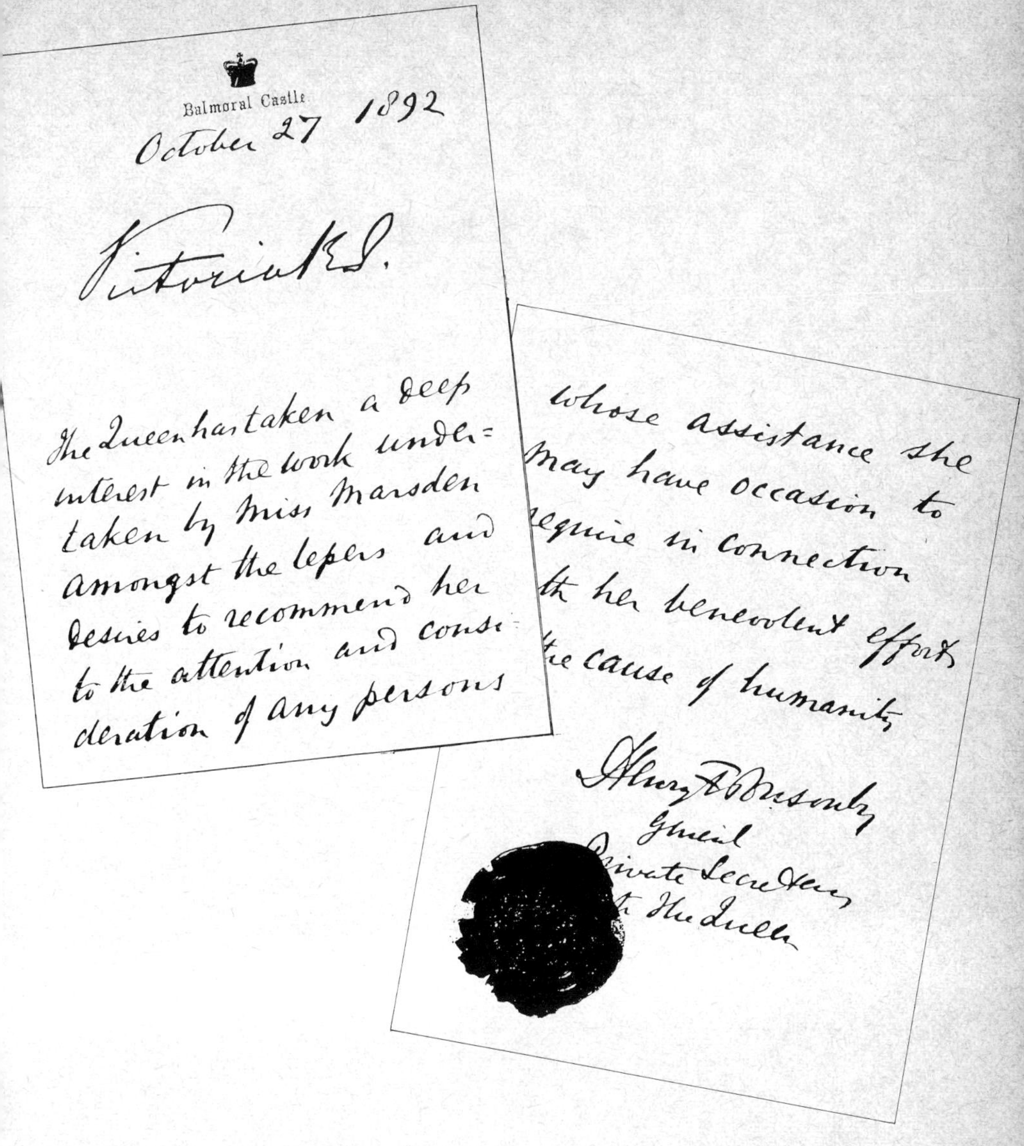

Balmoral Castle
October 27 1892

Victoria R.I.

The Queen has taken a deep
interest in the work undertaken by Miss Marsden
amongst the lepers and
desires to recommend her
to the attention and consideration of any persons

whose assistance she
may have occasion to
require in connection
with her benevolent efforts
in the cause of humanity.

Henry F. Ponsonby
Genrl
Private Secretary
to the Queen

Letter to Kate Marsden from Queen Victoria

DIPLOMA OF THE RUSSIAN IMPERIAL RED CROSS SOCIETY.

Diploma of the Russian Imperial Red Cross

The Princess Shachovskoy, the three
sisters who are already at work amongst
the lepers, and Kate Marsden

Kate Marsden in travelling dress with
a map of her route

The proposed leper colony

Our start from Yakutsk

The last stage of the journey before
the ice break-up in Siberia

My home in a cargo boat for the three
weeks on the river Lena

Edward, 1st Earl of Ellenborough

JANE DIGBY EL MESRAB

r Kenelm Digby (1603-
65), Jane's most spect-
ular ancestor - a swash-
ckling and colourful
venturer and intellectual

Chief Justice Sir Ed-
ward Coke (1551-1634)

Admiral Sir Henry
Digby (1763-1842)

Jane Elizabeth Coke,
Jane's mother

A view of Holkham Hall, Norfolk, seat of
the Coke family and Jane's birthplace

The imposing entrance hall at Holkham, with
its alabaster columns ans spectacular ceiling

Jane, about eight years old, with her brothers, Edward, six, and Kenelm, four

Jane at thirteen, painted in Switzerland when she was wintering with abroad with her family

Cruikshank cartoon (c.1820) of a Wednesday night ball at Almack's where London society gathered during the Regency and the reign of George IV

Innocent employment for Foreign Princes

Jane's partner in adultery, Prince Felix Schwartzenberg

Cartoon of 1830 depictin Schwartzenberg lacing Jane's stays

King Lugwig I of Bavaria, protector and
confidant of Jane, believed by some to
be her lover

Josef Stieler portrait of Jane, commissioned by Ludwig for his 'Gallery of
Beauties'

Baron Carl von Venningen, Jane's second
husband, who fought a duel over her

Portraits of the Theotoky family, Jane, Spiro, and their son Leonidas. Spiro was Jane's third husband

JANE DIGBY EL MESRAB

Portrait by Jane of Sheik Medjuel el Mesrab,
her fourth and last husband

ane's grave in the Protestant Cemetery in Damascus

Alexandra David-Neel and at right Lama Yongden

ALEXANDRA DAVID-NEEL

Alexandra David-Neel as the guest of the Tashi
Lama's mother in the Taspilhumpo Monastery

ALEXANDRA DAVID-NEEL

Procession around the Potala

Alexandra David-Neel seated in front of the Potala. Her face is smeared with Black Lac. Lama Yongden is on her right

lexandra David-Neel on a yak on the way to Shigatze

ALEXANDRA DAVID-NEEL

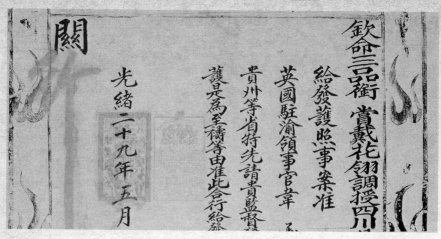

欽命三品銜賞戴花翎調授四川

給發護照事案准

英國駐渝領事官章　

貴州等省特先請貴監督

護是為至禱等由准此合行給發

光緒二十九年五月

關

Chinese passport

大英欽命駐劄漢口管理本國

給發護照事照得天津

往內地各處遊歷通商

地方如餒交出執照應

李貨物不得攔阻如其他

近送交領事官懲辦沿途

趙理明票稱欲由漢口

來據此本領事查該人

大清各處地方文武員弁驗

津局卡夆勿留難攔阻

一千八百九十六年九

光緒　二十二　年 X

大清欽命監督湖北江漢關

照　護

Tibetan passport

we find curious snow-white geese with curling feathers, turkeys, ducks, poultry, pigeons, guinea hens, and other pets. The whole is fronted and surrounded by a choice flower-garden. Upstairs is a suite of apartments which is elegance itself.

It does not appear, however, that Jane turned the garden into a clinic for the poor and sick of Damascus, as did Isabel Burton, her compatriot, Isabel writes; 'Our garden presented the strangest scene in the afternoon – fever patients making wry faces over quinine wine, squalling babies guggling oil, paralytic and rheumatic Bedawain being shampooed, and gouty old women having joints painted with iodine.'

Jane threw herself into Arabic life. She wore one blue garment, dyed her glorious chestnut hair jet black and wore it in two plaits and covered her head with the usual dark kerchief. She learned to milk the camels and submissively washed the hands, face, hair and feet of Medjuel, as an Arab wife should. When it came to riding, she was allowed to ride a horse, for she was as swift as the wind and a gifted horsewoman. Other Bedouin women were relegated to camels or dromedaries. She also built magnificent stables for the Arab horses and a visitor described the 'roaring and growling and groaning' which went on as eleven dromedaries were got ready for a long journey. But the greatest monument to Jane lay in her English garden of lily-ponds, herbacious borders and flowering shrubs. Many English travellers were to remember with pleasure the garden, although the site of the house has never been clearly defined. Apparently it was a short distance outside the city walls.

Jane rode with the tribes, fought alongside them, bought guns for them with her own money, and advised them on financial matters and the finer points of fencing with Arabs, who would do one down for a shekel. But she was always Jane Digby el Mesrab, tall, dignified, and supremely elegant.

Many people came to visit Jane Digby el Mesrab (the Hon. Jane Digby el Mesrab as she was called, for the rank of Baron's children had been conferred on her and her brothers and sisters in 1859) and all who were genuine friends, and not just curious sight-seers, were hospitably received. The house, the gardens, and the stables were tremendously admired and the hundred cats, which Eugènie was allowed to feed, had their own plates.

Jane saw her guests in the grand octagonal drawing-room where, one day, at 6 a.m., the Emperor of Brazil paid his respects and was graciously received. There was more to Jane's new life, however, than the reception of guests in a European drawing-room filled with family photographs and Victorian knick-knacks. There was another part to be played, that of the wife who could withstand the hardship of the wilderness with a husband whose responsibilities to the tribe were many, for in November the Mesrabs headed south to find the evergreens necessary for the camels.

There were often desert skirmishes lasting for weeks at a time in which Jane joined, galloping with Medjuel at the head of his Bedouin troops and routing the invaders with that same fearless spirit which had sustained her throughout her many adventures. With her money she bought guns and carried out reprisal raids upon those tribes which had invaded their area and carried off their camels. Sometimes the *Uttfa* was in the centre of the skirmish; this was a large camel-howdah made of bamboo, decorated with ostrich feathers; inside was an Arab girl singing the slow chant which it was hoped would whip up the fervour of the fighters. Some of the Syrian tribes used the *Uttfa* and the savagery invoked in the spectacle of wild shouts, clashing spears and the banging of old pistols must have struck terror into European hearts – all, that is, except that of the Hon. Jane Digby el Mesrab. If there were no raids to avenge there was the *fantasia*, a wild charge of the Bedouin horsemen, widely practised. Isabel Burton described one which she witnessed;

When I say the men are riding *djerid*, I mean that they are galloping about violently, firing from horseback at full speed, yelling, hanging over their stirrups with their bridles in their mouth, playing with and quivering their long feathered lances in the air, throwing themselves under the horses' bellies and firing under them at full gallop, yelling and shouting their war cry . . . The wildness of the scene is very refreshing but you have to be a good rider yourself, as they simply go wild.

Jane was also becoming adept at levying ransom on unsuspecting travellers. Isabel Burton tells us about the journey to Palmyra, which European travellers were just beginning to make. It was 'an awfully difficult thing in those days . . . First of all, six thousand francs used to be charged by the El Mezrab who were the tribe who escorted for that journey . . . There was no water, that is, only two wells on the whole way, and only known to them. The difficulties and dangers were great; they travelled by day and hid by night. You may say the camels were about ten days on the road and horses about eight days.' Jane, according to Isabel Burton, was 'more Bedouin than the Bedawi' and aided the tribe in concealing the wells and levying ransom on unsuspecting and bewildered travellers.

The winter of 1859 had been bitterly cold; hunger stalked the land, bringing starvation and utter helplessness from spring floods and a disastrous plague of worms which had threatened the food crops. Violence followed.

It all began with the murder of three men near the town of Sidon; the men were Druses, amongst whom Lady Hester Stanhope had lived early in the nineteenth century, queening it over them. Now she was gone and Muslim and Christian fought fiercely with each other. Four Christians were killed from a Maronite settlement and others were dragged from their homes and massacred in a blood-bath of stupendous proportions, while whole villages went up in smoke. In July, the terror spread to Damascus; Christians were put to the sword, dragged into the blood-soaked streets and left for the dogs. Medjuel was called to Homs as his first wife was dying but he would not leave Jane in Damascus, who felt the loss of his wife keenly, believing that her death 'did not mitigate my sin in having been the prime cause of Medjuel putting aside the wife of his youth'. For days the terror raged, finding a hero in Abd-el-Kadir, a true man of the hour, risking his life to help hundreds of Christians by leading them to his fortified house. Foreign diplomats did not escape the holocaust and all the Consulates of Christian countries were burned down; the American Consul reached the house of Abd-el-Kadir but the Dutch Consul was slain and the Greek Consul faced death with a certain panache, singing from the roof of his home.

Jane Digby el Mesrab was known and respected throughout Syria and she would have been in no danger if she had chosen to remain under Medjuel's roof; that she did not do so is vastly to her credit. At daybreak she ventured into the streets that were now a shambles, clad in her Bedouin garments and with a yashmak covering her fair skin, with only an Arab servant. She had no other protection, no loving Medjuel, no band of strong Bedouin followers to repel all adversaries at a single blow. She did what she could for the people left in the blood-soaked streets and when she could do no more she joined el-Kadir and helped to feed the twelve thousand-odd refugees sheltering in his house and courtyards by giving her own money. Jane's religion had never come between them before but the stand she had now taken on the side of the Christians had humiliated Medjuel in Muslim eyes; she was a *giaour*, an infidel who had disobeyed her husband and had spat upon the religion of Allah. Medjuel fled into the desert distressed and bewildered, with a situation which had never before arisen. Jane remained in Homs.

A new life began for Jane with the return of Medjuel and the freedom to practise her Christianity in the Missions; she made friends with the hard-working and self-sacrificing men and women of the Gospel who welcomed with open arms the *Sitt* Mesrab who sat so unostentatiously at the back of the Mission during the service, clad in Bedouin garments. She attended

Divine Service and bought her grave in the Protestant Cemetery in Damascus, for the long years of love and adventure had taken their toll and the tempestuous life of the Bedouin camps could no longer be entered into.

But if she had to subdue her craving for excitement with Medjuel, there were compensations in other ways. She was still beautiful; her body was like that of a young girl, her skin as fair, her hair, except for a few strands of grey as tawny under the black dye as when Balzac knew her, her mind as sharp and her intellect as keen as ever. As Damascus settled down, tourism developed in a small way with the arrival of those Europeans who had the time and money to visit ancient sites (and were prepared for danger and the payment of ransom-money). Baalbeck, Petra, and Palmyra were like magnets to the intrepid traveller, bored with Europe and ready for new adventures in the mountains and deserts of the Middle East. To Jane's house many visitors came, enjoying her hospitality and admiring the furnishings and the garden. There was Barry Mitford, later Lord Redesdale, who visited Damascus in March 1871 and was received by the Hon. Jane Digby el Mesrab. He wrote;

So many stories had been told about her and her strange life as the wife of an Arab chief, I expected to see a grand and commanding figure living in a sort of tawdry barbarism, something like the Lady Hester Stanhope of *Eothen* and Lamartine; an imposing personage, mystic, wonderful, half queen, half sybil O Semiramis and Meg Merrilies rolled into one, ruling by the force of the eye a horde of ignoble, ragged dependants, trembling but voracious.

He was impressed by her gracious old-world manners' and noted with a quick eye that she was a 'little old-fashioned, a relic of the palmy days of Almacks; dressed in quite inconspicuous Paris fashion and very nice to look upon'.

There was Count Louis de Thurhein, who told her that her daughter Mathilde (Didi) had now been married for nearly twenty years; there was the Scot, John MacGregor, who arrived in Damascus in his canoe, the *Rob Roy*, accompanied by seven men, two horses, and six mules. He had sailed down the Barada river from its source, paddled across Damascus, and finished up in a swamp in the middle of the Syrian desert. During his stay he met 'a charming Englishwoman, married to an Arab Sheikh'.

Sir Edwin Pears also paid a visit to Damascus in the autumn of 1876, determined to seek out Lady Ellenborough 'an elderly lady, granddaughter of "Coke of Norfolk" '. She had married an Arab Sheik and was, 'I imagine, thirty years older than he'. It was difficult to see her but Sir Edwin's friend had to visit Damascus twice a year to pay her her private income of £3,000 a year from the bank at Beirut and he promised to obtain an interview. Jane received Sir Edwin in the *salon*, evidently resented the intrusion, but was courteous enough to allow him to stay at one end while the money business was transacted. He admired the paintings executed by Karl Haag and this led to conversation and an invitation to tea, any afternoon he would be in Damascus at five o'clock. She was, wrote Sir Edwin in his book *Forty years in Constantinople* 'an excellent talker' and had much insight and wit and spoke to him of Arab women's life in the harem.

The women of the harem, she said, had about them the delightfulness of children. Their enjoyments were simple and genuine. Their passionate love of flowers constantly appealed to her, but there was another side to their character. There was the childishness of children which became imbecility when found amongst women. They had sudden outburst of anger, swift reconciliation, passionate affection, and even hate. The worst side of their character related to their sensuality. They had no pleasures corresponding to those found in European society, no music, no literature, no social intercourse with men. The results was that even amongst the most respectable classes there was a gross sensuality, which shewed itself in the language which well-dressed harem ladies would employ. Subjects were spoken of even in the presence of children about which all Christian races agree to be silent.

To Sir Edwin she told many stories of her experiences and was the only woman the Arabs would permit to ride a horse. 'I gained', wrote Sir Edwin, 'the impression that under different circumstances she might have exerted a most valuable influence in any society into which she had been thrown.'

Chief of all her visitors were the Burtons, Richard and Isabel. Richard Burton had been appointed to the post of Consul in Damascus, a position eminently suited to his talents and his knowledge of Arabic. They settled in a house at Salahiyyeh in the suburbs, where there was light and air and fresh water. 'In five minutes we could gallop out over the mountains, and there was no locking us up at sunset. Here then we pitched our tent', wrote Isabel. 'The people loved me', she continued, 'and my chief difficulty was to pass through the crowds that came to kiss my hand or my habit.' The people certainly loved Richard, but Isabel's high-handed methods in dealing with the Arabs evoked little feelings of genuine affection.

On Wednesdays Isabel held a reception for friends and dignitaries and after an evening meal guests relaxed on the flat roof of the house, settling down on divans spattered with cushions, smoking their nargilehs and eating sweetmeats between conversations lasting well into the night. The

Burtons liked her, although Isabel ignored the Arabic name and insisted on calling her Lady Ellenborough. Burton found her knowledge of Arabic life extremely useful and her candour in discussing bizarre sexual practices amongst upper-class women may have contributed in no small measure to the unexpurgated edition of *One Thousand Nights and a Night*.

In Isabel's *Life of Sir Richard Burton* we gain a glimpse of Jane Digby el Mesrab, for Isabel wrote of the 'large reception every Friday', which used to begin at sunrise and go on until sunset. The two most interesting and remarkable visitors were Abd-el-Kadir and Lady Ellenborough, although there were others on the house roof; Charles Tyrwhitt-Drake 'an indefatigable worker in the Palestine Exploration' and E. H. Palmer, afterwards professor of Arabic at Cambridge, and in 1882 murdered by the Bedawi in Arabia. Isabel was generous enough to write of Jane;

She was a most beautiful woman, though at the time I write she was sixty-one, tall, commanding, and queen-like. She was *grande dame au bout des doigts*, as much as if she had just left the salons of London and Paris, refined in manner and voice, nor did she ever utter a word you could wish unsaid. My husband said she was out and out the cleverest woman he ever met; there was nothing she could not do. She spoke nine languages perfectly, and could read and write in them. She painted, sculptured, was musical. Her letters were splendid; and if on business, there was never a word too much, nor a word too little. She had had a most romantic, adventurous life, and she was now, one might say, Lady Hester Stanhope's successor. She lived half the year in a romantic house she had built for herself in Damascus, and half her life she and her husband lived in his Bedawi tents, she like any other Bedawi woman, but honoured and respected as the queen of her tribe, wearing one blue garment, her beautiful hair in two long plaits down to the ground, milking the camels, serving her husband, preparing his food, giving him water to wash his hands and face, and sitting on the floor and washing his feet, giving him his coffee, his sherbet, his *narghilehs* [sic], and while he ate she stood and waited on him, and glorying in it; and when in Damascus they led semi-European lives.

Isabel also gave a picture of Jane which combined truth overlaid with a patina of Victorian smugness and upper-crust condescension;

She was the most romantic and picturesque personality . . . She was very unhappy with him Lord Ellenborough and she ran away with Prince Schwartzenberg when she was only nineteen, and Lord Ellenborough divorced her. She lived with Prince Schwartzenberg for some years, and had two or three children by him, and then he basely deserted her. I am afraid that after that she led a life for a year or two over which it is kinder to draw a veil. She then tired of Europe, and conceived the idea of visiting the East.

Isabel's potted biography takes no account of the fact that Jane's purpose in visiting the East was to purchase Arab blood-stock from Syria to replenish her stables; it was entirely co-incidental that she met Medjuel. 'At Damascus', Isabel continued, 'she blackened her eyes with kohl, and lived in a curiously untidy manner. But otherwise she was not in the least extraordinary.'

Of Medjuel, Isabel does not enthuse. She commented on his small stature and the fact that he was 'nearly black' and wrote; 'I could understand her running away with Schwartzenberg, but the contact with that black skin I could not understand . . . All the same I believe he was a very intelligent and charming man.' A grudging tribute.

Adventure came with inter-tribal warfare. In 1872 the Rowala and Saba tribes were at variance over pasture rights; the Mesrabs supported the Saba but suffered losses of men and cattle before the Rowala were finally overcome. Jane found the excitement she needed, fighting at Medjuel's side and alongside his Bedouin troops for here she could truly be his wife, sharing his defeats and battle honours, forgetting the humiliation she had inflicted upon him with her Christian apostasy and the pernicious doubts that his long sojourns without her in the desert induced in her. There were rumours that the chief's wife had been killed and newspapers of the day played it up; Jane was a well-known figure in Syria and obituary notices contained the grossest misrepresentations of facts about her life. Some were scathing in the extreme and one deliberately so; 'There has just died a noble lady who greatly used, or abused marriage.' Isabel Burton dashed off letters to *The Times* and other European newspapers and proved most loyal in her defence of Jane. She went to the Protestant Church 'often twice on Sundays' and 'had but one fault' (presumably Schwartzenberg was the 'one fault') the fall from grace. Tactfully, Isabel did not itemize the others: perhaps she was not aware of them.

Jane came riding back to Damascus, highly indignant and not a little amused. In a letter to the Pall Mall Gazette in March, 1873 Isabel had intimated that she possessed material relating to Jane's biography which Jane had wished her to write.

She wished me to write her biography, and gave me an hour a day until it was accomplished. She did not spare herself dictating the bad with the same frankness as the good. I was pledged not to publish this until after her death and that of certain near relatives.

In her life of Sir Richard Burton, Isabel wrote; 'She was my most intimate friend, and dictated to me the whole of her biography, beginning 15th March, 1871, and ending 7th July.'

Jane denied all knowledge of the biography; in a letter to her sister-in-law, Theresa Digby, she referred to the newspaper reports of her death and to the controversial biography; 'I was quite overset by the dreadful paragraphs in the papers, and as you may conceive, have been most *intensely* annoyed ever since.' With regard to the biography, one can fully sympathize with her attitude; 'I trust hers may be a correct view, but I certainly always deprecated every idea of ever publishing anything relating to myself or my former existence, as you can easily believe, and I never spoke to her at all upon the subject, excepting the answering of some of her queries as to what the world of that day knew, and positively denying some other histories that people had told, and as to *"begging* her remember *promises"* after my death of justifying me, it is pure error, and she knew the *horror* and *aversion* I have to that kind of thing.'

Although Isabel conceded without jealousy the fact of Jane's beauty 'even two years ago she was more attractive than half the young girls of our time', she was orthodox enough in her views, 'the romantic picture of becoming a Queen of the Desert and of the Bedouin tribes exactly suited her wild fancies, and was at once accepted'. She paints for us a picture of an impetuous girl who had put aside her sense of judgement in a moment of romantic passion; 'she was married according to Mohammedan law, changed her name to that of the Honourable Mrs. Digby El Mesrab, and was horrified when she found that she had lost her nationality by her marriage, and had become a Turkish subject.'

The Burtons left Damascus on the 13 September, 1871; Abd-el-Kadir and Jane accompanied Isabel on her night ride to the city gates, as she was 'determined to slip away quietly by night'. The farewell was 'affectionate' and the parting with Jane greatly so, 'I was the poor thing's only friend. As she wrung my hands these were her last words: "Do not forget your promise if I die and we never meet again". I replied; "*Inshallah*, I shall soon return".' A patronizing little speech.

Jane was now seventy-four, too easily tired for long desert rides with Medjuel and too concerned with the running of the Damascus home, for Eugènie had now left her employ and she found later domestics too trying; Gabrielle and Madame Marie were not of the calibre of her faithful Eugènie. Heribert, her son by Karl Venningen, had always kept in touch with her and he now had the unhappy task of sending her 'most melancholy intelligence' of the death of his father. 'My father died as he would have wished to die – in the saddle.'

But there were visitors to brighten up the long days; Admiral Sir James Robert Drummond, Commander of the Mediterranean Fleet, came to call and Jane lent him her best pony to compensate for the poor food. Then along came the Blunts, Wilfrid Scawen and Lady Anne. The meeting was secondary to the real purpose of their visit to Syria, which was to purchase horses of Anazeh stock for stud. In her book *A Pilgrimage to Nejd*, Lady Anne Blunt recalls her meeting with Jane; 'We have been spending the day with Mrs. Digby and her husband, Medjuel of the Mesrab, a very well bred and agreeable man, who has given us a great deal of valuable advice about our journey.' It was evident that Anne Blunt was greatly impressed by Medjuel and that the outrageous goings-on in Jane's past were of minor importance to the knowledge which could be gained from conversations with both she and her Arab husband.

In 1880 another visitor paid his respect to Jane Digby el Mesrab. Sir Valentine Chirol was an English diplomat who left for us a record of her charm and her wit;

When I made her acquaintance she must have been getting on for eighty, but so long as her Turkish yashmak concealed the lower part of her face, her ivory white and almost unwrinkled brow, her luminous eyes and the fine line of her aquiline nose still preserved traces of the beauty which had captured so many hearts in many lands and the highest places.

He suggested that she ought to write her memoirs but she replied that they would be 'a very naughty edition of the *Almanach de Gotha* and that a prayer-book would be more suitable for her declining years'.

In July 1881, Jane fell ill with dysentery and on 11 August, 1881, she breathed her last in the beautiful house she had so lovingly kept for Medjuel on his return from the desert. Most of her friends had left the heat of the city for cooler places in the mountains and only Medjuel remained. Jane Digby el Mesrab was buried in the Protestant Cemetery and this is where we return to the commencement of that strange story of love and sorrow which, shocked, delighted, and astounded so many people.

When the Burtons were in Damascus Jane visited Richard at the Consular Office with regard to her will. It was probated in London in April 1882; her estate was valued at £6,022 2s. 6d. She mentioned her house as situated near the Bab Menzuel Khassabb in the City of Damascus. The Blunts had settled near her when they sojourned in Damascus, living in a small house at the north-eastern end of the town on the road to Palmyra. On one side was the garden of a chief of the Damascus Ulema, and on the other side the garden of that 'amazing Englishwoman, Jane Digby, Lady Ellenborough, and her Arabian husband, "a very well bred and agreeable man", Mijuel el Mesrab'.

Margaret Fox Schmidt, in her book *Passion's Child*, traced Jane's children. Didi, who was the illegitimate daughter of Jane and Felix Schwartzenberg, had been baptized in the name of Mathilde Selden and was fifty-three years of age at Jane's death; she was living in Bohemia, very much a Schwartzenberg and still under the thumb of the redoubtable Mathilde Schwartzenberg. She was, like her mother, beautiful. Heribert, son of Karl Venningen, had lost both his father and his young wife, who had died from a fall. Poor Berthe had been committed to a mental home some years earlier. Leonidas, the son of her union with Count Spiridion Theotoky, crashed to his death from the balcony of the tall house at Bagni di Lucca – he was just a child. Of all her children, Leonidas was the one she seemed to love the best and the tragedy of his early death tore at her heart. She believed his death to be a retribution for her neglect of her other children.

The house in Damascus, incidentally, was destroyed many years ago to make way for tram lines. Jane's grave can still be seen in the Protestant Cemetery, but the damask roses described by Dr Wright have long since gone.

CHAPTER FOUR

Alexandra David-Neel

'Beyond the garden gate'

A LEXANDRA DAVID-NEEL was no ordinary child. 'Ever since I was five years old', she wrote in her book *My Journey to Lhasa* 'a tiny precocious child of Paris, I wished to move out of the narrow limits in which, like all children of my age, I was then kept. I craved to go beyond the garden gate, to follow the road that passed it by, and to set out for the unknown. But, strangely enough, this "unknown" fancied by my baby mind always turned out to be a solitary spot where I could sit alone, with no one near, and as the road toward it was closed to me, I sought solitude behind any bush, any mound of sand, that I could find in the garden, or wherever else my nurse took me. Later on, I never asked my parents for any gifts except books on travel, maps, and the privilege of being taken abroad during my school holidays. When a girl, I could remain for hours near a railway line, fascinated by the glittering rails and fancying the many lands toward which they led. But, again, my imagination did not evoke towns, buildings, gay crowds, or stately pageants; I dreamed of wild hills, immense steppes and impassable landscapes of glaciers.' Beyond the garden gate lay Tibet; the 'unknown' was Lhasa, the forbidden city.

Alexandra David-Neel was unlike any other of the Victorian lady travellers. She was not a protector of primitive, down-trodden and exploited races, like Daisy Bates; a globe trotter like Isabella Bird Bishop; a searcher after medicinal cures for leprosy, like Kate Marsden; an artist of rare talent, pottering round the globe, well-heeled and well-cushioned, sketch-pad in hand, like Marianne North; nor a searcher after love's fulfilment, like Jane Digby el Mesrab. She was an Orientalist and a scholar, a seeker after truth and a woman of great moral and intellectual qualities. At the age of fifty-six she had just completed an exhausting journey travelling from China to Lhasa in disguise, an attempt which would have overawed many men travellers; she lived with beggars, sharing the dirt, the filth, the intense hunger and the bitter cold of Tibetan life, acquiring knowledge and experiences, some of them bitter. She shared the lives of ordinary folk, who treated her with 'simplicity and kindness as one of themselves'.

Her book *My Journey to Lhasa* was well received, although one reviewer was distressed to read of the anti-British sentiments which were not wholly accurate. For forty years she wrote, a woman of disciplined energy, wasting not one second of her precious time, as articles for journals, books and magazines occupied her days. In her hundred and first year, she finally put down her pen *'Je ne peux plus écrire.'*

Louise Eugénie Alexandrine Marie David was born at Saint Mandé, a suburb of Paris on 24 October, 1868. Her parents were Alexandrine Borghmanns and Louis Pierre David, a native of Tours. Her father, as a young man, was a school teacher but had been forced into exile due to his revolutionary activities; at the age of forty he married Alexandrine in Louvain. Their marriage was not a happy one; after sixteen years they had a child, baptized on French soil at the request of her father, who applied to the authorities to grant his request in order that the child could become a French citizen. She had an unhappy childhood, this offspring of an unhappy marriage; the tension between her parents became more apparent with each passing year and the nurse deputed to look after her must have suffered under the strain of coping with a young mind eager to escape from a bourgeois home in which marital love had fled.

She was, like Marianne North, nearer to her father than to her mother. She thought her mother unacademic and interested only in middle-class society; her father was liberated and a true product of *La belle époque* but his age impeded a more personal relationship with his small daughter and he found it difficult to cross the bridge of years and enter into her youthful zest for life and knowledge. She felt neglected, unable to thrive or expand, inhibited and lonely and dreadfully vulnerable.

She found her escape in books of travel, absorbed in the exciting lives of explorers and fictional characters; Paul du Chaillu, probably a native of Paris, was forty-three years of age when Alexandra was a schoolgirl and his book *Explorations and Adventures in Equatorial Africa* was widely read; Pierre Savorgnan de Brazza created the capital of French Equatorial Africa and René Caillié had started his journey to Timbuktu in 1827. There were many, many more explorers to read about and wonderful far-away places to find on the map. Her longing to escape began from the age of five years and was the beginning of many attempts to cut herself off from a society which she found stifling.

One day, in the Bois de Vincennes, she toddled off to a life of adventure beyond the trees, followed by an anxious nurse and at the age of sixteen she actually got as far as the shores of England when her parents were on holiday at Ostend, an abortive attempt at women's liberation which the Reverend Mother at her convent viewed with horror. At eighteen years of age, she underwent a 'survival test' by sleeping in the open at the Saint Gothard Pass, a test inspired by Epictetus himself.

Always a searcher after truth, she became interested in Buddhism and the study of world religions and attended lectures at the Theosophical Society in London and in Paris. At the Musée Guimet in Paris a whole new vista opened up to her and in the library, enveloped by the 'noise of silence' she passed many happy hours, poring over Oriental manuscripts and books on Oriental mysticism, a quiet mouse tucked away in a quiet corner. 'Vocations are born', she wrote, 'mine was born there.' The Musée Guimet was founded in Lyons in 1879 by Émile Guimet and removed to Paris in 1888. In 1945 it became the Département des Arts Asiatiques des Musées Nationaux.

In her book *Le Sortilège du Mystère* Alexandra David-Neel wrote; '*Le musée Guimet renformait entre ses murs plus de mystère, d'estolerisme et de hauts secrets que toutes les sectes dispensatrices d'initiations imaginaires et puériles qui attirent et dupent tant de naïfs.*' The multiple effigies of gods and Oriental sages created, for her, an 'astonishing atmosphere', mystically reinforced by '*la petite salle de lecture*' of the Loge Pythagore, with its chapel dedicated to Marie Stuart.

It was fortunate for Alexandra that a chance came along for her to visit India; her godmother had left her a small inheritance, enough in those days to finance a trip by sea to the sub-continent and Ceylon. In her book *L'Inde où j'ai Vécu*, written some years later, we learn of her voyage and the effect that India had upon her, a child of the Paris of the *fin-de-siècle*. After her return from India, it was necessary for her to obtain some kind of work as her father was no longer in a position to subsidize her and pay for foreign travel. In future, she must pay her own way by earning a living.

Paris at this time was 'the right place in which to observe its manifold expressions'; there was so much building taking place, so many boulevards and avenues laid out, the Bois de Boulogne and the Bois de Vincennes converted into lovely parks, railway stations built, and over a hundred miles of subway lines leading away from the city to neat homes in the suburbs. The theatre was changing, too, feeling its way to the *Théâtre libre* of André Antoine with his innovations and more naturalistic style of acting. Paul Fort, a young poet of considerable talent stimulated audiences everywhere with his *Théâtre mixte*, where every kind of drama was presented, veering away from the 'boulevard theatre' of Feydeau and Scribe. Along with the growth of the city and the exciting and pulsating marriage of art and drama, Parisians were delighted by *La belle époque's* contribution to music and with the alliance of musical drama and word the Opéra-Comique was born, the child of the *Comédie-en-vaudevilles.* To many young French women the theatre and the opera were sheer magic; the great Sarah Bernhardt and the fascinating and redoubtable Madame Cossira had given them respectability and what was good enough for Bernhardt was good enough for them.

As a schoolgirl Alexandra had studied singing and the piano and had entered the finals for the *Prix de Rome* and with these talents she joined the Opéra-Comique, travelling in the name of Alexandra Myrial and at one point obtaining top billing as their *première chanteuse.* In 1902, she became Director of the Casino at Tunis and it was there that she met a distant cousin, Philippe-François Neel, chief engineer for La Compagnie du Chemin de Fer Bone-Guelma; he was seven years older than Alexandra, handsome and, according to Alexandra, 'very English'. On 3 August, 1904, they were married and on 8 August they parted, he to the south of France and she to Paris, to find herself at the age of thirty-six back in the Brussels home of her parents, lost and depleted after the death of her father, facing the coldness of her mother and a house full of memories. Of her marriage, we know little beyond her letter to Philippe in which she wrote, with a fatalistic acceptance of an irritating interlude; 'it was foolish, without doubt, but it is done'.

Many letters followed; letters full of self-analysis and self-recrimination, barbed darts, too, against a mother who could bring a child into the world as a symbol of supplication for a love grown cold. Marriage did not enter into her pattern of life, nor did the thought of children bring any comfort. 'Ah, my poor dear', she wrote to Philippe, 'believe me there is much wisdom, much foresight in my will not to be a mother.'

After the period of self-analysis and despair, in which at one stage suicide was contemplated, Alexandra lived in Paris and in London whilst Philippe returned to his work in Tunis. For Alexandra, it was never a conventional marriage; Philippe was kind and considerate, consenting to the terms Alexandra laid down for the continuance of their life together. He financed her, attended to all her business transactions, cared for the house she had bought in the south of France and continued to love her *in absentia.* Only her letters to Philippe remain, 3,000 typewritten pages of cold comfort for a man whose spirit yearned for her.

[110]

For eight years, from 1903, Alexandra studied and wrote and saw Philippe now and again. India beckoned once more and in preparation for her visit she studied Sanskrit at the Sorbonne and attended lectures at the Collège de France given by famous Orientalists. She was invited to lecture on a permanent basis but, apart from the lectures she gave at the Theosophical Societies in Paris and London, she had no use for formal teaching in class-rooms; she wished 'to live philosophy' and to learn from spiritual awareness 'on the spot'.

In France in the second half of the nineteenth century, there was a boom in publishing in the field of magic; the books of 'Eliphas Levi' made occultism and clairvoyance popular and by the late 1880s several Paris publishing firms were specializing in the cabbala, mysticism and spiritism. The Theosophical Society was founded in 1875 for the serious study of Buddhism and the ancient scriptures and in Paris Dr Charcot astounded the medical world by his experiments in hypnosis at the Saltpetrière. The second great Paris Exposition had put Orientalism on the map with its Chinese pagodas, Moorish mosques, Indian temple-dancers and tinkling eastern wind-bells. But Alexandra David-Neel was a professed Buddhist and a follower of Descartes and in the lectures at the Collège de France she gave her conclusions;

Everything that relates, whether closely or more distantly, to psychic phenomena and to the actions of psychic forces in general, should be studied just like any other science. There is nothing miraculous or supernatural in them, nothing that should engender or keep alive superstition. Psychic training, rationally and scientifically conducted, can lead to desirable results. That is why the information gained about such training – even though it is practised empirically and based on theories to which we cannot always give assent – constitutes useful documentary evidence worthy of our attention.

On 3 August, 1911, she left for India, a woman of forty-two years of age, a disciple of Descartes 'a master and possessor of Nature', a free soul, and at peace with herself.

'Well, then, it is understood. I leave Dawasandup with you as interpreter. He will accompany you to Gangtok.' Alexandra was at Kalimpong in the Himalayas, and Dawasandup was the interpreter given to her when she arrived. Early in 1912 she had given much thought to the idea of writing an article on the Dalai Lama for the *Mercure de France*. The Dalai Lama, ruler of Tibet, had fled from his capital due to struggles with the Chinese and had taken refuge in British Bhutan in a village called Kalimpong. At first, he obstinately refused to receive Alexandra, or indeed any foreign ladies, but Alexandra was different for she was first and foremost a Buddhist and an oriental scholar and knew a great deal of the ancient Tibetan literature; she also carried letters of introduction from important Buddhist personages of most exalted rank. 'It was quite an honour to be received, for no other woman, except Tibetans, had been thus honoured', she wrote.

She left Darjeeling 'in the early rosy dawn of a cool spring morning', with no other idea in her mind except a short interview and a brief excursion. As it happened, and to her own wonderment, her 'excursions' were to last fourteen years and take her finally to Lhasa, far beyond 'the garden gate' through which she had longed to go so many years ago in Paris. At Kalimpong she met the Dalai Lama; his suite was numerous and included more than a hundred servants, with officials and domestics, all looking alike in their greasy robes.

Around the monk-sovereign, I found a strange royal household of clerical personages, clad in shining yellow satin, dark-red cloth, and gold brocade, who related fantastic stories and spoke of a wonderland. Although when listening to them I wisely made a liberal allowance for legend and exaggeration, I instinctively felt that behind those dark wooded hills which I saw before me, and the huge snowy peaks which pointed their lofty heads beyond them, there was, truly, a land different from all others. Needless to say, my heart leaped with the desire to enter it!

There were other reasons from those of merely wishing to view the 'peculiar natural aspect' of Tibet which prompted Alexandra David-Neel to attempt a passage into Tibet. In her book *My Journey to Lhasa* she wrote;

Like many Oriental scholars, of whom I am but an humble colleague, I deeply regret the loss, in their Sanskrit original, of a number of Mâyânist Buddhist Scriptures. These are more or less available in Chinese translation and what original philosophic and mystic works have been written by Thibetan authors, either in accordance with Mahâyânist doctrines or contrary to them, is as much *terra incognita* as the land of Thibet itself. Thus, hunting after books and old manuscripts and seeking meetings with the *literati* of the country became my self-assigned task. Anyhow, things could not end there. The unsuspected is the daily fare of the traveller in Thibet, and my researches led me face to face with a world still more amazing than the landscapes I had beheld from the high passes through which one enters Thibet.

However, 'the solitudes of which I had dreamed since my infancy' were still a long way off; it was time to leave Kalimpong and take up the invitation of the Crown Prince, Sidkeong Tulka, who spoke English and Hindustani and was delighted to learn of her desire to further her education in Lamaism.

At Gangtok, in the beautiful country house which Sidkeong Tulka had built in the style of an English villa, Alexandra passed pleasant afternoons in the company of the Crown Prince and a real Tibetan doctor of philosophy from the University of Tashilhunpo, near Shigatze, talking of Lamaism and topics 'quite foreign to westerners' and listened patiently to the creeds expounded by the two philosophers, one of the 'Red Hat' sect and one of the 'Yellow Hat' reformed sect, taking tea flavoured with salt and butter in the Tibetan style.

In her book *With Mystics and Magicians in Tibet* Alexandra David-Neel explained many aspects of Tibetan Buddhism which had greatly interested, and influenced, her own thought; the 'ethereal double', the escape of the spirit upon death, the disposal of bodies in rare altitudes, the help given by the lamas to ordinary mortals who die, explaining to them the nature of the things they will meet upon the way. The science of death was as much a part of life as the science of life was a part of man himself.

The Dalai Lama was recalled to Lhasa in June 1912, the Kanchu Dynasty having fallen. At the foot of the Jelap Pass Alexandra went out to meet him in farewell, helping to arrange cushions for his bed as the furniture and rugs had failed to arrive; the 'assistants' told her that this would certainly bring her good luck in this life and the life to come. She left Sikkim, went on to Nepal and Benares, and stayed for a while with the Theosophical Society Members in a small apartment in their beautiful park where she studied anew the Vedanta philosophy 'somewhat forsaking Lamaism which I did not seem to be able to investigate more thoroughly than I had already done'.

In February 1914 the maharajah died and his son, Sidkeong Tulka succeeded him; it was no longer possible for Alexandra to acquire further knowledge by taking part in long and pleasant discussions on Lamaism and Tibetan Buddhism and the idea of leaving the Himalayas disturbed her. Life now was colourless, without the harmony which she had enjoyed; she felt the impact of hostile forces and the encroachment of invisible beings who 'incited me to leave the country'. Fever or neurasthenia may have been the cause of her fatigue, but it was now apparent that she must get away into quiet surroundings and in the monastery of Podang, near Gangtok, the new Maharajah offered her an apartment – an 'immense' room, from which she could hear the religious music which was played twice a day. 'The melody flowed as smoothly as the water of a deep river, without interruption, emphasis or passion.' She was happy at Podang and her innumerable questions were answered with the utmost patience by two visiting lamas, although in answer to her enquiry regarding the spirits of slaughtered animals, the *gomchen* was hesitant; 'Do not think I can answer your questions in a few words. The subject is intricate. Animals have several "consciousnesses" just as we ourselves, and as it also happens in our case, these "consciousnesses" do not all follow the same road after death. A living being is an assemblage, not a unity. But one must have been initiated by a proper master before being able to realise these doctrines.'

She made many excursions with the lama prince and his retinue and camped near the frontiers of Tibet, Nepal and Sikkim, but the Sidkeong Tulka left to return to Gangtok and Darwasandup could no longer stay. At her express wish, a personal attendant was found for her, a spiritual companion who was to accompany her to forbidden Lhasa, and to undergo vicissitudes, wretchedness, and torment of mind and body in the platonic friendship of two souls in earnest search for the truth. Yongden was a boy of about fifteen years of age, born at Mondo in Sikkim, but holding a British passport as Sikkim was then a British Protectorate. At the age of eight he had entered a 'Red Hat' monastery but Darwasandup had thought him to be eminently suitable for the position of Alexandra's companion. He became her adopted son and was registered in the name of Arthur-Albert David, a name not pleasing to Philippe, who would have none of him. As he grew older in wisdom Alexandra regarded him with respect, addressing him as 'Lama Yongden' and treating him as a spiritual companion, as well as a travelling one.

They went to the monastery of Chörten Nyima on the advice of a native official. 'The monasteries you have seen in Sikkim are very different from those of Tibet . . . since you cannot travel freely in Tibet, go at least to see Chörten Nyima. Though this *gompa* is very small, you will get some idea of a true Tibetan monastery.' Alexandra went to Chörten Nyima, and wrote;

It is impossible to fancy any more solitary site. The region in which the monks' houses have been built is not only uninhabited but the high altitude makes a desert of it. Sandy cliffs, curiously carved by erosion a large valley ascending toward a mountain lake, high snowy peaks, a limpid brook on a bed of mauve, greyish green or rosy pebbles formed around the *gompa*, an impassable, wholly mineral scenery from which emanated a serenity beyond expression.

She found only four nuns at Chörten Nyima ('Sun shrine') and isolated communities living at great heights, spending the long winters blocked in by snow.

The winter was approaching and she gave up all thoughts of further penetration into Tibet; it was extremely dangerous to cross the Sikkim-Tibetan border without a pass and there were penalties under the law. It was difficult, too, to travel to Europe; war had been declared between Germany and England in August 1914 and a safe journey was virtually impossible. She decided to go with Yongden to the hermitage at Lachen where the hermit lama was 'in residence' in his comfortably-furnished cave; he had thoughtfully sent her a black mare to ride and now he came half-way to meet them, stumbling along down the winding mountain paths. He led her to another hermitage near his own and offered her a large pot of buttered tea and ordered a fire to be lit in the centre of the room. She slept on the bare rock and ruminated on the hermit's life. 'I feel that the hermit's life, free of what we call "the goods and pleasures of the world" is the most wonderful of all lives' and with all her soul she cried; 'solitude! Solitude!' The solitude was to last for a winter, a spring, a summer and another late autumn, while Alexandra lived the contemplative life in a feast of self-negation and unfolding awareness of her own mystical powers.

The *gomchen* of the Lachen hermitage decided to admit her to the hermitage as a novice as she wished to experience the contemplative life for herself and a cave was found for her, with a rough cabin as an extension and a hut for Yongden, with his own small room. Servants were necessary for there was much fetching and carrying to be done before the winter snows set in. Winter came, and Alexandra shut herself in 'for a long reatreat', studying the Tibetan scriptures in the comfort of silence, while her one daily meal was brought to her door and left behind a curtain. Spring came at last; the rhododendrons bloomed below in the valley and letters came from Europe, written five months before. Summer came and went and the winter snows flurried round the hillsides as Alexandra talked for long hours with the *gomchen* about the lives of Tibetan mystics, pored over ancient books, and mastered the Tibetan language with the aid of grammars. 'I learnt a number of things', she wrote, 'but I never let myself be taken in by the illusion that my anchorite's home might become my final harbour. Sadly, almost with terror, I often looked at the thread-like path which I saw, lower down, winding in the valleys and disappearing between the mountains. The day would come when it would lead me back to the sorrowful world that existed beyond the distant hill ranges, and so thinking, an indescribable suffering lay hold of me.'

The suffering was of the spirit, the reality was of the moment that could not conquer time – the life of the hermitage had to be relinquished. The wilderness gave its savage love only to those, like the hermits, who could come to terms with it; the servants of those hermits had their roots in the gentler valleys and knew no destiny but that of the world they had left temporarily to serve the wise ones. It was time for them all to leave, for Yongden was young and the world beckoned.

Near the town of Shigatze lay the great monastery of Tashilhunpo, one of the two great religious centres of Tibet and the seat of the Grand Lama, the Panchen Lama, 'the precious learned man of the province of Tsang', whose rank equalled that of the Dalai Lama, but only spiritually; from a temporal point of view, the Dalai Lama was the ruler. Accompanied by Yongden and a monk who acted as servant, they left on horseback with a pack-mule on a four-day journey, not entirely pleasant, for the river Chi had to be forded, snow and hail overflowed into their temporary camp and the only sleep they could get was by standing up for most of the night on a small island, which was the only dry spot.

The suffering was well worth it. 'In the bluish gloaming, the enormous monastery of Tashilhunpo stood in the distance; a mass of white buildings crowned with golden roofs that reflected the last dim rays of the setting sun.' Alexandra was well received; there were formalities, of course, such as details which she had to give about her birthplace. Paris? Which Paris? She explained; it was 'beyond the sea, but could be reached by land', therefore she was not a *phiing* (foreigner). The mother of the Panchen Lama invited her to be her guest and, in return, Alexandra gave tea to the several thousand monks who lived in the monastery. The 'barbaric splendour' of the temples and palaces of the dignitaries greatly impressed her and the ostentatious display of gold, silver, turquoise and jade more than half convinced her that the lamas were not yet above human desires for worldly possessions. Alexandra thought it all 'unrefined and childish' and might have been disillusioned with Tibet if she had not become acquainted with those great minds living in 'calm solitudes'. But the Panchen Lama was kind and Alexandra spent happy hours in the palaces of Shigatze and its neighbourhood, visiting the largest printing press in Tibet, where religious books filled a huge building and where the printers sat upon the floor to work, chatting and drinking buttered tea. In a desolate place on a hill she met a *gomchen* in his anchorite's cave of many rooms who had never travelled but had spent his life 'walled in', receiving visitors but sleeping in a *gumti*, a square box about twenty-five to thirty inches long with one of the sides forming a back to recline against. He could not stretch his limbs, for a sash of woollen cloth passed under his knees and behind his neck, thus preventing him adopting any other position than that of meditation.

It was now time for her to return to the frontier with Sikkim; she had entered Tibet without permission and peasants brought her a letter from the British Resident at Gangtok ordering her to leave Tibetan soil. Entry without a pass was a very serious offence and could entail a fine of 100 rupees for the first offence, 500 rupees for the second offence or three months' imprisonment. It was a disaster for the small village about twelve miles down the hill from Shigatze for they had to pay immediately a fine of 200 rupees to the British Authorities for failure to inform them of Alexandra's departure. They crossed the Himalayas, turning southwards into India. 'How many things are left for me to learn! And I am leaving . . .'

Now followed many months of wandering. In Burma she spent days of retreat with one of the most austere sects of Buddhist monks; she refreshed her mind and body in the peace of the Tofoku-ji monastery where the monks were drawn from the aristocracy of Japan, and in Korea the 'monastery of wisdom' in the heart of the forest welcomed her and gave her temporary residence. Peking saw her next, living once again in a Buddhist monastery. But the far-away monastery of Kum-Bum called her and she and Yongden joined a caravan of two rich lamas and their retinues and a few monks and lay men. Alexandra was resolved to 'cross the whole of China to reach its north-western frontier into Tibetan land' and left Peking with high hopes of reaching the monastery in the wilds of Amdo in the Province of Kansu. The *gomchen* of Sakyong monastery had advised her to go to Tibet and be initiated by a Master of the 'Short Path' and had told her that 'many roads lead to Tibet' and that there were other, yet more learned, teachers in his own country of Eastern Tibet.

They left on 24 January, 1918, embarking on a journey which was to be full of interest. One day the head of their caravan made a bargain with one of the harlots they encountered at an inn; clad in green pants and pink coats she entered the lama's room along with several others of like ilk 'like a family of Tom Thumbs going into the Ogre's den'. The lama was a married man and a follower of a sect of magicians and the noisy bargaining which followed resulted in a payment of five Chinese dollars. Civil war, robbery and bloodshed were their constant companions on the journey; robbers and bandits made travelling extremely unsafe and at Tungchow the city was besieged and resembled a medieval battle-scene. Alexander herself escaped during the night by driving a cart at high speed, later taking tea with the Governor of Shensi while the enemy surrounded the city.

Seven months after leaving Peking she reached the monastery. It had been

established in the sixteenth century and had become one of the most important centres of Tibetan Buddhism, housing over 3,000 monks. She was settled
in the precinct of the Pegyai Lama's palace in a corner of a tiny cloister;
from her balcony she could see the golden roofs of the temples and the
grassy slopes beyond, where the shaggy yaks and the camels of the Mongolian caravans leisurely grazed. In the serenity of the evening hours, she
could listen to the harmonious music played by the lamas as they serenaded
the gods from the terraces of the Great Hall. In the 'subtle voluptuousness
of solitude and silence', she studied the books which had been taken for her
from the sealed bookcases, books carefully and lovingly wrapped in irides-
cent yellow brocade. 'It was delightful to study and meditate in such surroundings.' Women were not allowed to live in a monastery, but Alexandra
had the blessings of the Dalai Lama and the Panchen Lama, for she was a
scholar and a 'lady lama'. To Alexandra, it was all sheer bliss; she rose at
six; at nine she breakfasted, then studied the sacred books; at noon she
bathed and worked until four; at nine she was in bed. For Yongden, there
were no restrictions; he was a student and a monk. Kum-Bum monastery
was immense and the lives of its inmates strictly regulated. Later, in her book
With Mystics and Magicians in Tibet, published in an English edition in 1931,
Alexandra was to write in detail about the fantastic and magical world in
which the hierarchy of monks had their being, although Graham Sandberg
in *Tibet and the Tibetans* took a less lofty view than that of Alexandra David-
Neel. 'Amongst the Buddhist fraternity', he wrote, 'the highest ambition in
real life is not the attainment of Nirvana, but the acquirement of magical
powers.'

In all this time, Alexandra and Philippe wrote to each other. She was
appalled at the position of married women in various countries she had passed
through and, as a liberated woman herself she viewed with horror the sub-
servience of Indian wives and the lack of comradeship between many
French husbands and their wives. To Philippe she expressed her views,
clearly and frankly; he became her 'sole link' with the Western world and
she was sincerely grateful for the money he sent her, enabling her to live the
life she so desperately needed, the life that gave her happiness. In 1920 she
asked him to buy a piece of land for her in the south of France, where she
could live as she grew older, putting into book form all the material she had
gathered in her wanderings. In a strange occult way, she seemed to be
aware of the great age to which she would live and perhaps, in her mind's
eye, she saw herself putting down her pen with the words: '*Je ne peux plus
écrire.*' About this time she thought seriously of taking Yongden with her to

live in France; he was her adopted son and he could be useful in the house and help her considerably with her Tibetan studies. Philippe was totally opposed to the idea.

After Kum-Bum, her thoughts turned to Lhasa, although the city itself did not particularly interest her. 'Strange as the fact may appear', she wrote, 'I must confess that, unlike most travellers who have attempted to reach Lhasa and have failed to reach their goal, I never entertained a strong desire to visit the sacred Lamaist city. I had, as I have said, met the Dalai Lama, and as for researches regarding the literature, philosophy, and secret lore of Thibet, these things could be pursued more profitably amongst the *literati* and mystics in the freely accessible and more intellectual parts of north-eastern Thibet, than in the capital. What decided me to go to Lhasa, was above all, the absurd prohibition which closes Thibet. A prohibition – one could hardly think it possible – that extends over a gradually increasing area is now placed on foreigners who wish to cross territories over which they could travel at will a few years ago, and where, in a still more ancient period, missionaries have even owned properties.'

At the beginning of the seventeenth century the Headquarters of the Jesuits in the East was at Goa and the vital question was; were there not Christians to be found beyond the Himalayas? There had been Nestorian Christians some centuries before and tales of priests in black frocks and caps had circulated amongst merchants; an expedition to Tibet was organized in 1602 and after that date several Jesuis attempted the journey, Benedict de Goes dying at Suchow after great tribulation at the age of forty years (Mildred Cable saw his tomb which the Muslims built for him outside the Great Wall). In October 1661, the Jesuits Grueber and d'Orville journeyed from the Koko Nor Lake to Lhasa and later Ippolito Desiseri, perhaps the greatest of the early travellers to Tibet, entered that city with Father Freyre.

Until the end of the eighteenth century, only physical obstacles stood in the way of travellers entering Lhasa. Desiseri and Freyre arrived in the city, Desiseri to live there for thirteen years, a true spiritual ancestor of Alexandra David-Neel. After the Dutchman, Van der Putte, there is no record of a European reaching Lhasa until Thomas Manning arrived and stayed for four months. The French Lazarist missionaries Huc and Gabet reached Lhasa in 1846 and were the last travellers to enter Lhasa freely. In the second half of the nineteenth century, traveller after traveller had been turned back after attempting to reach Lhasa; Rockhill made two attempts in the guise of a pilgrim; Littledale reached a point only forty miles from Lhasa but he, too, was refused permission to enter. The British Expedition in 1904, under Sir Francis Younghusband, entered Lhasa and concluded a treaty with Tibet and extended the system of triangulation which finally determined the position of that city. Annie Taylor had served as a nurse at Base Camp in the Chumbi Valley, taking off her red Tibetan robe, putting away the yellow one given her as a mark of honour by the lamas, and adopting once again English dress. In the garden at the front of the small house, she had planted flowers. Captain Rawling surveyed 35,000 square miles of unexplored country in north-west Tibet in 1905, but after the British Mission, apart from officers and medical staff, no foreigner had been allowed to proceed to Lhasa. Alexandra David-Neel was determined to succeed where others had failed.

She left Kum-Bum with a sad heart. 'Joyous confidence and painful misgiving mingled and fought, for different reasons, in each of us. To start on a long journey, in this part of Asia, is always a step into the unknown', she wrote. With Yongden she travelled through Szechwan towards Tibet, then to Jaykendo, a monastery in northern Tibet. Her travels finally took her to Mongolia and the Gobi Desert, across which Mildred Cable and her colleagues were to travel on their way out of China a very few years later. With the faithful Yongden she soldiered on, living modestly, trying not to attract too much attention, her initial enthusiasm dampened by the pouring rain, landslides, flooded valleys, mud, dirt and damp of the inns of western China. 'I had the sacred fire of adventure, and no doubt, that sufficed to keep me physically as well as morally warm, for my health remained good and I escaped even the ordinary cold.' But it was a trying time, all the same, and lack of money almost made her give up the struggle; bandits and robbers were a constant threat and she dreaded death due to starvation and exposure.

China was a totally different question from Sikkim and India; there were check points to get by and watchful eyes of Chinese soldiers to elude. Food and beasts of burden were obtainable only by requests on paper to the Head Men or Magistrates of villages *en route* and at one point she almost turned back along the same route she had followed so laboriously. To suspicious soldiers she had an answer; 'Give me my revolver. I shall kill myself. Everyone will then believe that you have murdered me and you will suffer the consequences of this crime.' Alexandra could never accept the fact that it was well-nigh impossible to proceed to Lhasa and, at fifty-five years of age, was ready to show 'what a woman can do'.

In her introduction to *My Journey to Lhasa*, Alexandra David-Neel sets out the reasons for her determination to visit Lhasa; one of them was a practical one; 'I wanted the right to exhort others to pull down the antiquated

barriers which surround in the center of Asia, a vast area extending approxi-
mately from 79 to 99 longitude . . . if "Heaven is the Lord's", the earth is
the inheritance of Man, and that consequently any honest traveller has the
right to walk as he chooses, all over that globe which is his.' The prohibition
which closed Tibet seemed to her an absurd one.

My Journey to Lhasa was published in 1927 and well received. A reviewer
writing in the *Geographical Journal* acknowledged that 'Madame David-Neel
has performed a very courageous and a very difficult feat in travelling to
Lhasa from China. Those who know the terrible cold and the disgusting
dirt of Tibet can best appreciate the endurance it must have required to live
as she did for months in Tibetan houses of the poorest type and among the
lowest classes. The filth of the food would alone be sufficient to deter most
travellers.' The reviewer, however, deplored the anti-British sentiment
which appeared to run through some of the pages of the book and thought
that she could have written less disparagingly of the British who 'after all
have done more than any other people to open Tibet'.

The journey to Lhasa was different from all other journeys undertaken by
Alexandra David-Neel. It was the culmination of her life's work and it was
to be the proof that a woman could visit Lhasa and, with a fox's cunning,
outwit the Chinese Authorities. It was to be no longer Sikkim, with
peaceful stays at *gomchens*; it was China and Tibet, with terrifying sojourns
among Tibetan tribes, unaware of the true identity of the *philing* in their
midst. There were the Khams or Khamdo, comprising tribes of very
diverse characteristics, some of them independent and lawless; the Abors of
the extreme south-east, who had little Buddhism but powerful shamans; the
Mishmis of the mountainous tracts of Sadiya in Assam who were murderous
kidnappers of young people for the slave trade with the Tibetans at Zayul.
With rough maps stuffed into her boots which her friend, General Pereira, a
British explorer, had given her, she contemplated crossing the Tibetan
plateau into unmapped country, wild and inhospitable.

Her successive departures into Tibet had been very different from one
another. She wrote;

Some have been joyful, enlivened by the babbling and broad laughter of the
servants and country folk, the jangling of bells hung on the mules' necks, and that
rough yet gay fuss that the peoples of Central Asia so love. Others were touching,
grave, almost solemn when, dressed in the full lamaist garb of dark purple and
golden brocade, I blessed the villagers or the dokpas (inhabitants of the solitudes)
who had congregated to pay for the last time their respects to the *Kandhoma*'s
tragic departure, when blizzards raged in the solitudes, sweeping across awe-

inspiring white landscapes of impassable snow and ice, soon to be wrapped again in dead silence.

This time, with Yongden ('Yongden has travelled with me for eight years'), a small tent and two coolies, they had the appearance of holiday-makers taking a trip for a week or two and the villagers were in no doubt that some kind of a botanical excursion had been planned; many foreigners were interested in the plant life of the country and set off gleefully to collect lichens and flowers.

The foreign Mission House where they had stayed, begging the hospitality of the missionary for a few days, was soon out of sight and Alexandra's fifth journey into Tibet had begun. They had said nothing of their plans to journey to Lhasa, nothing of the hopes and fears of those unforeseen incidents which could wreck their schemes. Alexandra wrote;

What would be the end of this new attempt? I was full of hope. A previous experience had proved to me that in the disguise of a poor traveller I could escape notice. But although we had already succeeded in leaving quietly behind the baggage brought with us to cross China, we had yet to assume our full disguise and (most difficult task) to get rid of the two coolies whom we were compelled to take with us to avoid the gossip which would certainly have spread in the Mission House amongst the servants and neighbours, had they seen a European lady setting out with a load upon her back.

They had commenced their journey from the Gobi desert above the Koko Nor and travelled south to Szechwan, making a southern turn to avoid the regular caravan route from Peking to Lhasa. From the Mission House north of Lichiang they encamped on a sheltered tableland where they could see the Kha Karpo range, 'the vultures' cemetery', for once a year the Chinese slaughtered hundreds of the birds to collect their feathers which they sold.

The two coolies were got rid of by a ruse and over Tibetan tea they discussed the other 'personalities' which they were to assume once they had crossed over the Dokor Pass, where they would be in independent Tibet. They travelled light, as poor folk, with only one aluminium pot, which served as kettle, teapot, and saucepan; for Yongden there was one lama wooden bowl and for Alexandra one aluminium one, two spoons and a Chinese travelling case with long knife and chopsticks. Their meals were to be those of ordinary Tibetan folk of the lower classes, buttered tea and *tsampa*.

They travelled stealthily by night, leaving the villages behind them, trudging humbly along in the valley and covering themselves with dry leaves in the forest at night. The best disguise of all, they decided, was that of *arjopas* (mendicant pilgrims) who wander in thousands across Tibet, visiting the sacred places – it was an effective disguise and with Yongden along, should prove highly satisfactory. Alexandra was the aged mother of Yongden, undertaking a pilgrimage for religious reasons and her thorough detachment from worldy cares was 'the most blessed existence one can dream of'. Their only code now was 'to avoid detection' and to this end they devised a simple string of Tibetan words; '*Karma pa kien mo*!' which meant 'let us be off quickly!' They came to the foot of the Dokor Pass in the early evening, uttered the Buddhist wish 'May all beings be happy!' and descended. From then on, they were in constant danger. There was no village in which they could find shelter for it was not easy to escape detection as *philings*, although Alexandra had darkened her fair skin with cocoa and charcoal and had wound her hair with yak-hair. The ignorant villagers could easily be put off, but the monks had travelled for vast distances on their journeys and had met many *philings*. Sleep was not always comfortable; they eventually devised a plan of spreading their little white tent over the ground and then creeping in – from a distance it looked like winter snow. Sometimes it was necessary to forego the purchase of food and they went hungry, often for three days until Yongden, as a 'Red Hat' lama, could use his begging bowl. It was imperative that he walk in front of his 'aged mother', for her blue eyes could give her away as a *philing* (gray and blue eyes were the 'white eyes' of foreigners).

Their greatest fear was that of being found out as 'foreigners'; spies lurked behind every bush and rock and once, when they were seated by a fire which the cowmen had lit, the conversation turned on the despised *philings*. 'Yongden boasted of having met two of them in northern Tibet, but for my part I humbly confessed that I had never caught sight of any.' There were amusing patches, too, when Alexandra found a little 'fun' to lighten the way to Lhasa. A lama had requested Yongden to perform the rites for the dead for the relatives of some wealthy people living on the other side of the Salween. Alexandra was also asked if she would chant *Aum mani padme hum hri* at the door in return for food. Yongden declined as he had no wish to remain amongst the villagers as they were so near the border and there was always the danger of being sent back. Alexandra regretted that they could not stay; 'I would have enjoyed the fun of reciting *mani* "at the door".' The future was to give her many opportunities of chanting *mani* and, in fact, she became quite expert at it and was complimented twice for the 'nice way I had of chanting it'. *The Journal of the West China Border Research Society*, vol. XIII 1941, gives a very good explanation of this mysterious phrase.

Alexandra settled down to the life of the poorer classes. It was quite a change for her; she was no longer the 'lady-lama', the friend of the Dalai and the Panchen lamas, studying the ancient Buddhist scriptures in the quiet serenity of the monasteries. It was now incumbent upon her to obey local customs 'in order to preserve my incognito' and there were times when she longed to escape to the air of the forests and the mountains. Everything was done in public; the filth of the food had to be endured and the meal made from the decaying stomach of a diseased animal had to be commented upon most favourably and enjoyed with 'thanks'.

In the majestic Nu Valley her identity as a *philing* was almost discovered. In order to disguise herself as a Tibetan she had used Chinese ink to blacken her hair, but this dye wore off and had to be renewed from time to time. She still had dye on her fingers when a good housewife called them in for a meal. Curd and *tsampa* were prepared in a bowl and fingers were used to knead the mixture. As dirty streaks of black dye began to appear in the bowl, her white skin began to show. Luckily, Yongden came to the rescue and advised her to 'eat quickly!'

Sleep in the homes of the poorer classes was always a problem. If the housewife of a squalid, filthy dwelling offered her hospitality at night, it had to be accepted. After a meal of soup, nettles and *tsampa*, the family laid down on the earthen floor, Alexandra on a piece of sacking and Yongden, as befitting his rank, on a small piece of carpet. 'The lower classes in Thibet always sleep doubled up, like dogs, almost in the form of a ball, and they never possess carpets or cushions as long as their own bodies. To sleep with the body fully extended is regarded as a luxury pertaining to "the Quality" alone.' Luckily, Alexandra slept in her thick clothes and so was able to hide from prying eyes the belts containing their gold and silver, maps, miniature compasses, watches and thermometer. It was advisable to get up very early, before the others, for the dark hid her face and hands, which one perceptive Tibetan lady had once called 'foreign hands'; fortunately it was easier to travel with Yongden as her son for he was a 'Red Hat' lama and greatly respected as he was able to cast out demons and tell fortunes or foresee happenings. All this delayed them, but it was necessary and gave them a margin of safety.

And so she gradually assumed the *arjpo* and fitted her spirit into the body of the poor, downtrodden, dirty and ignorant peasant woman who would have jumped over the moon to have a meal of nauseating food and sleep on the earth floor in a communal room, with folk whose idea of privacy was non-existent. 'In a country where everything is done in public, down to the most intimate personal acts, I was forced to affect peculiar local customs which embarrassed me terribly. However, our way at times lay through large tracts of uninhabited land, and the greater freedom I enjoyed there somewhat relieved my painful tension.'

As they neared the high passes, the way became more and more arduous and the only sustaining meals they were lucky enough to have were made of water, bits of dry bacon and handfuls of flour and tea made with salt-butter, and *tsampa*; these warded off the intense cold and the freezing water of the streams through which they had to wade as best they could.

The pass was high, but they were lucky to find it open. It was bitterly cold and they were unable to light a fire, for the flint and steel which Yongden always carried were useless in the damp, dripping atmosphere, which had so enveloped them that they tramped until two o'clock in the morning to keep themselves warm. 'Jetsunma [Reverend Lady]', said Yongden, 'you are, I know, initiated in the *thumo reskiang* practice. Warm yourself and do not bother about me. I shall jump and keep my blood moving.' Alexandra had studied the art of *thumo reskiang* and resolved to use her knowledge to warm both herself and Yongden;

I put the flint and steel and a pinch of the moss under my clothes, sat down, and began the ritualistic practice. I mentioned that I felt sleepy on the road; the exertion while collecting fuel and pitching the tent, the effort to kindle the fire, had shaken my torpor, but now, being seated, I began to doze. Yet my mind continued to be concentrated on the object of the *thumo* rite. Soon I saw flames arising around me; they grew higher and higher; they enveloped me, curling their tongues above my head. I felt deliciously comfortable.

To acquire the mysterious heat of *thumo* which warms the hermits in the high altitudes of Tibet, it was necessary to be taught and trained by a master who was an adept; the 'empowerment' is preceded by a long period of probation. Alexandra, whose period of probation was shorter than that of the Tibetan hermits, was told by the venerable lama to bathe in an icy mountain stream in a lonely spot and to spend the night motionless in meditation, without drying her body or re-placing her clothes. The altitude was 10,000 feet and her description of the night as 'rather chilly' was a masterpiece of understatement. 'I felt very proud of not catching cold', she wrote. Many Tibetan hermits go safely through the ordeal each year, ascribing their endurance to the power to generate *thumo* and thus, at an altitude which varies from 11,000 to 18,000 feet and clad only in a thin garment, escape freezing to death.

The ice breaking in the river awoke her from her dream-state; the flames disappeared into the earth and fire seemed to burst out of her fingers and head. Yongden returned with cow-dung and branches of leaves and a fire was made. 'How have you done it?' he asked. 'It is the fire of *thumo*', she replied.

There were still more ranges to climb and valleys to cross in 'an immense space in which we were the only living beings'. In a mountain hut they encountered a place of the dead for bones littered the floor. Tibetans prefer cremation to other forms of burial. The great lamas are treated differently from the ordinary folk; they are incarcerated in huge cauldrons filled with butter. The common folk, being unable to afford such expensive fuel, are placed on the hills, where their bones are picked clean by the vultures and wild animals. When the bones are dry they are collected by the family and pounded into dust by a Lama, then mixed with clay and moulded into miniature *chortens*. These are kept by the family in caves or other places near the villages.

On the way to the upper Po snow began to fall; they found a shelter and slept, numb with cold, and awoke to find themselves practically submerged in their sloping shelter fixed with a few stones to a rock. They had no fuel and Yongden had sprained his ankle, but Alexandra found a 'peculiar charm' in the situation, so much so that it triumphed over all the physical discomfort. She remained seated and motionless, enjoying the 'absolute silence, the perfect stillness, of that strange white land, sunk in rest, in utter peace'.

After four months of hard travelling, they hit the old post road from Peking to Lhasa and crossed the final pass on the last stages of their journey. They had lived as beggars, sometimes going hungry for days; they had slept wherever a dry hut or cave presented itself; they had encountered rough hospitality and they had pitted their wits against Tibetan villagers and rapacious brigands. By superhuman guile, born of necessity, they had escaped detection as *philings*. Alexandra allowed no gloomy thoughts to distract her from her goal. At the commencement of her tremendous journey she had written; 'Whatever might be the future, I would not shrink from it ... Many travellers had been stopped on their way to Lhasa, and had accepted failure. I would not. I had taken the challenge by my oath on the "iron bridge" and was now ready to show what a woman can do.'

Alexandra had steadfastly refused to admit that they could never reach

Lhasa and now, as they crossed a river on a rustic ferry crowded with animals and men, her belief in her manifest destiny was fully justified. The roofs of the Potala glistened in the sun, but their view was not clear for a violent storm arose, enveloping everyone in sheets of lashing, dry dust which cut their faces with whips of stinging sand, as they bent double to escape the scourge.

It was the Tibetan New Year and the inns were full. In the wretched hovel where she and Yongden had found shelter for the night, her adopted son threw caution to the winds.

'Do you allow me now to say that we have won the game?'
'Yes'.
'*Lha gyalo. De Tamche pam!* We are at Lhasa.'

Alexandra meant to enjoy herself; there had been so much agony, so much hardship, so much wretchedness and physical discomfort, that she considered it was 'a well-won reward after the trials on the road and the vexations by which for several years various officials had endeavoured to prevent my wanderings in Thibet', and she intended that no-one should deprive her of the sights and ceremonies of the Tibetan New Year. Mingling with the happy crowds, she became one of them, watching the spectacles and pageants, the cavalcades of men dressed in the style of days gone by, the mail-clad infantry of ancient kings, and the violent and dangerous horse-races. The following day she watched several thousand men march in file around the Potala, carrying huge multi-coloured silk flags and state umbrellas, while several bands marched with the procession, the wailing Tibetan *gyalings* sending their solemn notes over the valley and the Mongolian musicians filling the air with sweet tunes and soft bells. 'Unforgettable spectacle which alone repaid me for my every fatigue and the myriad dangers that I had faced to behold it!'

But it was the Potala, the 'Tibetan Vatican', that she had come so far to see, with its suites of rooms, galleries and innumerable corridors, decorated by Chinese artists. The scenery of Lhasa would be unimpressive were it not for the two palaces erected on two summits of a ridge commanding a large valley. One of them is called *Chog Buri* and is crowned by the buildings of the Clerical Medical College; the other bears the magnificent edifice known as the Potala, a red palace capped with golden roofs thrusting to the blue sky. Vast, awe-inspiring and beautiful as it was with its dazzling white base and apartments too numerous to count, Alexandra lost no time in effecting an

[127]

entrance; the future was uncertain and she was extremely vulnerable to detection without the protection of the uncluttered wilderness. To be lost among a crowd of pilgrims was ideal. Conscious of the passing of time, she and Yongden moved amongst the sightseers in the hope of gaining admission. 'I was in Lhasa', she wrote, 'No doubt I could be proud of my victory, but the struggle, with cunning and trickery as weapons, was not yet over. I was in Lhasa, and now the problem was to stay there . . . All sights, all things which are Lhasa's own beauty and peculiarity, would have to be seen by the lone woman explorer who had had the nerve to come to them from afar, the first of her sex.'

Two country-men were selling barley before the entrance to the Potala and Yongden explained to them that by visiting the shrines they would achieve merit for themselves. As it was an honour to be instructed by a lama, they readily assented to enter the buildings, with Alexandra and Yongden as their companions. The long flight of stairs was climbed and the upper gate reached before ill-luck struck. 'I was about to follow humbly, when a boy, ten or twelve years old, a novice lama, short and fat, with a red face, flat nose, and large ears, looking like a gnome in a clerical robe twice too large for him, stopped me. He was acting as doorkeeper, and he ordered me rudely to take off my fur-lined bonnet, such headgear not being allowed inside the Potala.'

The bonnet had been a useful disguise in her Tibetan wanderings; it had screened her face and covered her hair, which she had dyed black. The dye had, unfortunately, worn away before she reached Lhasa and her own brown hair was now conspicuous under the black braid of Yak-hair. However, no-one seemed to notice and she followed the crowd along corridors and up steep staircases to the top, enjoying the view. The steep sides of the Potala were covered with colonnades, halls and tombs to a height of 300 feet, the whole being surmounted by five gold-plated concave cubes. From the entrance in the south-east there was a long hall and from here innumerable ladders take one through the entire height of the Red Palace, thirteen storeys of pure wonderment and magic. There were figures representing Tibet's warrior kings and their queens and an immense *chörten* of the fifth Dalai Lama in a huge edifice of several storeys erected within the Potala itself. Solid gold butter-lamps stood on every altar, and gold, silver and copper images of the Buddha and the saints were everywhere. There were rooms after rooms filled with porcelain, carved jade and oriental silks, the gifts of the Chinese royal house. On the lower floor were the offices of officials and in the Treasury were stored the gifts of centuries. In the upper storey of

Chokhang, the Cathedral of Lamaism, were stores of butter and supplies for the use of the monks within the palace and the visiting lamas, sometimes as many as twenty thousand. As a contrast to the dazzling display of Chinese porcelain and the lavish use of gold and silver ornaments, dark labyrinths and recesses contained images of the aboriginal gods and demons of the Tibetan religion before the introduction of Buddhism. 'So we went on, having reached the top of the dominating Potala, and enjoyed the beautiful sight of Lhasa, its temples and monasteries, lying at our feet like a white, red, and gold carpet spread in the valley.' Alexandra had reached her goal. 'All is well', said Yongden.

Alexandra left Lhasa quietly. She had gained enormous confidence as her identity as a foreigner had never been discovered, even when she became the object of the jokes of the market-traders. Now she departed with the faithful Yongden, no longer a lowly member of society but a middle-class woman with two horses and a man servant, in a garb befitting her station in life. She had decided to continue walking 'most of the time'. Even with a heavy load on her back, the wilderness trail to Lhasa had not been without enjoyment; with the horses as pack animals she could hunt for old manuscripts and books to add to her library. The river Kyi Chu 'The River of Happiness' led out on the south side and from there they ascended a small pass to gaze upon the Potala for the last time. 'Lhasa had forever gone from my eyes and taken its place in my world of memories.'

Lhasa had gone, but Tibet remained. Alexandra had wandered too long at her own pace to plough a straight furrow now; there were still monasteries to visit, shrines to gaze at, mysteries to ponder over – the field of the occult in Tibet is endless. The Samye monastery had an air of magic and mystery for it was the first Buddhist monastery to be built and contained a shrine ('House of the Vital Breath') where the breath of every being who had died on earth was conserved. At *Tag chen Bumba* she climbed the narrow stairs and gazed through an aperture in one of the two *chortensa*, a large one built over a smaller one. If she saw many lighted lamps it showed that her mind was pure; ordinary mortals saw no lighted lamps, for there was only darkness. 'I looked toward China, whence I had come', she wrote, 'but something made me feel that what I had done must be known.'

She arrived at Gyantze at dusk and went straight to the bungalow of the British Trade Agent, David Macdonald. In his book *Twenty years in Tibet*, published in 1932, he describes how he met Alexandra David-Neel. One afternoon in August 1923, he was informed that a lady in a white Tibetan dress and a man dressed as a lama wished to see him. He was told by the *chapprassi* that they looked like tramps, but the lady spoke in a peremptory manner 'just like Europeans'. The lady was Alexandra David-Neel. She was received in the sitting-room and gave a brief account of her long journey from China to Tibet, accompanied by Yongden. She had spent two months in Lhasa without detection, but now required a room in a rest-house and had requested the headmaster of the Tibetan Boys' school in Gyantse to accommodate her. He had sent her on to Mr Macdonald, as he alone had the authority. The eldest daughter of Mr Macdonald supplied her with lighter clothing, as she would be travelling in India and Sikkim after leaving Tibet. Mr Macdonald noted her frailty; 'to succeed as she had called for immense courage and vitality'.

Mr Macdonald also met another remarkable woman on the road between the Sikkim-Tibet frontier and Yatung at the Chinese Customs Post; Annie Taylor, member of the defunct Tibet Pioneer Christian Mission. At the time of the 1903/4 Mission to Tibet she was installed at the Trade Mart at Yatung as nurse; some years before she had attempted to reach Lhasa but had been turned back by the Chinese. With Miss Bella Ferguson, they were the only known Christian missionaries conducting mission work in Tibet.

There still remained the wilderness journey across the tablelands to the Tibet-India border, but in Sikkim she could assemble her thoughts and put her numerous writings in order, for the time was now ripe to present her experiences to the world; there were books to be written, magazine articles to be prepared, and a publicity machine to be put into motion. 'The first white woman had entered forbidden Lhasa and had shown the way', she wrote in her book *My Journey to Lhasa*. It now remained for her to acquaint the world with this fact.

Money was still a problem and she anxiously awaited word from Philippe; she had not heard from him since 1922, two years earlier, and a passage had to be booked on a ship to Europe if she wished to make good use of her publishing connections. It was not at all certain that her life with Philippe could be resumed; he sent her the money but was not at all enthusiastic about her returning to France. The First World War had left its mark on thousands of people and times were hard. Besides, there still remained the vexed question of Yongden and Alexandra's insistence that he return to France with her.

America was suggested, but that would have meant a plunge into the western world with a vengeance. Offers were coming along for her manuscripts and the French Consul and important French academics suggested that she return to Paris; with a logic born of necessity Alexandra decided to return to the west and in May 1925, after nearly fourteen years in Asia, she set foot on the soil of France.

From Le Havre she travelled by train to Marseilles and in the railway station she met Philippe in a confrontation which proved abortive. The adoption papers which would make Yongden her adopted son were duly signed by Philippe, although he would have preferred her to have stayed in Asia, along with Yongden and all her Tibetan and Chinese books.

She was now with honour in her own country. Awards were heaped upon her; she received the *Grande Médaille d'Or* from La Société de Géographie besides other distinguished awards. She lectured throughout France, Belgium and Switzerland and her talks at the Theosophical Society of Paris and that of London were enthusiastically received. She was fifty-nine years of age when *My Journey to Lhasa* came out in 1927 and her book *With Mystics and Magicians in Tibet* reached a vast reading public in 1931. At the age of sixty-eight, she published *Tibetan Journey*.

Reviewers of her books were kind, although one gentleman drew attention to the anti-British sentiment not founded on facts. 'But Madame Neel acknowledges that she takes little interest in politics. If she studied them at all she would know that the Dalai Lama is as independent of Great Britain as is the President of the French Republic, and has, and exercises, the right to admit or refuse to admit to Lhasa whom he will . . . If Madame Neel had been more fully aware of this she might perhaps have written less disparagingly of the British, who after all have done more than any other people to open Tibet.'

Philippe and Alexandra were still in touch with each other; Philippe, as always, was loving kindness itself, giving her money and arranging for the storing of her Oriental books and purchases. In 1927 she bought a house at Digne, near Nice, and here she gathered up all her treasures; there was a room for meditation, a Tibetan altar, a figure of Buddha and, in the large garden, chestnuts and acacia trees. She named the house *Samten Dzong*, 'Fortress of Meditation' and, later on, Philippe visited her from time to time, helping her with her manuscripts.

Soon she was restless again. Giuseppe Tucci, the Italian scholar and Orientalist, was about to publish his work on the translation of *Tsong Khapa*, which Alexandra herself was also translating. It was necessary that she find a Tibetan scholar who could assist her with the translation. On 9 January, 1936, three years before the beginning of the Second World War, she left with Yongden for Western China, taking the Trans-Siberian Railway from Moscow. The Japanese had invaded Manchuria and the time was not propitious for travellers to visit China; Chinese spies were everywhere and all foreigners were suspect. To get to Hong Kong from Chungking was out of the question; the Japanese had sealed the railway leading from the coast to Yünnan (Kumming) and, as she had no money to venture further, Alexandra decided to try to reach Tatsienlu on the high road to Tibet.

Three months before her seventieth birthday, she and Yongden reached Tatsienlu after having been carried in a sedan chair up the mountains while a storm raged for ten days and blinding rain soaked them to the skin. It was July 1938. She was happy in Tatsienlu; there were missionaries there and it was cheap to live (always an important factor with Alexandra, dependent upon Philippe). The air was bracing and pure and with better health Alexandra wrote avidly about every aspect of life in China at that time. Even a terrible winter snowstorm did not deter her or dampen her rising spirits; she was near her beloved Tibet and the language was spoken – she felt at home. In January 1941 Philippe died at the family home in the south of France where he was looked after by his niece. Her letter to Alexandra was received belatedly; 'I have lost the best of husbands', she said many times.

Towards the end of the war in Europe, the Japanese were dangerously near Tatsienlu; Alexandra and Yongden loaded their meagre possessions on to the backs of two tired mules, joined the stream of refugees and pushed on, hoping to find the French Military Mission and induce the authorities to fly them both out of China. The lack of food, the wretched weather, the hardship and the long marches had held no terrors for them, but Alexandra was now no longer young and Yonden had a destiny to inherit. The Mission was found and they left China by plane, one time when they neither foot-slogged, nor jolted along on the backs of weary mules.

Back at Digne, Alexandra lived peacefully, surrounded by her Oriental treasures, which included many weird and wonderful things, including the ashes of Yongden who had died at *Samten Dzong* at the age of fifty-five. She was looked after in her declining years by Marie-Madeleine Peyronnet, a young French girl from Algeria, who acted as companion and housekeeper and was happy to take Yongden's place as a student, sitting at the feet of the lady lama, now suffering from rheumatism and irascibility. Alexandra refused to think of age and made plans for further travel, proposing that she and Marie-Madeleine should visit Moscow to note the progress Russians were making on the building of Red Square: Marie-Madeleine could drive them in her little red car. Fortunately, Mademoiselle Peyronnet had the good sense to cry off, making a reasonable excuse.

Alexandra retained all her faculties; she was sharp and alert, especially where money was concerned and the foibles of publishers and business men were handled with that same degree of adroitness that had seen her through her Tibetan adventures. She was particularly adept on the question of royalties on her books. At a ceremony at Digne in May, 1964, she was promoted to a Premier Commandeur in the Légion d'honneur and thus received the final accolade which was her due.

She died on 8 September, 1969, just short of her 101st birthday, putting down her pen for the last time. '*Je ne peux plus écrire.*' She had come home at last.

Glossary of Terms

CHÖRTEN A religious monument of the kind that the Buddhists of India call *stupa*

DOKPAS People of the solitudes. Herdsmen who live in tents in the grass wastelands of Tibet

GOMCHEN A contemplative hermit

GOMPA Tibetan name for monastery

GYALING Long Tibetan horn

JETSUNMA 'Reverend lady'

MANI Current expression for the sacred formula *Aum mani padme hum!*

TSAMPA Flour, with which soup is made

THUMO RESKIANG A way devised by the Tibetan hermits to increase bodily heat in very low temperatures

TULKUS Those individuals whom foreigners incorrectly call 'Living Buddhas'. The reincarnation of a former individual. TULKA literally means 'an illusory body' created by magic

TULPA An ephemeral creation which may take different forms at the will of the magician

CHAPTER FIVE

Marianne North

A Lady who worked hard at what she liked best?

IN THE YEAR 1880 Sir Joseph Hooker planted the Chestnut Avenue in the Botanic Gardens at Kew and in the autumn of the following year 2,630 Alpine plants graced the rock garden. He was particularly impressed with the fine display of flora and in a letter to his son-in-law wrote; 'The Rock Garden is gorgeous!' Another event also took place in 1881; the announcement in the Director's Report of the completion of the structural work of the gallery which was to house the plant and flower paintings of Miss Marianne North.

On 8 June, 1882, the gallery was officially handed over to the Director, and on 9 July, 1882 it was opened to the general public. It contained 848 of her paintings, meticulously and formally arranged in tiers, the result of nearly twenty years of globe-trotting to far-away places in search of rare and beautiful flora, birds and insects. Sir Joseph Hooker, formerly President of the Royal Botanic Gardens at Kew said of the flora depicted; 'Very many . . . are already disappearing, or are doomed to disappear, before the axe, and the forest fires, the plough, and the flock of the ever-advancing settler and colonist. Such scenes can never be renewed by Nature, nor when once effaced can they be pictured to the mind's eye, except by means of such records as these.'

There was little attempt at artistic grouping, or geographical arrangement; the pictures were painted as representations of flowers as they blossomed, or fruits as they hung from the boughs, but the careful studies of moths and butterflies, birds and insects were faithful records rendered with almost scientific accuracy and attention to minute detail. There were harmonious combinations of colour in the paintings of Bornean orchids and climbing shrubs of Java, and the Jain Temple at Chittore shows Indian landscape faithfully reproduced. Each painting was executed 'on the spot' and often in much physical discomfort. It is a pity, though, that English

[134]

flower paintings were not included (in her book *Recollections of a Happy Life* she mentions that she often went to Chiswick Gardens to paint, but these do not appear to have been exhibited at any time at Kew). The only European one which graces the collection is that of the papyrus plant, which she painted in Sicily. Miss North wished her paintings to represent an 'integral whole'.

Less than two years after her death, her book *Recollections of a Happy Life*, edited by her sister, Mrs John Addington Symonds, was published: *Further Recollections* followed. The books give an account of her travels and of her studies of fauna and flora, which resulted in the paintings to be seen at Kew.

Marianne North was a painter and a traveller; she set up her easel on the plains and mountains of India; in the dense forests of Brazil; in the arboreal magnificence of California and the rugged terrain of Canada. She carried her palette and brushes in all sorts of harsh conditions, often in great physical suffering and ill health. She was more than just an amateur delineator; she was a botanist of rare intelligence, endowed with pertinacity and courage and more than her share of humour. The distinguished men and women she knew in her lifetime were countless; Joseph Hooker, President of the Royal Botanic Gardens at Kew; Wallace; Darwin; Francis Galton; the Erskine-Mays; the Benthams; and Edward Lear, who brought a breath of fun and a touch of springtime and lighthearted youth into the scientific circle meeting at Hastings Lodge. Lear was enchanted with her; and described her as 'a great draughtswoman, and Botanist; and is altogether graciously clever and delightful'.

Although she had a conventional upbringing; she was a person of joyousness, never bored, interested in others and in making friends with people and animals, which she loved. She did not set out on her travels with any purpose; she was a happy young lady content with family life and the knowledge that her ancestors had been delightful members of the English middle-class, leaving their legacies of art and music to their descendants. The countries of Europe were her early playgrounds and her universities; in company with her father she acquired that training of ear and eye which was to stand her in good stead in later years.

Of all the lady travellers of that era, perhaps Mrs Isabella Bird Bishop was the one with whom she had least in common, and an illuminating view of Marianne's reaction to her is shown in her book *Recollections of a Happy Life*.

I saw her first at a party, given by some relations of hers, who sent out cards – 'to meet Mrs. Bishop née Bird!' I found her seated in the back drawing-room in a big armchair, with gold-embroidered slippers, and a footstool to show them on, a petticoat all over gold and silver Japanese embroidered wheels, and a ribbon and order across her shoulders given her by the King of the Sandwich Islands. She was being interviewed in regular Yankee fashion; and I was taken up to her the moment I came in. Miss Gordon Cumming put her great hand on my shoulder at the same time, on which Lady A. joined our three pairs of hands and blessed us – 'three globe trotteresses all at once!' It was too much for the two big ones; and we retreated as fast as we could, leaving Miss Bird unruffled and equal to the occasion.

'It began in Hastings in 1830', she wrote in her book, 'but I have no recollections of that time, the gap of unreason shall be filled with a short account of my progenitors.' There were many, beginning with her ancestor, the Hon. Roger North, sixth son of Dudley, Lord North, Baron of Kelting. He was a noted lawyer and statesman, but is probably best remembered for his contribution to historical biography; his memoirs of his three elder brothers, Frederick, Baron Guildford, Lord Keeper of the Great Seal under Charles II and James II; The Hon. Sir Dudley North, a Commissioner of the Treasury to Charles II; and the Hon. and Rev. John North, Master of Trinity College, Cambridge, published in 1740 and 1742, rank with the diaries of Evelyn and Pepys and his own life written by Clarendon. He retired to the Old Hall at Rougham in Norfolk, built a library, covered his walls with pictures and lived to a ripe old age. Marianne North's father was his great-great-grandson. There was also a Squire of Rougham who ran away to sea to escape his father's constant floggings and a niece of Roger North, Dudleya North, 'whose great knowledge of languages would have been remarkable in any age'.

Marianne was born on 2 4 October, 1830 at Hastings Lodge, a fine house on the London Road. Round about the turn of the century, and after Marianne's death, it appears to have become a Hydro and Spa Hotel; later still, the finest rooms were rebuilt and incorporated into a convent. Marianne's father was Frederick North, Esq., M.P., of Rougham, Norfolk, and Hastings. He was successor to three generations of country squires, none of whom seemed to have inherited the talents of their ancestor, Roger North. He took an active interest in politics and in 1830 successfully contested the borough of Hastings and took his seat in the Commons as Liberal M.P. Marianne was wont to say years later that her earliest recollections were of the Hastings Reform Dinner given in 1831. Her mother, a stately beauty of Saxon type, was the daughter of Sir John Marjoribanks, Bart.; upon the death of her first husband, Robert Shuttleworth of Gawthorpe, she married Frederick North. Frederick North was much esteemed in the community; a local writer, who knew him well, wrote; 'for seven Parliaments the honest friend of the people' and the Vicar of Halton, the Rev. John Parkin, said of him; 'Mr. North is such a perfect gentleman that I am sorry that my politics prevent me from voting for him.'

Marianne had two sisters and a brother; the brother, Charles, educated at Eton and Oxford, lived on the estate at Rougham as Squire; one sister married John Addington Symonds, and the other became the wife of Kay Shuttleworth, the educationist.

Hastings in those days was a mere fishing village and St Leonards was truly a part of old England, for its name appeared on a map dated 1291. The old 'White Rock' was later removed piece by piece. As Marianne grew older, she became the constant companion of her father, whether trudging along the lanes at Rougham, or walking over the breezy Sussex Downs; Frederick North was hardly ever to be seen without his beloved 'Pop' and the Hastings fishermen long remembered their Member of Parliament as he strode down to the beach to see the nets drawn and the fish put up for auction, carrying Marianne upon his shoulders.

Marianne was devoted to her father, although she does not appear to have inherited a great deal from him; her passion for musical and pictorial art came to her from her ancestor, Roger North, for her mother cared little for music and her father had no ear for it. It was, to him, 'a horrid noise, which must be submitted to for the sake of others who like it'. Music was the love of her life in her young days; she played most of Beethoven's sonatas by heart and sang the best songs of the best composers in her fine, contralto voice. Amelia Edwards, writing in the *Hastings and St Leonards Observer* of 20 August, 1898 wrote; 'How she sang these songs, with what charm of tone, and with what breath and beauty of style, will not readily be forgotten by those who were privileged to hear her.' In her tours around Europe with her father, she cultivated her love of music, practising many hours during the winter in their Brussels's lodging under the guidance of Herr Kufferath, a pupil of Mendelssohn.

Painting went hand-in-hand with music; she had an admirable eye for form and colour and was passionately devoted to all forms of animal and insect life, although her delight in floral painting was eventually to take pride of place. Each summer on her journeys she filled her folio with sketches of flowers, lakes, mountains, and glaciers and in a letter from Thebes (dated 11 February, 1866) Lady Duff Gordon wrote; 'They are absolutely true in colour and effect, and are the very first I have seen that are so.' After the death of her mother, and after taking a few lessons from the artist, Valentine Bartholomew, she abandoned water-colours for oils.

Her home life was happy and settled; she lived a good deal apart from domestic chores, dividing her time between riding and painting, bubbling over with good spirits as she entertained the numerous guests who called at Hastings Lodge. Edward Lear was a frequent, and delightful, visitor, settling himself in the gardener's cottage and painting his pictures of the quarries of Syracuse and Thermopylae 'with our fig-tree in the foreground of the former, a group of ravens in the latter, all of them painted from one old specimen with a broken leg, which was fastened to an apple-tree opposite his windows.' He would let the children watch him at work and sing the songs of Tennyson 'for hours', concluding by singing out nonsensical patter words to the same tune. On one occasion when they visited Kew, Sir William Hooker gave her a bunch of the *Amherstia Nobilis* 'one of the grandest flowers in existence'.

During the winter of 1863–4 'we had a succession of nice people staying with us, whom our cousins in the Croft used to describe with youthful flippancy as "Old Couples without Encumbrances" '. There was Sir Edward Sabine (President of the Royal Society); the Benthams; the Francis Galtons; the Erskine-Mays; and Lady Hawes 'with a queer household of polyglot servants'. There was also a sprinkling of eccentrics, such as the lady who was interested in schemes of philanthropy for the improvement of the working classes (a subject very little touched upon), who carried models of drains, ploughs, and machines in her pockets, bringing them out whenever the conversation lagged.

She took flower-painting lessons from a Dutch lady, Miss van Fowinkel, who taught her the art of flower arrangement, colour and grouping although she would have much preferred tuition from old William Hunt who passed his winters in a small house under the East Cliff, making little sketches of boats and fishermen. A Madame Stainton-Dolby also gave her lessons in singing, cultivating her fine voice. The happy home-life, however, was fast drawing to a close. In July 1865 her father lost his seat in the Commons by nine votes and during that winter he and Marianne spent their days on a Nile boat, returning to England by way of Carinthia and the Tyrol. The season of 1867 was spent in Hastings for the garden was 'much of a weedery'; three glass-houses were built, water-pipes laid to irrigate the soil, and sick plants looked after, with the help of a young gardener from Wiltshire and a boy from Rougham. More travel followed, but at Salzburg Mr North fell ill and was brought home. He died at Hastings on 29 October.

Marianne was alone and bereft and wrote to a friend; 'He was far too tender and delicate to stand the rough ways of this world. It is well that he is now at rest; but for us the trouble is very great, and, for myself, all seems gone. I shall leave England as soon as possible.' She left the house at Hastings 'for ever' and went a-roving once more, taking with her the old family servant, Elizabeth, and settling down in the flat in Victoria Street, London, to resume her life. 'I could not bear to talk of him or anything else, and resolved to keep out of the way of all friends and relations till I had schooled myself into that cheerfulness which makes life pleasant to those around me.' The flat was cluttered with objects collected in travels with her father; stuffed birds in glass cases; butterflies in cabinets; collections of shells and musical instruments, which were now dust-gathering and lifeless and no substitute for the sun and warmth of spirit that she longed for. Without the vast circle of talented friends which had filled Hastings Lodge with the urgency of life, the Galtons, the Layards, Edward Lear and the Brasseys (who had given a fancy dress ball at Beauport 'the great event of the winter'), day-to-day living became a mere existence, a catalogue of routine perambulations between the stuffed *aves* and the cold comfort of beautiful, but inert, forms of necrophilia.

In 1871 she embarked at Liverpool for Jamaica and Brazil by way of the United States and Canada. 'I had long had the dream of going to some tropical country, to paint its peculiar vegetation on the spot in natural abundant luxuriance; so when my friend Mrs. S. asked me to come and spend the summer with her in the United States, I thought this might easily be made into a first step for carrying out my plan, as average people in England have but a very confused idea of the difference between North and South America. I asked Charles Kingsley and others to give me letters to Brazil and the West Indies, his book, *At Last* having added fuel to the burning of my rage for seeing the Tropics.' There was little tropical magic in North America, but there were a great many things to wonder at; the wooden house at Boston, of three storeys being moved on rollers; the home of Mr and Mrs Adams at Quincy Street, where whole volumes of Washington's letters and all his precious books were lovingly kept in a stone fire-proof library; Niagara, where 'The falls far outstretched my grandest ideas', (Isabella Bird had also been impressed by the falls; 'I do not care for any waterfall but Niagara').

In Washington she went to the opening of Congress.

We drove to the Capitol after breakfast, a really handsome white marble palace with a large dome over its centre; then wandered up and down, asking our way till we got to the gallery reserved for diplomats in the Lower House, and were told to take the front seats by Mr. P. the publisher to whom I had a letter, and who seemed to be a universal busybody, and most important personage. The House looked twice as large as our House of Commons; all the names were read over to 'the Bar of the House' (though there was no Bar). The oaths were decidedly calculated to keep truth-telling Southerners out, as they swore they had never counselled nor helped in any rebellion against the Government of the U.S. etc. etc. There were two black M.P.'s particularly well dressed (not a general fault in the assembly), and there was a very ample supply of bald heads, as well as some preposterously young-looking men. There was a female reporter among the others in gold bracelets and a tremendous hat and feathers; the messengers were all boys, who dashed about continually among the members below, sitting between whiles on the steps of the Tribune.

The White House was her next port of call;

I had a card brought me the next morning, 'The Secretary of State' and Mr. Fish followed it, to whom I had a letter of introduction. He was a great massive man, with a hard sensible head. He said he would call for me in the evening, and take me to the White House. So at eight o'clock in he came again after another big card, I being all ready for him in bonnet and shawl, and in no small trepidation at having to talk *tête-à-tête* with the Prime Minister in a small brougham. However, I found there was no need, as he did it all himself. We were shown in first to the awful crimson satin room in which Mrs. G. had described to me, with a huge picture of the Grant family all standing side by side for their portraits. Then we were told to come upstairs, and passed from staterooms to ordinary everyday life up a back staircase, which was the only means of reaching the upper storey allowed by the architect of seventy years ago. We were shown into a comfortable library and living-room, where a very old man sat reading the newspaper, Mrs. Grant's papa, who did not understand or hear any of the remarks Mr. Fish or I made. Then came Mrs. Grant, a motherly, kind body; then at last came the President, also a most homely kind of man.

They all sat 'rather wide apart' at first but Mrs Grant showed Marianne a book of dried grasses and she put on her spectacles and knelt at Mrs Grant's knee to look at them. 'They began to find out that I was not a fine-lady worshipper of Worth, and we all got chatty and happy. Mrs Grant confessed she had no idea "Governor Fish had brought me with him, or she would not have let me upstairs, but didn't mind now".' They went in to dinner in the blue satin oval room, where the President and Mrs Grant, Mr Porter, aide-de-camp, two Senators and the Secretary of Foreign Affairs sat down to dine.

After a terrible five minutes, dinner was announced, and to my horror the President offered me his arm and walked me in first (greatness thrust upon me). I looked penitently across at Mrs. G., who looked highly amused at my confusion, and did not pity me in the least. I was relieved by finding the great man did not care to talk while he ate, and General Porter was easy to get on with on my other side. He seemed to know every place, inhabited and uninhabited, in America. He gave me some curious accounts of the few remaining Indians, some of whom are as near animals as mortals can be, too lazy to look for food till the strong pangs of hunger seize them, when they sit down in a circle and beat down the grasshoppers with whips, gather them up and crush them in their hands, eating them just as they are, and then sleep again till the next fit of hunger seizes them. The President drank tea with his dinner, and had every dish handed to him first. He seemed an honest blunt soldier, with much talent for silence. His wife had a funny way, when shaking hands with people, of looking over their heads, and appearing to read off their names out loud from some invisible label there . . . General Cameron promised if I would come back in spring to take me to a place in Pennsylvania only eight hours off, where they still talked pure Elizabethan English, and to another where they can talk nothing but Dutch, having kept themselves apart from their neighbours. Miss Nelly got scolded for not playing the piano. She was kept very much at home, and not allowed to go with any of the fast girls of the day.

Christmas Eve saw her in the West Indies, arriving 'alone and friendless'. For four pounds a month she hired a house set amidst a deserted botanical garden of early settlers and with an old black woman and a 'coal black mortal with a gray head and tattered old soldier's coat', she painted all day, almost submerged by a tangle of tropical flora – lemon-verbenas, orchids, daturas, and hundreds of varieties of ferns. She was 'in a state of ecstasy'.

People always ask how I fed there. I used to buy two pounds of beef from the soldiers' rations at the guardhouse a mile or two down the valley every Saturday. The meat was tough at first, but every day we stewed it up with fresh vegetables; the black people brought eggs and vegetables, and a woman went once a week into Kingston and brought out any shopping I wanted. I was advised to buy some tins of turtle soup, and was amused to find they were made at Glasgow.

On 24 May, 1872 she embarked on the *Cuban* for Haiti, but was home in London on 16 June, to sample once more the dubious delights of the Victoria Street flat and the companionship of stuffed fauna and friends who could not give her the *rapport* she so desperately needed; they were no compensation for freedom and sunshine. On 9 August she was off again, 'in a most comfortable cabin, quite like a little room'. She did not land on

Madeira, which looked to her like a 'great cinder itself', but at Pernambuco she fetched her umbrella and braved the great sea-swells into the harbour. 'Friend', a Quaker from New York told her, 'a walk on shore will do thee good; my husband hath work to do there, and where he goeth I can go, and where I can go thee canst also.'

One must admire Marianne North, for the well-heeled Victorian lady from Hastings Lodge, accustomed to travelling in bourgeois comfort with her father, came face-to-face with great physical discomfort; the way up from Rio to the Morro Velho, where she was to stay with her friends, the Gordons, was in a carriage dragged by four mules for two miles at full gallop downhill. At Petropolis she took her place in the coach for Juiz de Fora and afterwards described it all in her book;

It rained all night, and was still raining when we packed ourselves into the coach at six on the morning of the 28th October, and four splendid mules, after their usual resistance, started suddenly at full gallop, with the swinging rattling old vehicle. A violent jerk brought us to the door of the other inn, and there our fourth place was filled up by a very important person in these pages, Antonio Marcus, commonly called the Baron of Morro la Gloria, who had been for forty years in the service of St. Jose del Rey Mining Company, to whose mine I was going. This old gentleman generally commanded 'The Troop' which brought the gold up to Rio every two months at least; he was a great character, full of talk and pantomime, either grumbling or joking incessantly, or sometimes even doing both at once.

In rain and mud they floundered on, looking like a scene from a Fellini movie, the loaded mules 'with their bare-legged black drivers, then the Baron in the shabbiest of straw hats, any quantity of worsted comforters, and brown coat and gaiters'. Marianne fitted into the scene perfectly, with her short linsey petticoat, long waterproof cloak and old black straw hat. At the Casa Grande of Morro Velho Marianne's life fell into a pattern of painting, walking, and botanical excursions for new wonders, 'I never found the dreary montonony Rio friends had talked about.'

Just below the flower garden was a perfect temple of bananas, roofed with their spreading cool green leaves, which formed an exquisite picture . . . Masses of the large wild white ginger flowers were on the bank beyond this temple, and scented the whole air. This was a grand playground for the Hector and Morpho butterflies; here, too, I used to watch the humming birds hovering over and under the flowers, darting from bush to bush without the slightest method.

Here is the Marianne North whose sense of colour and arrangement was first awakened by Miss Fowinkel's painting lessons at Hastings Lodge and whose keen eye as a draughtsman was inspired by Edward Lear as he let the children watch him at work in the garden, painting his masterpieces and uttering his nonsense patter with unaffected delight.

For the first time in her travels she encountered slavery. Although the anti-slavery movement had gained momentum since its inception in Britain in 1823, Brazil, Cuba and the southern states of America still maintained slave systems. In 1872, during her sojourn in Brazil, she accepted without question the presence of black slaves in the households and on the land.

It was an odd sensation living in an English colony which possessed slaves; but this company existed before the slave laws, and was with some others made exceptional. As far as I could see, the people looked as contented as the free negroes did in Jamaica, and, thanks to the new Brazilian regulations, they have the happiness of being allowed to buy themselves at a fixed price, if they can save sufficient money. The girl who brought me my coffee in the morning had bought two-thirds of herself from her own father, of whom she was hired by Mrs. C., as he was said to be such a brute that it was a charity to keep her out of his hands . . . If they have abundant food, gay clothing, and little work, they are tolerably happy: seven years of good conduct at Morro Velho gave freedom, which they had just sense enough to think a desirable thing to have.

It is doubtful whether Isabella Bird Bishop and her sister Hennie would have taken this detached viewpoint; Isabella wrote in her book *An English-woman in America*; 'Slavery, though under modifications which rendered it little more than the apprenticeship of our day, was permitted under Mosaic dispensation; but is contrary to the whole tenor of Christianity, and a system which lowers man as an intellectual and responsible being is no less morally than politically wrong.' Marianne's world was that of the naturalist and the artist; the socio-political questions of the day affected her but little and she willingly left them for others to solve. 'It is a mistake', she wrote, 'to suppose that slaves are not well treated; everywhere I have seen them petted as we pet animals, and they usually went about grinning and singing.'

March saw them in the Highlands, in a veritable wilderness of tropical vegetation where they stayed at a *Casa Grande* and played whist in a ghost-like old hall with hooks on the ceilings from which chandeliers had once hung and upon which a late superintendent had committed suicide.

From the Highlands back to Rio, where she was received everywhere with great hospitality and talked with the Emperor himself, who was greatly interested in scientific attainments. When His Majesty came to England in 1877, he toiled up the six flights of steps, attended by a single equerry, to visit Marianne in her London flat and pay her a farewell visit before leaving England.

One spot especially attracted me, where an old companion of Humboldt's had settled himself in an unpretending cottage. He had planted all sorts of rare plants and palms around it, and the real virgin forest sloped down to it at the back, while a glorious view of blue mountains was seen from the front window, with some few great forest giants left as foreground, their branches loaded with parasites and festooned with creeping plants.

The Emperor found the old German naturalist a pleasant companion but he was dying and the cottage would soon be in ruins. 'Already his treasures of moths, books, birds, and butterflies were half destroyed by mould and devouring ants; even the bridge which crossed the cascade and the path up to the house were falling away. I never felt anything more sad. Did I not paint? – and wander and wonder at everything? Every rock bore a botanical collection fit to furnish any hothouse in England.' But the time came to return to England; the gorgeous birds and butterflies, the strelitza, the daturas, the trumpet-trees, all had been lovingly transferred to canvas for the delight of future generations. During that winter in London she took lessons in etching on copper and visited her cousin, Dudley North, in hospital at Netley; the Queen went several times to enquire about the captain's health, calling him 'Major', which amused him as he said that he earned his promotion.

As the winter was a cold one, she determined once more to 'follow the sun' and in the summer of 1875 visited Chicago 'that gorgeously-slovenly, machine-made, and inflammable city', went to Salt Lake, where she had an interview with Brigham Young, 'horrid old wretch! my hand felt dirty for a week after shaking hands with him', and left for the big trees of Mariposa Grove. In San Francisco she saw the exhibition and the seals from Cliff House, but there was a wind, made worse from the lack of trees on the hills and she found the streets 'not agreeable'. It was no better in Japan, for the cold defeated her, although she saw much to paint. 'Latterly I suffered much from an attack of my old pain, brought on by the cold.' Singapore was her next stop; the gardens and rare plants were a source of great delight and she took tea with the famous Mr Wampoa 'whose hospitality and cordiality to the English have been so well known for half a century in the Straits'.

He showed us all his curiosities; but his garden was to me the great attraction, rare orchids hanging to every tree, and the great *Victoria regia* in full bloom in his ponds, as well as the pink and white lotus, and blue and red nymphaeas. Many of his plants were cut into absurd imitations of human figures and animals, to me highly objectionable, but amusing to the children. He had also several live creatures and birds of great beauty. He showed me a tortoise from Siam with six legs.

There was so much to paint for the great *Poinciana regia* in full scarlet blooms grew in his front garden at Government House. A branch was begged and hung up to paint but, unfortunately, Marianne had hung it up the wrong way 'a most absurd mistake'. It was some consolation, however, to learn that the Dutch lady, Madame von Nooten, had done the same thing and had published the painting. From Mr Wampoa to the 'White Rajah', Sir Charles Brooke and the Rani in Sarawak, to 'a most luxurious room' and a mounting admiration for the Rajah for his determination of character and his sense of justice which he had displayed in his handling of some Dyaks, who had come some distance in their canoes to ask his permission to take the heads of another tribe. They were politely told that 'they must not have that pleasure'. She went on to Kuching, where she found the custard-apple 'very difficult to paint', and Java, where she met Dr Burnell, to whom she wrote many letters in her later life.

He also contradicted me flatly when I talked of the *Amherstia nobilis* as a sacred plant of the Hindus. I said Sir W. Hooker told me it was so, and he said Sir William had been a great botanist, but was not a Hindu scholar. I had made a mistake, and I began to look at the little man with respect, and found he was Dr Burnell, the famous Indian scholar and Judge of Tanjore, making a pilgrimage to Boro-Boro during his short spring holiday; so we became friends, and continued so till he died.

Dr Burnell was the recipient of her thoughts and of her wit and her ability to sum up people and situations. She found no difficulty in expressing her reactions and her passionate belief in those ideals which she had found fast disappearing. 'It is a pity clever women make themselves laughed at, and I do not see the necessity for so much talk – quiet work is far more feminine, and the really great have had very little machinery to educate them.' In another letter from Coonoor, India, in 1878 she neatly summed up her views with a logic of outstanding clarity; 'there are certain things man must not reason upon and cannot understand, but which must be taken with faith and humility – I used to be told – a dictum I always resented, as it was treating "man" like a fool'.

The deep sorrow she had felt upon the loss of her father found an echo in a few pages penned to Dr Burnell, 'I have drifted with his sweet smile in my memory, merely painting to keep myself quiet and not to worry my neighbours more than I can help'; from Cochin she wrote straight from her heart to Dr Burnell; 'Thank you for your kind words about my father – you have had an escape in never having felt the loss of such a friend and yet I pity you your never having had the joy of possessing one – it quite compensates for the pain – and even now when I feel dull I can fancy his quiet old smile and voice and get comfort out of the very thought of it – sometimes as I sit and paint, he seems to come and watch me, and the very thought of him keeps me from harm.'

She was impressed with Java and the 'strong rule of the Dutch', and went on to Ceylon, which she reached at the end of 1876. At Kalutura she met Julia Cameron, the photographer, who lived on a small hill, surrounded by animals and birds and monkeys with gray whiskers. Julia was most anxious to photograph her;

The walls of the rooms were covered with magnificent photographs; others were tumbling about the tables, chairs, and floors, with quantities of damp books, all untidy and picturesque; the lady herself with a lace veil on her head and flowing draperies. Her oddities were most refreshing after the 'don't care' people I usually meet in tropical countries. She made up her mind at once she would photograph me, and for three days she kept herself in a fever of excitement about it, but the results have not been approved of at home since. She dressed me up in flowing draperies of cashmere wool, let down my hair, and made me stand with spiky cocoa-nut branches running into my head, the noonday sun's rays dodging my eyes between the leaves as the slight breeze moved them, and told me to look perfectly natural (with a thermometer standing at 96)! Then she tried me with a background of breadfruit leaves and fruit, nailed flat against a window shutter, and told *them* to look natural, but both failed, and though she wasted twelve plates, and an enormous amount of trouble, it was all in vain, she could only get a perfectly uninteresting and commonplace person on her glasses, which refused to flatter.

She left Kalutara on 21 January, 1877, taking a French steamer to Naples and then on to London to prepare a catalogue of her 500 plant studies for the Kensington Museum; 'I found people in general woefully ignorant of natural history, nine out of ten of the people to whom I showed my drawings thinking that cocoa was made from the cocoa-nut.'

In September 1877 she was once more on her travels – this time to return to Ceylon and then on to India. India afforded her a long tour, with visits to temples and painting excursions; there was so much to see and so many strange and beautiful experiences to write about – and all in the midst of flood, fever, and starvation. She saw Dr Burnell and his friend at Tanjore;

rode in many strange modes of conveyance, like the small, open carriage 'with two ponies to drag it, not much bigger than cats', and the bullock carts with their horns painted blue, yellow, red, and green and a steamer bound for Bombay swarming with red ants. At Madura the railway was washed away and she passed the time by smoking opium; 'every one was taking opium, so I followed the fashion, prevention being better than cure'. During the weeks that passed, she wended her way to Bombay with her sunshade and her easel; letters of introduction and influential people smoothed her path by providing accommodation and servants, and money was obtained by letters of credit, although an elderly clerk at one bank refused to honour them.

'It cannot be done.'
'How funny. Why not?' said I.
'Because it is a most irregular proceeding.'

People were generally much in evidence; at one place, in a fairy dell, she had to pack up her easel during pouring rain and return to the bungalow, only to find it occupied with cooks, coolies, litter, and ladies drying their hair. If the questions were trite and often naïve, Marianne was always equal to the occasion.

'You only sketch it on the spot and paint it indoors?' one beauty said, pointing to the poor thing which was covered with raindrops that it looked as if it had the smallpox. 'Yes', I said, 'that's what I do. Then I take it out to be rained on, which makes the colours run faster, and that's the way I paint, as you say, so quickly.' Those un-thinking, croquet-badminton young ladies always aggravated me, and I could hardly be civil to them.

Then she was home again, ready to entertain friends with tales of India, and eager to arrange her paintings. She wrote to Dr Burnell; 'I have just taken a Gallery at 9 Conduit Street for my Indian sketches and shall be in all the agonies of hanging and quite dead by the evening of the 30th and unable to attend to my guests with any degree of politeness ... I am ignorant of advertising – but it must be done to pay the rent! General MacMardo is arranging everything about the hanging for me and will I believe come down with hammer and nails and help me himself.'

Out of this grew the idea of a permanent building at Kew and from Ross she wrote to Dr Burnell; 'Have you seen the bits in the Spectator, Times, Pall Mall, and Gardiners' Chronicle, etc. etc. about my Exhibition? they all admire and abuse different things and are amusing as a whole – but give me credit for truth which is one thing I aim at – I opened the Gallery *free* on

Bank Holiday and 170 people went – who wanted to know if it was *hard* work. 69 people went the day after the Times notice. I should like to build a Gallery close to the pleasure grounds (or in them) at Kew, hang my pictures and have coffee and tea for all the poor tired visitors – with a cottage attached to boil the kettle in – and a spare room for myself to go and sulk and paint in when I want rest and green trees. If Sir Joseph could find me a bit of ground I would build this – and leave it to him and future directors of the gardens cups and saucers and all pictures – do you think my scheme will ever come to pass?'

Sir Joseph was in full agreement with the idea, but was dubious about supplying the public with refreshments (77,000 possibly on a Bank Holiday). The site, however, was chosen and the architect set to work.

'I chose the site myself', she wrote, 'far off from the usual entrance-gates, as I thought a resting-place and shelter from rain and sun were more needed there, by those who cared sufficiently for plants to have made their way through all the houses. Those persons who merely cared for promenading would probably never get beyond the palm-house. There was a gate and lodge close to my site for those who drove there straight, and that gate was kept shut then, I hoped to get it opened by means of the *vox populi* in due time – perhaps not in my lifetime. I also obtained leave to build a small studio for myself or any other artist to paint flowers in at any time, as there was no quiet room in the gardens in which a specimen could be copied, away from the sloppy greenhouses and traffic of visitors.'

A visit to Australia was suggested to her by Charles Darwin whom she considered the 'greatest man living' and on 18 April, 1880 she departed from Marseilles for the Antipodes, in company with Rajah and Mrs Brooke. In Queensland there was much to see along the shores of Australia; the 'blacks'; the 'Bottle Tree' Plains; the animals left behind by the tide of evolutionary progress. At the house of her host, one of the first settlers, she heard many stories;

He told me a story of his having to speak at the Geographical Society on his election as a Fellow, and how there was a map of Australia on the walls which he did not know was the work of Sir Roderick Murchison himself. He began by telling his hearers they must carefully erase from the map the big lake in the middle, a good many rivers, and other mistakes, and that perhaps on the whole it would be as well to whitewash it all, it was so full of blunders!

To his surprise, Sir Roderick good-naturedly apologized for the map. Her host also remembered Mr Darwin's visit in the *Beagle* and said that, 'he was the most agreeable and the ugliest young man he ever met'.

Australia fascinated Marianne; there was so much to see and so many tales to listen to, that it was impossible to be bored. Above all, there was the sunshine. She had sampled so many different modes of conveyance that the coaches of Cobb and Co. came as quite a pleasant surprise. Cobb and Co. gave the travellers a good ride; Marianne and the other ladies were told that they were the first ladies who had ever travelled on that road alone in a Cobb's coach – an extra lot of beef was always ready for them at the halting place, but Miss North, true to her own predilections, never favoured the ubiquitous double-bedded room. Cobb's coaches were the Wells Fargo of Australia, with the best horses and vehicles 'of every shape and size'.

Miss North kept her eyes and ears open and was often vastly amused and fascinated; the recollection of 'the old couples without encumbrances', who cluttered up Hastings Lodge from time to time, must have developed in her that ability to 'get on with people' and overlook their idiosyncracies. At Merriwa she stayed with a certain Mr C. and his wife. Whilst painting an opossum a shearer came in to see Mr C. about a 'union'.

Well, Sir, me and that girl down at the overseer's, we was thinking of commencing a union. You know, sir, it's very hard to come in tired to a cold hut, have to blow a fire, and to cook rations after a long day, all oneself, and I was thinking that girl *could* cook, and she *could* blow, and she would be as good as any one to commence a union with [an Australian way of announcing his intended marriage!]

'All servant-girls went the same way; Mrs C. was quite worn out with drilling fresh ones', Marianne added.

In Sydney she went to concerts and was delighted to visit a museum of Australian natural history, where the owner gave her a rare red parrot. 'Every stranger', she wrote, 'is so much bored everywhere by the question, "How do you like Sydney Harbour?" that some English naval officers at a picnic printed up over their tent, "We do like Sydney Harbour!"' She considered going to Perth, and got there by the kindness of the Governor, who gave her the use of police horses and a driver with nothing to pay.

Although she grumbled at the delay in fixing a broken axle, the 'wonderful things' she passed more than made up for the horror of the journey, which included a seven-hours drag over sand and a furious ride of eighteen miles at full gallop. From Vasse she had a nightmare journey, for O'Leary, the Irish police driver, lost the road twice through sand and swamps and they were saved only by the man with the lead horses, 'O'Leary was only good as long as he did not think; when he tried to do that he lost his head entirely.' Vasse was named after the botanist of the ship *La Perousse*, who lost his way in the woods and the ship sailed away without him. Marianne was much amused in Vasse for the wife at the rambling farmhouse where she stayed ran the whole place with only an orphan from the Perth Orphanage; when she was told to do anything she put her arms akimbo and laughed. A Christmas pudding was voted 'first-rate'.

On 20 January she crossed the Straits to visit Tasmania, but the cold and drizzle and the 'English' country were a disappointment; she suffered from a gumboil and a swollen face and was driven around the country but could find nothing to paint there, although the tree-ferns were the finest she had seen. On to New Zealand, 'No wonder it was cold, with no land between us and the southern ice-cliffs!' She wrote;

The scenery was all bare and savage. Not a place to land on for miles after Queenstown, and no plants or trees to be got for foreground within three miles of walk, except a few lots of flax. My bones already began to ache with rheumatism, so I contented myself with finishing a sketch of the lake from my window on the ground-floor, with only the road between me and it . . . people come to Queenstown for consumption.

She left Queenstown for Dunedin for the cold was raw and the small suburb where she spent the night depressed her, 'I felt I could never rough it in such a climate, and my aching limbs could not crawl fast enough to warm me. I sat and wondered if I should ever get home to England and see my gallery finished.' The sight of her cousin, John Enys, cheered her immensely and his house of single-roomed huts joined by a verandah was just the place to house his museum and 'cheerful little parlour full of curiosities'. With a sample of the 'vegetable sheep' – tiny daisy plants looking for all the world like lost sheep as they nestled amongst the rocks – to take home for Charles Darwin, Marianne turned for home by way of Honolulu and California.

Honolulu had little to offer her in the way of plants and trees and a visit to Hilo (which Isabella Bird Bishop had made) was not possible owing to an outbreak of smallpox. On 20 April she reached San Francisco, stayed at a hotel, 'perplexing in its vastness', and finally reached the redwood forests, which she described in detail, being much taken up with the trees and their great height. 'One had a room formed in the hollow trunk, and a ladder up to it and great prayer-meetings had been held there year after year.' She returned to Yosemite but did not submit to the 'barbarism' of sitting in a coach and four while it drove through the great hole in the trunk of a Mariposa tree; there was more comfort to be obtained from the Pullman-Car on the Santa Fé railroad, which took her by way of the Rockies to New York City, Kansas City, St Louis, and Philadelphia. She had a 'capital dinner' and was the only woman starting on the train along with some 'intelligent and agreeable diggers'. At Cincinnati she saw the Mississippi, after having been woken up by the train conductor. 'I guess you will be wanting to see the Ohio Bridge at two o'clock in the morning, that's what you'll be wanting next?' But 'Old Man River' inspired her but little, for she could barely see it under the moon's light and it was cold and chilly. In New York there was little time for painting; she was lionized until she grew tired, but was pleased at the interest shown in her Australian paintings by Mr Church, whom she considered 'the greatest of living landscape painters'.

She reached Liverpool on 13 June and started to unpack her paintings. Without delay she drove off to Kew to inspect the work on her gallery.

The building had been designed by James Fergusson, the architectural historian and was a fine example of Greek lighting. The site was the one she had chosen 'far off from the usual entrance gates' and 'a resting place and shelter from rain and sun', as she had written in her letter to Dr Burnell. As far as the bare walls were concerned, she found the building finished and pronounced the lighting 'perfect'. A year was spent in sorting out her pictures, but finally the gallery was opened to the public on 9 July 1882. Although delighted with the lay-out, she was much concerned about the cartographical aspect of her work.

I had intended putting an enlarged map of the world on the ceiling, coloured according to the geographical distribution of plants, in different shades of green and brown, the sea also shaded as it is in nature – clearest turquoise in the tropics, indigo in the middle seas, and green near the ice. I meant to add an index of fruits painted by myself, on the cornice, and twelve typical trees between the windows, but everyone was against such an unconventional idea, except my old friend Mr. Fergusson, and he wanted some good geographer to make a model, and suggested consulting Francis Galton or Mr. Wallace. The first was most kind and helpful as usual, but covered the map he started on with level lines and curves from 500 to 10,000 feet, and that was of no use on so small a scale.

Eventually, a map was made by Mr Trelawney Saunders, but it was not at all what she wanted, although it was 'a most exquisite piece of hand-shading'; she abandoned it but paid for the maps. It gave her a great deal of pleasure to come into contact with people who showed interest in her gallery. 'One day', she wrote in her *Recollections*, 'when the door was accidentally left open, some ladies and a gentleman came in. He was rather cross at not finding Sir Joseph, whom he was seeking. He turned rather rudely to me, after getting gradually interested in the paintings – "It isn't true what they say about all these being painted by one woman, is it?" I said simply that I had done them all; on which he seized me by both hands and said, 'You! then it is lucky for you that you did not live two hundred years ago, or you would have been burnt for a witch.'

H. V. Barnett, writing in *The Magazine of Art* for 1882, was greatly impressed.

I may say at once, however, that the collection is not to be judged from a purely artistic standpoint, though its aesthetic merits are occasionally anything but insignificant. Its chief interest is essentially scientific; and, since there are few things in creation which appeal more pleasantly and constantly to the human mind than flowers, it is also essentially popular.

He thought that the collection suffered from 'the necessities of geographical arrangement' and that the narrowness of the margins did not improve the view to the 'sensitive eye'. But he conceded that many of the paintings were full of charm and he particularly liked the Darjeeling flowers, the colour contrasts in the Bornean orchids and the 'quiet harmonies' in the shrubs of Java.

She was anxious that the gallery should be a place of delight to coming generations and wrote to Dr Burnell; 'I shall leave the money for the building with Trustees here, so that even if I am drowned the work will go on, and it will be a great pleasure to think I leave behind something which will be a help and pleasure to others, as the world goes on.'

One summer day she went to Bromley Common, to visit Charles Darwin, now no longer the young naturalist of the *Beagle*. He hardly went away from home, but spent his time walking on the verandah in the unpretentious old house, his home, wife and children his constant joy. He seemed 'so full of fun and freshness' and sat under a shady tree and talked 'deliciously' to them all for hours, turning over and over again her collection of Australian paintings which she had brought for him to see. He afterwards wrote to her; 'I am glad that I have seen your Australian pictures, and it was extremely kind of you to bring them here. To the present time I am often able to call up with considerable vividness in various countries which I have seen, and it is no small pleasure; but my mind in this respect must be a mere barren waste compared with your mind.' He packed the paintings for her and insisted on taking her to her carriage; 'He was seventy-four: old enough to be courteous too. Less than eight months after that he died, working till the last among his family, living always the same peaceful life in that quiet house, away from all the petty jealousies and disputes of lesser scientific men.'

In August 1882 Marianne North set sail for Africa, the one country which had no representation at Kew. There was plenty to paint and soon there were two baths full of plants and flowers and she could not paint fast enough, 'We can all work hard at what we like best.' Flowers, plants, animals, and birds filled her days with delight; she travelled by ox-cart; in a coach pulled by six horses, and on the railway. Friends gave her hospitality in beautiful homes and lonely farmhouses where, on one occasion, she discovered that the woman of the house was 'a regular Queen Bess or Boadicea for ruling men'. The naïvety of the ladies afforded her some amusement and their remarks were carefully stored away to appear later in print. One lady was curious to know how she painted – were they all 'hand-work' or did she use a machine, and the answer of one lady to her friend almost made her explode with merriment; 'She just takes a flower and does it all at once in colours.' With her usual detachment to the influence of politics, she remained aloof from 'Zuluism'; the portrait of Cetawayo on the wall of Bishop Colenso's house did not fire her with enthusiasm and she was glad to leave the home of 'Zulu mania'.

Another room had been planned for her gallery at Kew by Mr Fergusson and so on 27 September 1883 she set off once again in her quest for rare plants, this time to the Seychelles and Chili, painting all the time, even in the pouring rain, excitedly sending off to Sir Joseph Hooker the flowers of the Capucin tree which he called *Northea seychellana*, after Marianne North. Smallpox broke out in Mahé and her health broke down.

Doctors say my nerves broke down from insufficient food and overwork in such a climate. There being no banker, Coutts had sent me £200 in notes, which were stitched into my clothes, and for two days and nights I tied up my door, barricaded my window, and was in fear of my life, hearing things said behind the low divisions, which they tell me never had been said. The ship came at last, and we got home; but the same troubles followed me till I reached England, when I was among friends, and able to enjoy finishing and arranging my paintings in the new room at Kew, trying to forget all that dreadful time.

But one more country remained to be visited; the *araucaria imbricata* did not appear to be represented in any book of travel about Chili and so, with her usual spirit and determination, she obtained a cabin 'all to myself all the way to Valparaiso'. But the voyage out dampened her spirits and increased her nervous tension and deafness. Her hatred of the cold on this last journey invalidated her and her search for the blue puya high up in the mountains, riding on a hired horse and attended only by a guide, was a contributing factor in her increasing ill-health. The ascent was steep;

We tied up our horses when it became too steep, and proceeded on foot right into the clouds; they were so thick that at one time I could not see a yard before me but I would not give up, and was rewarded at last by the mists clearing, and behold, just over my head, a great group of the noble flowers, standing out like ghosts at first, then gradually coming out with their full beauty of colour and form in every stage of growth; while beyond them glittered a snow-peak far away and I reached a new world of wonders, with blue sky overhead, and a mass of clouds like sheets of cotton-wool below me, hiding the valley I had left.

In a boggy valley she found her araucarias and returned to England, anxious to re-arrange her paintings in order to keep them geographically together and this entailed the arduous task of re-numbering. After all her efforts to paint the most beautiful flowers and plants in the world, and all the cold, heat, tropical rain and savageries of travelling she had endured in order to obtain them, 'a garden to make after my own fashion' was finally all she desired. She found one, and an old house at Alderley in Gloucestershire.

To a friend she wrote that there were very few of her father's old friends left and that Hastings was 'very sad to me. I am glad to be in an unspoilt part of old England, I have turned gardener, having found a most beautiful spot to end my life in, with a comfortable house, some 250 years old, attached to it. I am making one of the most perfect gardens in England. Everyone helps me and sends me rare plants. I have put nearly 1,500 different species in since I came last year and few of them are dead. The climate is delightful, and the poor people are only too happy to be employed. They are nice, gentle, old-fashioned people about here, and take everything one can do for them kindly.'

The old-fashioned old stone house hidden away in the Cotswolds was her refuge; with increasing deafness and continuous noises in her head she slaved in her English garden, planting with loving care the flowers and bulbs which friends sent her. During the summer of 1890, she battled on for eleven weeks but in the end she became too weak to read, or to be read to; on 30 August 1890 she died, after only five years at Alderley. 'There was never any real hope', her sister wrote to a friend, 'the beautiful home here, so lately made, must again be broken up.'

After her father's death in 1869 Marianne North began her life of painting. She was 'Intolerant of Rules', scornful of the laws of composition and draughtsmanship and 'painted as a clever child would, everything she thought beautiful in nature'. Her friends who visited her in the Victoria flat always imagined that she had never known illness of any kind and that she bore a charmed life. The malarious rheumatism of a swamp in Japan; the dry heat of Agra; the misery of illness in New Zealand; the nervous exhaustion in the Seychelles, were private sufferings, borne with courage. She had no sense of fear; in northern India, when the rivers were in flood, she laughed in the face of an official who demanded toll for a bridge which had been swept away, and she painted for hours on the rough edges of stones which were in danger of loosening at any moment, hurling her over a sheer precipice.

Perhaps the truest assessment of her character is that given by the old pilot of a Nile boat;

This Bint was unlike most other English Bints, being firstly white and lovely; secondly, she was gracious in her manner and of kind disposition; thirdly, she attended continually to her father, whose days went in rejoicing that he had such a Bint; fourthly, she represented all things on paper, she drew all the temples of Nubia, all the sakkiahs, and all the men and women, and nearly all the palm trees; she was a valuable and remarkable Bint.

Her name has been given to five plants; *Northea Seychellana, Nepenthes Northiana, Crinum Northianum, Areca Northiana, Kniphofia Northiana.*

CHAPTER SIX

Daisy Bates

A T THE OOLDEA SIDING of the Australian Trans-Continental Railway which runs dead straight across the Nullarbor Plain, is a bronze memorial to Daisy Bates. It reads;

1859–1951

MRS DAISY BATES C.B.E.

DEVOTED HER LIFE
HERE AND ELSEWHERE
TO THE WELFARE OF
THE AUSTRALIAN
ABORIGINES

In the North Road Cemetery in Adelaide is another memorial; it was unveiled on 27 July 1952 by the Minister of Defence, speaking on behalf of the Federal Government of Australia. To the assembled crowd he said;

She has now passed into the legends of the tribes amongst which she worked for so long and with such devotion. It is probable, while I speak to you of her, somewhere in the Northern Territory, in Central Australia, Western Australia or South Australia, some tribal elder is sitting under the shade of a tree telling children inspiring stories of 'Kabbarli', of the grandmother, the wonderful white woman who spent the best years of her life amongst the tribal aborigines.

The District Council of Loxton put up a plaque to her on 9 August 1964;

DAISY BATES C.B.E.
'KABBARLI' (Grandmother)
BORN TIPPERARY IRELAND 1860
LIVED HEREABOUTS IN A TENT 1936–1940
MASTER OF 188 ABORIGINAL DIALECTS

Erected by
District Council of Loxton
9th August 1964

Daisy Bates came to Townsville in Queensland, Australia, in 1884, a fresh, fun-loving, ebullient Irish girl, whose forbears could be traced back to Edward III and whose family and relations were considered as 'gentry'. By the time she attained middle-age, she had devoted a part of her life to the welfare of the Australian aborigines and when her frail body could no longer survive the melancholy of fading life, her devotion to them in their declining years rounded out her own few remaining days and gave to her in full measure that which she had so willingly and selflessly extended to them. She became known as 'The woman who lives with the blacks'; there were other terms, too, such as 'The Great White Queen of the Never Never'; *Kallauer* (sister) and, most treasured of all, *Kabbarli* (grandmother). Over thousands of square miles of Australia, in burning, searing heat, and in terrifying drought, she trudged with the groups, looking after them in sickness, caring for them when the white man's diseases brought them low and when leprosy, tuberculosis and measles ravaged their unresisting bodies, comforting them in life and praying for them when death became more than a stranger. Over the vast wilderness of half a continent she set up her little tent only a few yards away from their camps, while she dispensed her stock of medicine in the immaculate clothes of Victorian refinement – the long skirt, the clean, white blouses, the buttoned boots, the hat with the fly-veil, the white gloves to keep out the dirt and disease, and the black umbrella. She lived frugally and gave her own food to always-hungry natives. Bread and rice, and sometimes an apple, were luxuries to her and the bad times of hunger were appeased by handfuls of fried wichity grubs and lizards.

Over the long, wandering, cruel years, parted from her husband and her small son, she learnt about the aborigines, those poor, neglected outcasts of the 'Never Never', trailing along in the wake of progress, grubbing about in the dustbins on the outskirts of the growing townships, looked upon as little better than Neanderthal Man by the whites. By her gentleness and perseverance she won their confidence, learnt their age-old rituals and languages, compiled a dictionary of over 2,000 words and wrote down in her many note-books the lore and legends from the 'dreaming time', as she worked through the long nights by the light of a lamp until she could barely see. *Kabbarli* she became to the tribes and from her oneness with them she unravelled the complicated kinship within the various circumcised and uncircumcised groups until she carved for herself a niche in the new anthropology, not because she possessed scientific training or based her observations upon academic deductions based upon strict attention to socio-ethnographic groupings, but because she trod the wilderness with them and shared their lives. As she grew older she returned to Perth and to Adelaide and wore for a time the soft cloak of a gentler life, but she always returned to her blacks. In the sixteen years between 1919 and 1935 she set up her little tent on the edge of the Nullarbor Plain and there, by the side of the four 'fettlers' cottages at the Railway Siding, she ministered to the pathetic remnants of the great tribes, scattered like seeds in the wind into the twentieth century, a friend of the blacks and an embarrassment and figure of fun to the whites passing by in the well-appointed trains. When she was seventy-five years of age, she returned to Adelaide and began the sorting of her voluminous writings, but she returned again to the old tribal grounds to find her friends; they were no longer there, for after the Second World War they were dispersed and mostly lived in 'settlements', receiving education for their children and welfare services for their sick and old. The able-bodied men were employed in industry and on stock-farms and English gradually supplanted the old dialects. It was a sad day for the aborigines when *Kabbarli* died; when the natives at Ooldea were told of her death in 1951 at the age of ninety-one or thereabouts, one of them shook his head; 'Poor *Kabbarli*, she finished.'

She was no missionary, no do-gooder, no anthropologist, although she knew the tribal laws, social and sexual practices far better than many of the observers and writers of her time. She was the expert who became a prodigious writer and gave ninety-four volumes of notes to the Australian government; they are now available to students and researchers in the Canberra Collection and various libraries. She became a member of the British and Australian Anthropological Societies, a lecturer and writer and a Justice of the Peace for two states. She was also awarded the C.B.E. The languages and dialects of the aboriginal tribes were a constant source of interest and study and she claimed to speak 115 of them. Money meant little to her, except for hand-outs of food, clothing and little presents to the dying, and at one time she struggled along on a miserable pittance of ten shillings a week. The aborigines were her life's work, but she saw no future for them and in *The Passing of the Aborigines* she wrote; 'I have tried to tell of their being and their ending and the cause of their decline. Nothing is ever lost in this world, and if the slightest impression of anything I have said or done by example or in devotion, remains with them in comfort for the past or hope for the future, I shall be content.' Now the grave in the North Road Cemetery in Adelaide is lovingly tended and flowers are brought each year on her birthday, 15 October. The ethnologist, the writer, and the martyr became a trinity which wove itself into a legend and the *Kabbarli* of the blacks of those early years passed into the history of a continent. The post-war blacks remembered her and so did the elderly whites. One schoolgirl, now herself a grandmother, recalled the day when Daisy Bates visited her school. 'She was brought into our classroom by the Headmistress and we stood up and gazed enraptured at the little figure dressed in such old-fashioned clothes. She stood there so quietly, her hands together on her black umbrella and her long skirt touching the floor. Afterwards, when we were told who she was, and how she had devoted the greater part of her life to the blacks and had travelled with them under the most gruelling conditions, we were all deeply touched.' To many of the whites she was just 'The woman who lives with the blacks', but to the blacks she was *Kabbarli*, the grandmother.

Daisy Bates was Irish, born in Tipperary at Ashberry House, and she was christened Daisy May O'Dwyer. Her actual birthdate is uncertain; one memorial plaque gives the date as 1859; another at Pyap as 1860; the chronology of her marriage certificate gives the date as 1863. She came from solid Protestant stock, although centuries ago the O'Dwyer chiefs were Catholic and saw service in the armies of Europe. Her grandfather, a magistrate, made a profound impression on the young Daisy May and his hard-drinking habits and decided opinions about politics and the Church of Rome coloured her formative years. Daisy's mother was 'a fragile beauty' and tuberculosis, the Victorian scourge, carried her off shortly after Daisy's birth. She left to Daisy her translucent skin, chestnut hair, bright blue eyes, an ebullience of spirit, and a susceptibility to weakness of the lungs which later led her to Australia in search of health. Grandmother Hunt brought up Daisy May and her two sisters and a brother and, slightly embarrassed by the O'Dwyer surname with its overtones of liquid conviviality shed upon it by the male side of the family, tacked on her own name of 'Hunt', thereby conferring a degree of refinement and breeding which obviously came from the gentry. The children were 'the O'Dwyer Hunts. and were raised by grandmother Hunt in a manner befitting to their station in life. Grandmother Hunt lived at Ballycrina and spent a great deal of her time spinning and weaving clothes for the "unfortunates' of the Irish countryside, the

'Hovel Irish' who were always in the need of care, clothes and food. They stole potatoes and poached salmon and, in ragged disarray and unclean shiftlessness, roamed the magical Irish roads which led nowhere, except perhaps to America. Grandmother Hunt was a matriarch; she had faced life in the time of the Great Hunger and had fed and doctored the dispossessed beggars of the southern counties, while the O'Dwyer Hunt children, carefree as leprechauns, wandered the hills and made friends with monsters, fairies, and ghoulies. In spite of bad times in Ireland, there was plenty of magic in the soft shadows of the untilled countryside and the treacherous bogs and rippling brooks held monsters and goblins and a whole panoply of Gaelic gods.

Childhood at Ashberry House and Ballycrina ended, for Grandmother Hunt died and the family home was broken up, the farm sold, and the children ushered out to relatives, except Daisy May who no doubt enjoyed the change of scene under the eye of a kindly, but illiterate, nurse. She disappeared from her early life and Daisy's father sent her on a visit to the widow of the Dean of Ripon in North Wales, where a Mrs Goode taught her the elements of that Victorian gentility and ladylike behaviour which she was later to carry into the Australian bush. The lady-like behaviour stood her in good stead in the grounds of Balmoral Castle, where she inadvertently strayed while on a Scottish visit and where she came face-to-face with Queen Victoria herself. A hasty curtsy was dropped and Her Majesty moved on with regal composure, matched only by that of Daisy May, who never forgot the incident. She was ever after a staunch supporter of the Crown and the British Raj and treasured all her life the black umbrella which she had accidentally dropped at a soirée attended by King George V, who had graciously picked it up for her. It became 'King George's umbrella' and its tip rested elegantly on many a patch of green lawn at Government House parties. It also kept off the fierce heat of the Australian sun whilst Daisy tended to her blacks – but all this was still a long way off.

Daisy was fast growing up. At five feet four inches, with a lithe body (the result of walking, riding, dancing, and swimming) and good natural manners, she entranced all who met her and intrigued those who had not. Her father, sensing perhaps that her 'loneness' was detracting from her social chances, sent her off to the family seat of Sir Francis Outram near Balmoral and the Outram's, with four girls themselves, were delighted to have Daisy as companion for Grandmother Hunt had been a close friend of the family for many years. The 'Outram girls' were lively as crickets, cultured and well-travelled and it was now a part of Daisy's education that she explore the art of elegant living without too much concern for those lesser mortals who supplied the wherewithal for her to do so and hurried and scurried to serve the 'gentry'. The family of six travelled all over Europe with French and German governesses and, in Daisy's own phrase, she received at that time a 'funny travelling kind of education'. A Finishing School in Belgium appeared to have had little or no effect on her and if she acquired those polished manners which were considered the hall-mark of the upper-classes, it was due as much to her own inborn breeding as to any patina of lessons arduously learnt. She read much and studied the German language and philosophers and became interested in the elements of science; she observed more, noted more, and took cognisance of the great capitals of Europe – Rome she called a 'smelly city, clammy and damp and cold', but the capital of France was 'the gay and dainty Paris of the seventies'. Her father died and left her a small inheritance; he left her much more for he told her that character was more important than brain and that she must keep her private life to herself. Her old friend, Bishop Stanton, now Bishop of North Queensland, wrote to her offering her hospitality and for Daisy the chance was pennies from Heaven; so many Irish had left their hapless country for good to try their luck in America, or, like the Durack Brothers and the Hennings, pulled up their roots, travelled half-way across the world, and hacked their homes out of a sun-burnt wilderness. Daisy developed consumption and kicked her heels in Dublin, balanced on a knife-edge of doubt, loneliness, and indecision while she effected suitable introductions and bought elegant and fashionable clothes which would brighten a long sea voyage and add gaiety and colour at the parties and balls which would almost certainly come her way when she had once set her feet on Australian soil as a guest of Bishop Stanton's family. She waited a long time in Dublin, but at last she stepped on board the *Almora*, enjoyed with her usual vivacity and high spirits the games and travelling companions provided by a thoughtful shipping line, and delivered herself to the Australian landscape at Townsville in Queensland. The year was 1884.

Townsville was a burgeoning township of cattle drovers, cotton pickers, 'blackbirders' and gold-miners, but Daisy stuck to her own kind, delighting prospective hostesses with her letters of introduction from important dignitaries; the rough and tough days were still to come and the blacks were as yet totally unaware of her presence on their shores. She was, however, no tender flower of beauty and frailty, for she incorporated herself into the pioneer life by helping on the farms and swimming her horses over unbridged rivers; she learnt how to muster cattle and how to kill and skin them and how to cook the evening meals for the family and the hungry hands. She met the local gentry and indulged in those flirtations with those young men of her own generation and her own class who had been attracted to the new Australia and had, by this time, exchanged their first 'grass castles' for more comfortable homesteads. Their devotion to their new life, their grit and determination to 'make a go of it', were just the ingredients Daisy admired and it was not long before one of them, Philip Gipps, may have appealed to her as a suitable husband. There is, however, no record of any serious affair between her and Philip Gipps; it may have been to meet him once again that she left Queensland and Bishop Stanton's protective, but irksome, presence and travelled south in a Cobb's coach.

The coaching business of Cobb and Co. had been started in Victoria in 1853 and had developed rapidly. Four Americans imported several American coaches suspended on leather springs (much more comfortable for long journeys) and soon the business returned a handsome profit as it served the goldfields. The original partners sold out their interests to a new company, including one James Rutherford, an American; he opened up in New South Wales and fixed his Headquarters at Bathurst, sending 'an imposing caval-cade' of ten coaches, 103 horses, and two feed-wagons from Bendigo to begin the service. By 1870 Cobb and Co. were using 6,000 horses a day and travelling 28,000 miles a week; their annual pay-sheet exceeded £100,000. The partners left the business, retired, or died, and Rutherford alone remained as the sole surviving partner. During the eighties the service developed in Queensland where 4,000 miles of route were controlled by Cobb and Co. Although the coaches were often 'bush-whacked' the drivers were skilled and popular and many courageous deeds were woven into the legends of early travel in the Outback. When the railways came, the coaches were gradually supplanted, but not until 1924 was the last coach taken off the Queensland run. In the early twenties, the coach was exhibited in the Queensland Museum and another one was also preserved at Vaucluse near Sydney. Rutherford had other interests; he bought pastoral properties and imported prime stock. He died at Mackay in 1911. In Daisy's time, 6,000 horses a day were used to pull the coaches imported from America and driven by men trained in the service of Wells Fargo.

Daisy travelled down to Sydney, wide-eyed by tales told to her as she sat 'up front' by the driver, and even more wide-eyed as she left the coach at the Sydney depot, for here was no Townsville, but a raucous, mush-rooming city, where down-and-outs, swagmen, squatters, and child slaves of industry, crowded the streets. It was a city breathing the air of a new world whose gifts to those it loved were freedom and opportunity, which Daisy was to grasp with both hands. As usual, she mixed with the whites of her own class, caught up in the challenge of the new intellectual drive; here in Sydney she could attend lectures and classes, borrow books and fling herself into the life of the mind – the image of the Queensland pioneer woman was beginning to fade a little. She stayed with the White family, and, according to one member, got herself engaged to Philip Gipps, but he died shortly afterwards and Daisy must have looked round at that time for a companion with whom she could settle on land offered by the Queensland Government. She found him in the person of Jack Bates, with whose family she was then staying on their farm at Pyree, ninety miles south of Sydney. It was Christmas, 1884, when they met, the Victorian lady with the 'upper class' English accent from an Irish Protestant family and the practical man-of-action, the 'lean Australian' of popular fiction, the Catholic stockman and drover who spent much of his time in the saddle away from home. He was a quiet man of the outdoors, a drover who had once been Head Stockman on the 'biggest woolshed in the world', a man not given much to talk, a roamer of the cattle trails which led across Australia's sun-fired land. He typified for Daisy the indigenous Australian that the pioneer women married, suffered under, and finally buried under the vast, empty skies. Daisy was attracted to him, although he had a younger brother, Charlie, of a more academic and studious turn of mind, and soon she was riding in his company on outings covering many miles, listening to his tales of a drover's life and of survival in a savage land where it was 'every man for himself' when the cattle stampeded and the wells ran dry in the long droughts. 'What heroines these pioneer women were!' Daisy wrote, and no doubt she imagined herself as a homesteader, married to a practical man of few words, bearing his children, and watching for his return in the golden sunset. There was little talk of the blacks; Jack Bates regarded them as unreliable and, on the whole, unsatisfactory, and dismissed them as savage survivals, unlike the Duracks, who strove to understand them. Jack's attitude towards the blacks was to prove a bone of contention between him and Daisy for the rest of their lives; at this stage, though, she had no intimation of the great part they were to play in her later life.

After an impetuous courtship, Daisy married Jack Bates in the old Anglican Church at Nowra. It was 17 February, 1885 when they entered the church in their riding clothes, filled out the necessary papers, and walked out as man and wife. It was romantic, exciting, and sudden, but Daisy afterwards described it all as 'an error of judgment' and his immediate departure on a six month's droving trip left her plenty of time to dream of her 'pioneer' life on a good property. When he returned, she handed over to him the major part of her inheritance with a view to his finding a suitable station. He never found it. He was a cattleman, now saddled with a Victorian young lady who was obviously becoming disappointed in him and in his inability to adapt to a life almost foreign to him. On 26 August, 1886, Daisy gave birth to a son, Arnold Hamilton, and her dismay led her to become a householder in Sydney with a companion and nurse; Jack returned to the trail and the conjugal rites were never renewed. 'But I don't want a baby!' was Daisy's cry, and the offspring from the union of Daisy and Jack Bates saw little of either of them as the years passed. They rarely met, but Daisy had cause to be grateful to Jack Bates for he taught her many things on the cattle drives in which they both took part. Daisy was no desert flower; she was tough and resilient, willing to learn and from the man she had married so impetuously she learnt the art of survival in a wilderness. She made damper from flour (this became her staple diet in later wanderings with her aborigines) and mastered the art of pitching a tent and making a fire with 'kindlers'. She took Jack's advice when he told her never to be without a face-veil as protection against the marauding flies and as the days passed on the trail she mastered the art of keeping warm during the cold nights and nursing the cattle through bitter winds and sandstorms. Rivers were often flooded and many cattle could be drowned. In 1904, no fewer than 300 head of cattle were lost in crossing the Georgina River, 'There's lots of other trouble we have to look out for', an old drover told Daisy, 'There's poison weed . . . then cattle get footsore in rocky country.' If it all became too much for Daisy, she was grateful to Jack for the invaluable lessons he had taught her, but her disappointment in Jack as a domesticated animal accepting his responsibilities in a cosy homestead kept neat and tidy by Daisy, finally convinced her that the marriage had been a mistake. He was 'happier in his aimless wanderings' and her attempt as catalyst ended in failure. They went their separate ways.

In the rainy month of July 1892 Daisy took part in a rabbit drive at a station on the Lachlan River, an eighteen-hour journey from Melbourne, writing about it ten years later. Rabbits, said old settlers, were brought to the country by settlers in the early days of the colony and the first attempt by the government to check their advance from South Australia was to send a large number of cats to the West Australian border. It was not effective, for the cats seemed to have settled down in the burrows with the rabbits. Then fencing was tried and, ultimately, some 2,034 miles of fencing were constructed, with patrols over a vast area. The rabbits were driven into an enclosure by dogs and finally 4,000 rabbits were destroyed. The idea was for each rider to make the biggest outcry he could, thereby frightening the rabbits into the enclosure. Daisy seemed to have enjoyed it all and the Riverina Rabbit Drive passed into history. A year later, she visited Tasmania, taking Arnold, now a little boy of six, with her. He was a shy, reticent boy, with little of his mother's warmth and vivacity but Daisy had enough vitality and charm for two and she never had any difficulty in securing hospitality and doors were always open for her. She stayed with the Mac-Kinnons of Dalness, a pioneer family, and her unaffected interest in the early struggles drew a ready response as the women told her of their grim life in the past, of their dealings with convict labour, and their staunch will to survive in some of the worst climatic conditions in the world. Through them she learnt of the 'Black Wars' of 1804 and the extermination of some 12,000 aborigines.

It began in 1802, when a party of French naturalists disembarked on the banks of a river in south-east Tasmania; they had been sent by Napoleon to explore the lesser parts of Australasia and for two months explored Tasmania, meeting the natives, making maps, collecting specimens, and recording the manners and social customs of the natives. François Péron, the *anthropologue*, together with the artist Charles-Alexandre Leseuer, brought back 100,000 animal specimens and portraits of the inhabitants. They did not always find them friendly; spears were thrown at them and they were often assailed by stones from savages who were just as brutal to their women, 'almost all of them covered by sores', wrote Péron. Upon the return of the expedition, the specimens were housed in the Museum at Le Havre. The natives were ripe for exploitation for they appeared to have degenerated from their early state, habitaully going naked, wearing no garments except kangaroo skins, and keeping out the cold with seal grease as they were unable to make fires.

The founding of the British Penal Settlement in 1803 provided the opportunity to hunt down the aborigines and the usual story of murder and rape, cruely and torture followed. The absconded convicts hunted both men and women and took the women as slaves and concubines. After the Napoleonic Wars, settlers began to arrive, bringing sheep and the kangaroos and wallabies left the main hunting grounds; without them the natives were doomed and a Government Proclamation of 1828 gave the settlers the power to hunt them down to extinction. George August Robinson went on expeditions all over Tasmania to collect them at government expense. The aborigines lingered on until 1847, when a few remaining ones were taken to Oyster Cove near Hobart. A portrait of Truganina, the last Tasmanian, hung on the wall at Dalness; she died in 1876, aged seventy-three. After her short visit to Tasmania, Daisy returned to the mainland to find Australia in the throes of a depression, with banks closing their doors and her own capital swallowed up. Daisy could no longer afford to take extended tours around Australia, for it was now imperative that she co-ordinate her life, obtain money, and see Arnold safely boarded with the right people. She placed him in a Catholic Boarding School in Campbelltown, where his paternal grand-mother and his father could look after him during the holidays. Jack, away on his droving trips, content with his 'irresponsible driftings', was a negligible factor in Daisy's life. After nine years in Australia, Daisy boarded the ship *Macquarie* on 18 February, 1894 and left for England.

Daisy arrived in London penniless; here her hopes were further dashed, for the bank was unable to advance her money and it appeared that her own meagre funds had been swept away in the crash. She thought of Ireland, that delightful demesne where her numerous O'Dwyer relatives would surely take her in; it might be intriguing for them to welcome back an errant member of the far-flung family who had sidled off to Australia and, further-more, married an indigenous Australian in romantic circumstances. She was welcomed back into the fold, and the cloak of Irish comfort settled once more on her shoulders as she rode to hounds, went to dances, and regaled her numerous cousins with tales of the Antipodes. But it didn't last. Money was in very short supply and 'in grief and suspense' she returned to London, contacting a General Brownrigg, a relative by marriage with her sister Kathleen. He took her to see W. T. Stead, the famous editor of the *Review of Reviews* and the interview with that 'giant of a man' changed her life. She took along some of her poems ('we don't accept poems for the *Review*') and offered to do anything from scrubbing the floor to dusting the books. The young man who popped his head round the office door looked pleasant. 'Go with my son Willie, will you? He will fit you in.' And fit her in he did. With the sum of one pound a week in her pocket she arranged accommoda-tion at St Gabriel's, a home for gentlewomen in Cavendish Square and, with soaring spirits, divided her time between her apartment and Mowbray House, where she threw herself into whatever task she was given to do, exulting in her office work and going to concerts and lectures and readings from Dickens with an impoverished 'Bohemian', one James Grun. More than anything else, she adored W. T. Stead 'The Chief', as he was always called, for he was a crusader and a fighter and the office at Mowbray House was a bright light which drew to itself many of the great ones of the time; Rhodes, Gladstone, Madame Blavatsky, the 'Hallelujah Lasses' of General Booth's Salvation Army, Carlyle and Matthew Arnold – all were welcomed. Estelle Stead, in her book *My Father: personal and spiritual reminiscences*, published in 1913, presents a portrait of the great man and quotes his profound belief that; 'In the world's great field of battle, no duty is higher than to keep the ranks of the forces of Light well filled with recruits. It is to no holiday that our offspring are called – rather is it a combat long and stern, ending in inevitable death.' W. T. Stead was born in the Congregational Manse at Embleton, Northumberland. As a young man he edited the *Northern Echo* and in 1883 he took over the *Pall Mall Gazette*. *The Review of Reviews* was 'an attempt to render accessible to all, the best thought to be found in the periodical literature of the world', and it was this journal which used the talents of Daisy Bates in the two years between 1894 and 1896. Cecil Rhodes and Cromwell were Stead's heroes; when Rhodes returned to England in 1891 from Africa 'he came round to Mowbray House and talked for three hours concerning his plans, his hopes, and his ideas', wrote Estelle Stead in *My Father*. Stead was wholly against conscription and at the *salon* of his Russian friend, Madame Novikoff, he became interested in fostering a more amicable understanding with her country. At Symonds Hotel in Brook Street Madame Novikoff held her little court and here Stead met, and crossed swords with, many of the literary giants of the time. This was the world into which Daisy had precipitated herself and into which a new element was creeping. Before the period of his life in the 1880s Stead had evinced no interest in Spiritualism, but after he came to London he attended his first séance and was told; 'Young man, you are going to be the St. Paul of Spiritualism', a prophecy which had far-reaching consequences, for it led to the founding of a quarterly journal called *Borderland*, from which later, articles were printed in book form as *Letters from Julia*. About 1890, Julia A. Ames, an American journalist, paid a visit to Europe and descended upon Mowbray House and Cambridge House, Wimbledon, where she took tea with Stead and his family. After her return to America, Julia died at Boston and Stead, to quote his own words, 'never had the slightest idea I should hear from her again'. Automatic writing was begun, and Stead steadfastly and patiently persisted in attempting communication with the now defunct Julia; the 'letters' were published in *Borderland* and the office was moved from Cambridge House to Mowbray House, where Daisy acted as 'stand-in' to a Miss Goodrich Frece, who was sub-editress. To Daisy, with her practical mind and dislike of charlatans, the 'new journalism' was becoming far too wrapped up in spirits and spiritism; Madame Blavatsky, Annie Besant, Eusapia Palladino, the Fox Sisters in the United States, and a host of intelligent and responsible persons were trickling into the office at Mowbray House, but there were also many other lesser lights, hovering on the grey fringe of spirit 'doubles', fake photographs, and clouds of ectoplasm that looked surprisingly like cheesecloth.

The death of Willie, Stead's son, at the young age of thirty-three was a bitter blow for he had been his right-hand man. 'His was a noble life, brief in span, but full of service from his boyhood up.' The séances continued, with Miss Goodrich Frece herself acting as medium; in the Mausoleum at Mortlake Isabel Burton, Richard's widow, anxiously awaited those words of comfort from her explorer husband, but the automatic writing recorded only a message predicting Isabel's own death. Daisy was sceptical and determined to expose the phony mediums and mis-guided charlatans, thick on the ground as the leaves of Vallombrosa, and lost no opportunities in informing Stead of their deception of him. Daisy began to loathe the 'spooky little quarterly' and the last issue published in October 1897 must have given her a great deal of satisfaction and contributed directly to her break with Stead. She was grateful to him for his acceptance of her, and his high-principled views of life and love beyond the earth-plane evoked no expressions of cynicism, but she had no stomach for further penetrations into the unknown and Mowbray House saw her no more. She took a job as librarian with Jarrolds, the publishers in Norwich, and took up the life she was used to; Norfolk's 'gentry' were a fry cry from the spirits of *Borderland*. She was offered re-marriage, but Australia once more intruded into her life and, as the Bank of Australia offered a refund to her of a shilling in the pound and Jack Bates had written to tell her that he had found a property for them, she boarded the ship *Stuttgart* and sailed for Perth. The year was 1899.

She met Jack and Arnold, whom Jack had brought from east Australia, on the quayside at Perth. If Jack was overawed by her formal behaviour, Daisy was equally overawed by his appearance. The meeting was 'a shock' and she wrote about it in the form of an autobiographical short story, sparing nothing of her feelings. 'This creature with the weak hanging underlip, the man who was to win success for her? This unkempt untidy soul, the man in whom she thought great possibilities lurked! His very form and features had moulded themselves to his character and had become loose and flabby and common – above all common!' She was equally disappointed in her son, Arnold and found him 'Dirty, unmothered, neglected, incongruous'.

She set about finding a school for Arnold and obtained a place for him at the Christian Brothers' College in Perth. Daisy, with her new-found status as a journalist, was offered membership of Perth's most exclusive women's clubs and delighted her audiences with her interesting lectures. The grand occasion was an invitation to the Governor's Reception and a chance to meet the Premier, Sir John Forrest. Forrest was a trail-blazer for the Indian-Pacific line and a man who had a vision of a Trans-Continental Railway crossing Australia to link the west with the east. He left Geraldton on 1 April, 1874 with six men and twenty horses. In May they entered a country of hostile blacks and even more hostile desert. The land was in the grip of drought and on 2 August Forrest wrote; 'Much troubled about our position.' They pressed on under the grimmest conditions in the world and Governor Weld wrote; 'Should he succeed in this journey, his name will go down to posterity as that of the man who solved the last remaining problem in the Australian continent and whatever may come after him, he will have been the last of the great explorers of this continent.' On 27 September 1874 John Forrest and his companions rode into Adelaide, convinced that the railway must link west with east actoss the Nullarbor Plain. His courageous crossing of the parched and empty land had earned for him the first peerage to be conferred on an Australian and his later championing of the idea of a railway across south Australia's waterless vastness upheld the vision of his youth. The Trans-Continental Railway was built, linking up with the narrow gauge of Western Australia. 1,950,000 sleepers were used, and 126,000 tons of steel and a team of track-layers from Thursday Island slogged their way through the deepest railway cutting in the Antipodes. This was the Sir John Forrest Daisy was later to admire, not only for his tremendous vision of a nation linked by modern communications, but for his views on the empire and his understanding of the aborigines, akin to Daisy's own.

Arnold was installed in his new school, Jack left for droving in the north, and Daisy pulled up her roots once more and boarded the S.S. *Sultan* for Cossack and Roebourne, then south to Carnarvon on a pony-trap journey of some weeks, afterwards writing it up for the *Journal of Agriculture*. Back in Perth, she contacted Bishop Gibney, an Irishman, and a man of determination; she had met him and his colleague, Dean Martelli, on her voyage back to Australia in the *Stuttgart* and through their tales of the sufferings and exploitation of the blacks had resolved to give to the world the truth about their treatment. She was now an accredited journalist, with a scientific bent, her standing greatly enhanced by her association with W. T. Stead and her later articles for Australian magazines. Bishop Gibney would be visiting the

Trappist Mission at Beagle Bay at the end of August, along with Dean Martelli. It was to be an official visit to prove to the Government that the subsidy given to them was yielding a good return in the improvement of the 10,000 acres which the monks leased; otherwise, the subsidy would not be renewed. Bishop Gibney agreed to take Daisy along on the journey to the Trappist Monastery; perhaps with some misgivings he saw the neatly-clothed and fastidious lady board the *Sree Pas Sair* on the first leg of the voyage up the coast to Broome. Daisy had no such misgivings; she was undaunted by the fact that the bullock dray which met the small boat at Broome almost sank in mud and that 'the horses were trappists, too, skin and bone in their poverty'.

Bishop Gibney had founded the Beagle Bay Trappist Mission ten years before his meeting with Daisy, when he bought a site, under lease, of 10,000 acres. He found one after a long trek through the prickly bush; a wonderful site with ten acres of springs and natural wells, and a native reserve of 600,000 acres. The two little pioneer priests and the sixteen ordained men who had followed them from the old French Monastery had endured years of unbelievable hardship in a remote wilderness. Some had died there, under the saddest conditions. Others, blind and emaciated, had been rescued from their fate and invalided home. Daisy Bates, fresh from her period of journalism in London, now faced another life 'back to the stone-age nomads whom I had but glimpsed on my first visit to Australia, but among whom the rest of my life was to be cast'.

When she arrived at the Mission she found 'a collection of tumble-down, paper-bark monastery cells, a little bark chapel and a community room of corrugated iron'. Only four monks were left on the station, with Frère Jean, the stockman who had never seen a white woman, other than his mother in his whole life. 'I was the first white woman to appear among them at the Mission, and the first that the natives of the region had seen', she wrote in *The Passing of the Aborigines*. She was even allowed to sleep in the Abbot's bed, 'he wasn't in it and besides it wouldn't hold two', she wrote with disarming Irish humour, and continued, 'and I went through their cells and talked and made them talk to me and all through those months they were perfect little gentlemen.'

It was the meeting with the aborigines which introduced her to her life's work. The sound of a conch shell awoke her in the mornings, heralding breakfast; all the women of the Nyool-Nyool tribe surrounded her and it was a case of 'no bath, no breakfast'. 'Father Nicholas had told us that they ate dirt in handfuls, and that the women sometimes ate their new-born babies, but that since the advent of the Mission, with its admonitions and its daily distributions of pumpkin and rice and tea and flour, cannibalism was not nearly so much in evidence.' Later, Daisy was to base her controversial opinions that cannibalism existed among the aborigines on her findings begun at Beagle Bay and as the women worked and played, they told her of their laws and taboos. They frankly admitted that they liked 'babymeat' and Daisy deduced that, among the Central Western peoples, cannibalism was rife. 'In one group, east of the Murchison and Gascoyne Rivers', she wrote, 'every woman who had had a baby had killed and eaten it, dividing it with her sisters, who, in turn, killed their children at birth and returned the gift of food, so that the group had not preserved a single living child for some years. When the frightful hunger for baby meat overcame the mother before or at the birth, it was killed and cooked regardless of sex.' When she visited the town of Eucla in later life, it was in decline. 'Cannibalism', she wrote, 'had been rife for centuries in these regions and for a thousand miles north and east of them', and at the last manhood ceremony at Eucla in 1913 the Koogurda, 'fine sturdy fellows', told her that in their own country they were 'cannibals to a man', frankly admitting that they shared 'kangaroo meat and human meat'. It was a controversial subject, and one which haunted Daisy for the rest of her life; at Ooldea Siding, when she returned once again to minister to her blacks, she encountered again the promiscuity, the hunger, the half-caste children, and the cannibalism which she had proved existed among the tribes. 'There were sometimes as many as 150 natives in the vicinity of Ooldea. Every one of these Central natives was a cannibal', she wrote, 'Human meat had always been their favourite food, and there were killing vendettas from time immemorial.' 'Victims were shared according to the law. The older men ate the soft and virile parts, and the brain; swift runners were given the thighs; hands, arms or shoulders went to the best spear-throwers, and so on.' 'Every one of the natives whom I encountered on the east-west line had partaken of human meat, with the exception of Nyerdain, who told me it made him sick.' The sight of a *lubra* (female black) tearing away at her new-born infant so affected Daisy that she went almost blind.

Daisy had the greatest admiration for the Trappist monks; she attended the religious ceremonies and the many weddings and baptisms among the tribes, for they were sources of wonderment and delight, with the black brides wearing wreaths (a relic from early Spanish customs) and veils above masses of tangled, matted hair 'a delightfully ludicrous touch'. After a survey of the Mission land, they travelled to Disaster Bay to convert the unconverted, but they found no water and the horses were bad-tempered. The survey itself had been a challenge to Daisy; with a few helpers the Bishop slogged round the 10,000 acres, repairing buildings and digging wells, his only guidance a ship's compass and a measuring chain. She wrote;

The Bishop and I were the chainmen, walking in steamy heat of 106 degrees at times, sometimes twelve miles a day. Over marsh and through *pindan*, now lame from stones and prickles, now up to our thighs in bog, the Bishop throwing down a small peg to mark the chain limit, I always in difficulties because of my high-heeled footwear. We were always hungry.

To get back to Beagle Bay, Daisy and the Bishop, with four natives, walked nine appalling miles through shallow waters of mangrove flats, where Daisy's feet swelled with poison. When they finally boarded the *Sree Pas Sair*, waiting for them on the beach, the Bishop collapsed from exhaustion and was laid on the flattened sail for the voyage back to Broome. Broome was created by the pearling trade and was the largest pearling centre in Australia. In the 1900s it was a place of contrasts; the galvanized wood and iron buildings, erected on cement blocks, looked crude and ugly, but the vegetation was green and pleasant. In the pearling season, which lasted for three months, luggers employed white men, aboriginals and Orientals; there were six men in each lugger, Japanese or Manilamen or aboriginals. Virtually no white man went down 'in the dress to dive'. Diving was done by Australian blacks, men and women, without diving dress. A maximum of forty feet in depth and fifty-seven seconds as the average time to be spent under the water was insisted on by the government; the membrane of the ear had to 'crack' before the man could do much diving and blood frequently poured from his ears. 100 feet to 120 feet was the lowest depths in which a man could remain under water and work – the shells were taken between those markings. In shallow water the divers could remain under for two to three hours at a time. Bishop Gibney had seen many human wrecks as a result of pearling; aboriginal women went down when pregnant and some had had their hands crushed by spades and such-like tools when they clung to the sides of the boats too long before diving again.

There were dangers all the time; deep chasms into which a man could fall without hope of recovery; depressions on the sea bottom; accidents caused by jagged coral and, the greatest danger of all, the Tiger Shark. The men were paid £2 per month and £25 a ton for all the shell they could collect; experts could gather about 5 tons each year. Superstitions abounded. The Japanese refused to go down without a written charm about their necks and the Malays sported a talisman, a piece of wood called a 'poori-poori'. The nights were fast and furious in this prosperous pearling port in Daisy's time. A polyglot population demanded excitement and it was duly provided throughout the night by, to quote Daisy's words 'continuous revelry' and the comings and goings in the infamous China Street. Daisy adjusted well to the mixture of races and the quick tempo of port life, although at one time she was locked in her room from 'danger of unpleasantness'. A far cry from the gentle Trappist monks.

Broome, however, was the starting point of her work with the aborigines and the next eight months were spent among the Koolarrabulloo where she observed them at rather closer quarters. About thirty giggling women watched her dress and mimicked her actions. 'Every motion of mine, as I laced my corset and eased my shoes on with a shoe-horn, brushed my hair and adjusted my high collar and waist-belt, was greeted with long-drawn squeals of laughter and mirrored in action, though the slim black daughters of Eve about me had not even a strand of hair between the whole thirty.'

In *The Passing of the Aborigines* Daisy wrote; 'The tribes of Australia may roughly be classed as circumcised and uncircumcised. Certain it is that all the tribes came from northward, and that the uncircumcised were in the first hordes, later driven down south, east or west by the encroachment of the circumcised.'

From Broome she went to Roebuck Plains and here she joined Jack Bates in September 1901. It is doubtful whether Jack appreciated her work with the blacks at the Mission, or her aboriginal name of *Kallauer* (sister); for him the aborigines were 'The Blacks' and he resented the fact that they had 'robbed him of a wife'. Jack was stationed on the cattle-run at Roebuck Plains and had staffed the house with domestic help, probably hoping to entice Daisy back into a more solid and comfortable world, but Daisy entered more and more into the aboriginal mind, noting their languages, their customs, their loneliness and misery. There was, for Daisy, so much to learn and note, so much to wonder at, so much to write down and assimilate. Roebuck Bay was the stamping ground for all the salt water tribes and with a native guide she searched them out, sat down with them, listened to their tales, collected vocabularies, learnt of the totems and the forbidden relationships and the *Ngargalulla*, the spirit-children waiting to be born, but when the corroboree season was over the natives went back to the stations; Jack's cattle station needed re-stocking and Daisy prepared to ride side-saddle alongside 770 well-fed Herefords, together with a Maori half-caste cook. 'My equipment', she wrote, 'was a good English pig-skin side-saddle with ordinary stirrup; three pairs of laced wallaby-skin shoes; three habits; a felt hat; three pairs of riding gloves, and plenty of fly veiling.'

Daisy was always dressed *de rigueur*. Although she was always 'band-box fresh' and a delight to the hardened drovers, she was fast becoming a thorn in the side to Jack, head drover; the men resented her interference with the blacks, regarding it as 'black-fella business' and Jack and Arnold, who was with them on the long drive, suffered a degree of embarrassment which Arnold never forgot, and probably never forgave. The mob of Herefords travelled down the West Kimberley's 'on a golden day in the Australian April', with Daisy riding behind them with eight of her own drovers, finally covering a distance of 1,000 miles, although, to Daisy, it seemed more like 3,000 with all 'the zigzagging'. The drive took six months and for most of it followed a nightmare pattern; there was drought and a bad stampede and Daisy was often in the saddle for eighteen hours a day. Eighty-mile Beach was where the wells began, but they were in a bad state of repair and far apart. Finally, the circle of the Eighty-mile east to Roy Hill and then to the Hammersley Range and the Tablelands brought her to the parting with Jack and Arnold, her son. Jack stayed with the cattle, Arnold remained at the Christian Brothers' College to continue his further education, and Daisy awaited an opportunity to take ship at Port Hedland for Perth, where her life's work was about to begin.

In Perth, journalism occupied a great deal of her time; she wrote many articles and obtained a paid job with the Registrar-General's Office, compiling notes and recording the dialects and customs of the aboriginals. They called her 'The Office Flower' and extended her period of employment. Although her interest in the aboringes never wavered, she found time to take up the cause of the white settlers in her beloved 'new' state of Western Australia; she still identified with the pioneering families of the middle-class and that the men from good families and backgrounds could neglect or ill-treat those lower orders for whom they were responsible was far from axiomatic to her. On 8 April 1904, a letter appeared in *The Times* of London accusing the settlers of crimes towards the blacks. Daisy wrote in answer; 'I have journeyed throughout the whole of the district from Beagle Bay to Perth, giving myself ample leisure to observe the mode of living of the natives in the various districts, of their treatment by their white masters on the various stations . . . For Mr Malcolmson to describe indenturing as slavery and to assert that the aborigines are worse off than the American negro slaves is ridiculous . . . there is no hope of the station owners ever growing into plaster saints, yet the majority of them are humane and will not wantonly ill-treat their natives.'

In 1905 a chance came for her to 'get out among the blacks herself', for it was now necessary to live amongst them, to refute some of the ideas of the new breed of anthropologists which conflicted with her own findings. A few miles from Perth was the Maamba Reserve and here Daisy pitched her little white tent on a winter's day in July, watched by the derelicts, the forgotten, unhappy remnants of the great Bibbulmun race. Her tent was fourteen feet in diameter and her 'kitchen' was outside in the break-wind; her table was an up-turned case and an open fireplace boiled her billy cans of tea. She never wandered into the camp of the blacks for 'you must not go indiscriminately into a native camp if the friendship of the occupants is valued'; 100 yards was her dividing line.

The Bibbulmun race was the largest group of aborigines in Australia; they had once roamed the coastal plains with their own clans, totems, and tribal grounds and they were the last of the uncircumcised hordes, driven on by a fiercer race. There were more than seventy groups in the Bibbulmun area, but when Daisy pitched her little tent at Maamba only a few remnants remained. The landing of the white man on the Swan River was the beginning of the end for the Bibbulmun; the aborigine, Yalgunga, did not know that the date was 1829 as he dozed in his camp by the little spring called Goordanlup, smilingly giving away his spring and his land to the white strangers 'the spirits of the dead who had come back as white men'. As the years passed, they were compelled to change their mode of life. In *The Passing of the Aborigines* Daisy Bates wrote; 'Their age-old laws were set aside for laws they could not understand. The younger generations, always wilful, now openly flouted the old, and defied them, and haunted the white men's homes, protected by his policemen. A little while, and they reverted to thieving – where theft had been unknown – and sycophancy, and sold their young wives to the depraved and foreign element. Half-castes came among them, a being neither black nor white, whom they detested. They died in their numbers from the white man's diseases; measles, influenza, whooping-cough, and the results of their own wrong-doing. Can we wonder that they faded so swiftly?'

From her little tent on the Maamba, Mrs Bates faithfully recorded their legends and folklore and wrote down sheaves of notes as she toiled away half the night under the light of a lamp, straining her eyes and subjecting her frail body to a hardship it was never intended to endure. 'Civilization was a cloak that they donned easily enough', she wrote, 'but they could not wear it and live.' With great fairness of mind she recalled the efforts of the pioneers in their treatment of the aborigines. 'The pioneers of Australia were noble men and women, and nearly all of them were above reproach, and more kindly in their treatment of the aboriginal. There is evidence that they did everything in their power for the preservation and betterment of the race.' Bishop Salvado founded the great Benedictine Mission at New Norcia in 1846 and clothed and fed the natives of the dingo-totem tribes, building a village for them of stone houses, laying out streets, and giving each man an allotment of land. He taught them and educated the children in handicrafts and stockwork and took five aboriginal boys to Rome to study for the priesthood. All died in Europe, except one, who returned to the Bush and died there.

Daisy lived at Maamba for two years, her little tent 'sagging about me in the wet and ballooning in the wind' in the midst of a bushland bright with flowers. She was on duty all the time, collecting 'scraps of language' whilst the dampers were cooking by the campfire, adhering to a spartan routine of early rising and attention to her natives in their camp 'the remnants of the once mighty Bibbulmuns', now so dependent on her. She wrote continuously, happy to receive the pittance which Australian magazines sent to her for her articles and, in between, she visited other camps. These were the years leading up to the First World War and were, for Daisy, happy and successful ones for she lectured and wrote and obtained the support of dignitaries for her views on the future of the aborigines. She spoke to the Geographical Society and to the Historical Society in Perth and women listened to her lantern lectures and talks and became aware of the blacks as they had not been before. She had 'arrived'. Jack came down to Bunbury on occasions and Arnold visited her in the camp and in the holiday of 1909/10 she was elected by the Perth Carnival Committee to round up some natives who were adept at spear-throwing and the use of the boomerang. The natives left on 5 January 1910, Daisy seeing them onto their trains with full tummies and pockets bulging with coins. It was not, however, the end for Daisy.

Malcolm Fraser, the Registrar-General of West Australia, had long been anxious to record the customs of the aborigines. On 3 May 1904, Daisy had been appointed to the position of recorder and had been given an office in Perth in which to edit all her notes and all the various reports from government departments which dealt with the aborigines. Besides her work at Maamba and the camps she devotedly prepared her great work on the languages and dialects of the 'sections'. There were additional chapters to be written, for Fraser himself had presented a title for the book; *A Short Authentic Historical Record of the Habits, Customs and Languages of the Aboriginal Natives of this State*. It was a portentous title and one which attracted the interest of anthropologists in England, as well as other parts of the world. However, all was not plain sailing for the subject was a complex one and Daisy's findings were hampered by the necessity of putting her source material into correct anthropological and scientific order, a task which she found frustrating and irritating, as she was not a trained ethnologist. Twice she completed a lengthy manuscript and twice she began again; Fraser's request to the authorities that her small salary be increased to the princely sum of ten shillings a day was summarily dismissed. Chapter after chapter of her book was completed, and in her room in Perth she strove to finish it. It needed editorial revision and Daisy felt that a visit to England to consult the more academic authorities would be useful and enlightening, but before she could put her plans into execution, news reached her of an anthropological expedition under the auspices of Oxford and Cambridge Universities which was to visit the State of Western Australia in the following year. As it happened, the Oxford representative had dropped out and the position was offered to Daisy; this was just what she needed, for it offered her a chance to join an anthropological expedition and establish herself on a more scientific footing. It required only a degree of co-operation on her part with the leader of the expedition.

A. Radcliffe-Brown arrived in Australia to take up his post in 1910. He was young, good-looking, and had been known as 'Anarchy Brown' at Cambridge. He was strong-minded and noted for his condescension to women, Margaret Mead had described him as 'impenetrably wrapped in his own conceit'. His assistant was a newly-qualified zoologist, Grant Watson, a quiet and impressionable young man who quickly summed up the explosive situation in which he, Daisy and Brown were soon to find themselves. 'Daisy was made for Brown's exasperation and he for hers', he wrote in his book; *But to what purpose?* Radcliffe-Brown considered that Daisy had amassed a great deal of information which would be of 'immense value' in the work of the expedition and he appointed her as 'travelling protector, with a Special Commission to conduct inquiries into all native conditions and problems'. It is doubtful if Brown really thought of her in this way and it was soon apparent that Daisy had some tough fighting to do after he and Grant Watson had politely called at her office with introductions. Daisy found that co-operation with Brown was difficult; she had an extra desk put into her Perth office in order that they could work together on her manuscript and was gracious enough to pay him homage for his help as an anthropologist of considerable standing. Daisy had considerable standing, too, but in another direction; her ethnological knowledge had been acquired after long, gruelling years in the wilderness with her blacks, laboriously compiling their languages and social and sexual customs. Their trust and friendship had been won only by long years of devotion.

The expedition lacked funds and Daisy proceeded to obtain them from her old friend Sam McKay. He was generous and Daisy handed over to Brown a cheque for a thousand pounds; Daisy was to be attached to the Expedition another six months and Brown was to continue to undertake revision of her work, which he was no doubt glad to do, for he considered her mind to be 'a well stored sewing basket after half a dozen kittens had been playing there undisturbed'. Two days before her forty-seventh birthday, Daisy left for Bunbury to meet the two men; horses were hired, a cook taken on, and a camp pitched on the edge of the aboriginal settlement. The differences between Brown and Daisy over her manuscripts were overlaid with laudatory and diplomatic reportage; the *Mirror* gushed; 'Her exceptional and unique knowledge of the natives as well as the mysterious influence she holds over them . . . will be of invaluable assistance to her companions', and the *West Australian* was of the opinion that the situation of a woman in an all-male scientific expedition was 'unique', so far as could be called to mind.

They left the aboriginal settlement before any real work could be done and Brown told Daisy that she could stay behind if she wished to do so. Grant Watson was non-plussed; he was intensely loyal to his chief and yet he admired Daisy and her work. Sadly he wrote; 'And so it was that we went our way', Daisy remaining at Sandstone and the two men proceeding to Bernier Island, where Daisy caught up with them on 11 December. The expedition found that the Laverton and Lancefield Camps had 'transgressed the bounds of every native law'. In his book *Where Bonds are Loosed*, Grant Watson described their stay at Bernier Island and of the 'broken and helpless pieces of humanity who lay still all day and looked out across the bleak expanse of sand dunes under which they were destined to be buried'. Shortly after 11 December, they celebrated Christmas on Dorré Island, Daisy experiencing the full force of a 'cockeye bob' gale, with the hospital roof blown away and her own tent shredded into ribbons.

Christmas passed on Dorré Island, with pudding and sweets provided for the natives. A few days later, however, a consignment of about 133 disease-ridden blacks was camped outside the town of Carnarvon, brought in by Corporal Grey from all parts of the state. 'Shall I ever forget the surge of emotion that overcame me as they saw me, and lifted their manacled hands in a faint shout of welcome, for many of them recognized me?' Daisy wrote.

Due to the passing of time, the breaking-up of the groups, and the demoralization induced by contact with the white man's way of life which they did not understand, venereal disease was spreading; sufferers were brought in to Dorré and Bernier Islands, to the 'Lock' Hospitals, where devoted staffs did what they could. Chained, humiliated and with bodies sometimes covered in sores, they were lucky if they survived the journey. In *The Passing of the Aborigines* Daisy Bates wrote; 'Restlessly they roamed the islands in all weathers, avoiding each other as strangers. Some of them cried all day and all night in a listless and terrible monotony of grief. There were others who stood silently for hours on a headland, straining their hollow, hopeless eyes across the narrow strait for the glimpse of a loved wife or husband or a far lost country, and far too often the smoke signal of death went up from the islands. In death itself they could find no sanctuary, for they believed that their souls, when they left the poor broken bodies, would be orphaned in a strange ground, among enemies more evil and vindictive than those on earth.' When pronounced cured, the natives would find their own way back to their homes, slogging it for hundreds of miles, often through the territory of tribes who were hostile and strangers.

Daisy became postman for the Islands, carrying the *Bamburu*, the letter-sticks, crudely-carved pieces of wood which were the only means by which the natives could send messages to their loves ones and to their friends. The *Bamburu* were returned, bearing greetings and messages of hope and comfort. 'I did what I could among them with little errands of mercy', Daisy wrote, 'distributing rations and blankets from my own government stores when boats were delayed; bringing sweets and dainties for young and old, extra blankets in the rain, and where I could a word of love and understanding. To the grey-headed, and the grey-bearded, men and women and children alike, I became Kabbarli, the Grandmother. I had begun in Broome as *kallauer,* a grandmother, but a spurious and a very young one, purely legendary. Since then I had been *jookan*, sister, among the Bibbulmun; *ngangga,* mother, among the scattered groups of Northampton and the Murchison, but it was at Dorré Island that I became kabbarli, Grandmother, to the sick and the dying there, and kabbarli I was to remain in all my wanderings, for the name is a generic one, and extends far among the western-central and Central tribes.'

Daisy stayed for nearly a year, helping the living and comforting the dying, the leprous, the insane and the blind. 'The horrors of Dorré and

Bernier unnerve me yet', she wrote and poured out her heart in her book. 'There was no ray of brightness, no gleam of hope . . . To question the poor shuddering souls of these doomed exiles was slow work and saddening, but as I sat with them in the darkness of their *mias* at night, the torture of hospital routine was forgotten, and harking back to thoughts of home, they were, for an hour or so, happy.'

In April 1911 Brown went to the north again and Daisy returned to her old camp in the Bush, moving around from one aboriginal settlement to the other, jubilantly engaged once again on the work of recording vocabularies and legends of the tribes. Now that she had split up with Radcliffe-Brown, she trod the old, familiar round with greater heart, for here she was on ground that she knew was her own, with the blacks who were 'just simple children' to her – not specimens for ethnological study to be discussed and tabulated. Her book was now ready for publication, but many difficulties still remained; one copy was sent to Andrew Lang in England and the other copy was with Brown. Lang had contacted Professor Rivers and Professor Hartland to help with the editing, but he died in 1912 and Brown returned to England without Daisy's manuscript. Unfortunately, the publishers had received only portions of the manuscript from Lang's executors and the other copy had been, according to Daisy, 'mutilated beyond recovery'. Daisy was antipathetic towards Brown 'the father of Australian anthropology' and and by the time he left for England they had quarrelled. The story of Daisy's manuscript is a complicated one, with Brown showing Daisy a letter written to him by Lang in which he said that 'a red pencil would be needed' on the 'long and wandering work'. Daisy told Malcolm Fraser that 'the mutilated portions are useless' and that she feared 'the whole thing would have to be re-written'. His answer was; 'Oh Lud!' In the government files kept in the Battye Library of Perth are diaries and correspondence between the government and Mr A. R. Brown. The manuscript remained unrevised and unfinished.

In 1912 Daisy returned to Perth and made the decision to dedicate the rest of her life to the 'fascinating study' of the Australian aborigine. It was 'a glorious thing' to live in a tent and wander round the camps with no fear of loneliness. 'The ever-open book of Nature has taught me more of wisdom than is compassed in the libraries of men.' She once again pitched her tent near the Maamba Reserve, amongst the few half-castes and mixtures, and made occasional visits to Rottnest Island, which had become an aboriginal prison in 1838. Ignorant of the white man's law, the prisoners were shipped in batches after their trial and sentence in Perth and died in great numbers a few attempted to swim to the mainland but very few must have made it and there is no known evidence that any one of them succeeded.

The name itself came from Rats' (wallabies') nests which were seen by the crew of the *Geelvinck* and two other ships commanded by William van Vleming when they landed on 29 December 1696. The first cell was a cave, but soon offenders from all over the State were kept there, five and six to a cell, undergoing hard labour for five to ten years, wrecks of humanity, outcasts from their aboriginal homelands. Cattle and sheep killers were caught and punished and native prisoners shipped to the island to work in the salt plant. For the killing of a white man there was no reprieve. Daisy wrote; 'It was only another tragic mistake of the early colonists in dealing with the original inhabitants of a country so new and strange to them.' Rottnest Island is now a nature reserve and a place for families and children; 'plane or ferry take the holiday-makers the twelve-mile crossing and the clean beaches, the caves, and the swimming hole among the reefs make the once convict settlement a veritable paradise for tired city dwellers. There are flowers, plants, and roughly sixty species of birds; the quokkas, the rat-kangaroos, are friendly creatures and forage into the tents and picnic sites as they 'thump' along by their tails. Fishing parties are popular in March as the herring migrate and 'Daisy Day' in early spring brings tourists in hundreds as the blue bloom covers miles of the northern area.

Events were now moving towards Daisy's eligibility as the first woman Chief Protector of Aborigines. Bishop Gibney wrote in 1912;

That a woman inspector is needed cannot be questioned for a moment and that the position has not long ago been created is a dishonour to ourselves. That male inspectors should be commissioned to examine native women and children under well known conditions is a blot on our civilisation.

Daisy was suitably qualified for she understood the blacks and they loved and trusted her and it was now evident that there was little hope of the publication of her book on the aborigines, that portentous volume which had taken so many gruelling years to write and which had been so cruelly misused in its long passage from unedited notes to final compilation. Daisy applied for the position, backed by the past Premier, the Commissioner of Police and other dignitaries. She did not get the post. It was pointed out to her that a woman would be subject to great risks and that a police escort would be needed to protect her. To Daisy, this attitude was one of 'inconsistency' on the part of government and she particularly resented the offer of an unpaid job as honorary protector for the Eucla District of south-east

Australia. It was a disastrous time for Daisy for the new Premier told her that her book was not a commercial proposition and the withdrawal of the eight shillings a day which had just about sustained her whilst engaged on her researches left her penniless. She was a severed limb, for Jack Bates had settled on a property near Darwin as overseer stockman and her son Arnold had gravitated to New South Wales where he found a bride. She went to Eucla, as unpaid Protector of the Aborigines and set herself up in a home lent to her by a friend, Beatrice Raine. The house was on a tree-less plain 'well beyond civilization, right in the heart almost of the continent. On the plateau formed by the extensive cliffs which so impressed Eyre on his East West journey.' She went on a 'dogging' expedition with her black friends and kept an illuminating account of the measures they took to destroy the predatory wild dogs which savaged sheep and their lambs in a holocaust of cruel and brutal killing. With renewed vigour she resumed her work on the social organizations of the various aboriginal groups and wrote to a friend; 'My sole desire is just to live among my black friends . . . I have not a particle of personal ambition or self seeking beyond my desire to impress upon this native race that there is one woman who is absolutely their friend, without thought of self advancement.'

With the publication of her great book now not possible, and with no hope of reconciliation with Jack Bates, she made her final home with her blacks on the Nullarbor, living as one with them, and continuing her researchers. The little town of Eucla was a mere handful of buildings huddling around the telegraph station and, beyond the usual recreation centre, general store and station master's house, there was nothing but the enveloping mantle of sand. The Nullarbor, named from the Latin (*nulla arbor*) by Alfred Delisser, was one vast limestone plain which had once been under the sea, a plain shot through with blowholes from underground caves; the blacks believed that one of the caves was the home of Ganba the serpent and that he sucked in the water when he was thirsty. Daisy noted everything, although she explored only with the blacks as guides, for the Nullarbor was a place of terror where 'to be lost in the Plain meant almost certain death'. When Daisy set up her little tent in 1913, the tribes were fast diminishing. The manhood ceremony that Daisy saw was the last in the area; the kangaroo had been virtually exterminated by the white man and the groups existed on government hand-outs which kept alive the old people, the children, and the half-castes. It was the light of the half-caste children which affected Daisy; 'The heritage of suffering and woe that a white man leaves his half-caste child!' she wrote in her diary, 'Set apart as children of a Ghetto, with every avenue of advancement except that of servitude and prostitution closed to them, they see themselves – those of them who read and think – left out of account or absolutely ignored by those leaders who shout for a white Australia.' She stayed with the tribes which were left, sharing their lives, keeping their laws according to the old traditions, and making sure that her own standards were above reproach and at the end of 1913 she moved to Jeegala Creek to be present at the gathering of a huge grouping of natives at an initiation ceremony. 'They hold the mystery of life', she said, 'No native knows more than that.'

With the outbreak of World War I came an invitation to attend the British Association for the Advancement of Science in Adelaide on the strength of her now-acknowledged status as an anthropologist. With her friends Gauera and her fourteenth husband, Balgundra, she plodded by camel buggy across the Nullarbor to Yalata, putting up her own tent at night and greeting with smoke signals the wandering groups of bewildered and lost natives. It was a surprise to Daisy that she had become a celebrity and that her views were topics of conversation and discussion. Her writings in Australian newspapers and journals had focussed attention on the aborigines, but the fact that her own views were non-orthodox made her enemies. She had always regarded the blacks as a doomed race, to be loved and tended, but not to be assimilated into the white man's world – the pathetic half-caste she pitied and wept over.

She had no wish to bring them into the twentieth century, to reform them, or 'missionize' them, or regard them as subjects fit only for the microscope of the scientist. She only wanted to record their languages and their legends, understand their social groupings and help them gently along their thorny path to extinction. The pure poetry of her prose enchanted the women journalists on the occasions of her many interviews; and to one interviewer who asked about her life in the bush she replied that she was 'really happy in the bush'. 'I love the space and the peace and the freedom . . . the light of early dawn in the scrub and the twittering of birds . . . the wonder of sunsets and the peace of lengthening shadows.' The shadows lengthened for many of her black friends, especially for Jeera who had become the 'wife' of a white man and had inherited venereal disease during the temporary absence from the group. Daisy wrote of Jeera in a letter to William Hurst.

'Where's my firestick, Kabbarli? Where am I going?' she asked.
I ventured a word, 'Did you ever hear of the white man's God?'
'Oh, yes, Brophy [the wretch who had brought her to this state] often told me about his God Jesus.'

Well do you know, I simply could not claim the same God as Brophy. I said to Jeera, 'You know Kabbarli loves you and tried to make you better?'

'I've only you, Kabbarli. No one else would be good to me.'

'Well', I said, 'you're going on a little journey only and to a place where my Father is. I've asked him to look out for you and he'll take your hand as I'm taking it now.'

'Your father, Kabbarli. Then Jeera will be all right.'

And she died so quietly that I did not know she was dead until her poor small hand was cold in mine.

Daisy's own health gradually worsened and by September 1918 she had to rely on the generosity of the store-keeper at Yalata for any food she needed. The government sent her fifty pounds and the offer of the Matronship of a retired soldiers' home in Adelaide. Life became difficult and complicated in Adelaide and she stayed at the home only three months before she was off again, after having made enemies over her views on the 'survival' of the aborigines. In October she made her first camp on an extension of the railway line at Ooldea Soak, 427 miles north of Port Augusta; her natives were lost and sick, helpless without their *Kabbarli*, wandering disconsolately along the railway tracks, some of them blind, many of them ill with the white man's scourge. Ooldea sheltered her for the next sixteen years of her life.

There were hundreds of derelict tribes at the Sidings, begging from the passengers on the trains at every stopping-place; they had been forbidden to use the wells and could only use water from the taps. Daisy found them 'a diversity of creatures'. In *The Passing of the Aborigines* she wrote;

Numbers of white derelicts and camp followers were still on the line, strike-agitators, foreigners, pilgrims of one kind and another, 'jumping the rattler' between the capitals, or recklessly walking the whole thousand miles, throwing themselves on the hospitality of each succeeding camp of fettlers. Some of them cut the telegraph wire in the throes of thirst, or held up the passing trains in starvation, and most of them stirred up trouble wherever they went. Prostitution of native women was rife, sought by the blacks and encouraged by the lowest whites, and many unfortunates had already reaped the wages of sin.

Her *Kabbarli* camp became home once again; in her bough shed was the precious tin trunk containing her manuscripts, and under the bed her portmanteau protected the only wardrobe she had ever known whilst with the tribes. The wide-brimmed hats, with their tiny veiling, the button boots, the long skirts and underskirts and the many pairs of white cotton gloves (now supplied to her by John Martins, of Adelaide) were neatly folded. She had come to Ooldea partly for the initiation ceremony for which the tribes were gathering and she gladly walked the three miles to and fro between their camps and her own little tent. Unfortunately, she fell foul of the Department for Aboriginal Affairs; she was now a public figure, with her sparse frame clothed in old-fashioned Victorian 'get-up' and as she passed in full view of the trains there were many strange faces peering at her from the windows;

'There's Daisy Bates. The one in the funny clothes.'
'How can she touch those filthy blacks!'
'Fancy, gloves in this heat!'

and so on.

Her pleas for more money to feed and clothe the blacks fell on deaf ears; she was encouraging the aboriginals to depend on public money, they cried, and by her constant requests and badgering for increased rations she was looked upon as an eccentric. She further shocked the Adelaide Women's Guilds by her unorthodox view of missionizing. She regarded mission prayers as 'pitter patter parrot fashion' and wrote; 'our consanguinous marriages would be punished by instant death ... our lenient divorce system ... reduce us below their own level ... our drunkenness, misery and vice – though so often tragically adopted – receive their contempt'. This was not the way to win friends and influence people. Her old statements regarding the practice of cannibalism had cropped up again with the release of the first of her reports; a case as recent as 1920 had occurred at Ooldea which was mentioned in A. G. Bolam's book *Trans Australian Wonderland*.

But her natives continued to wait patiently for her outside her camp, sometimes letting two days elapse before they summoned up courage to call on her for they came from all over, from the Musgrave and the Petermann Ranges and from far across the north-western borders of the State. 'Some-times', she wrote, 'two years on the journeys zigzagging in the desert for food and water they followed the tracks of those who had come in before them ... at last the remnants arrived on the rim of civilisation outside my break-wind. My duty, after the first friendly overtures of tea and damper, was to set them at ease, clothe them, and simply explain the white man's ways and the white man's laws.'

Daisy was constantly in demand at Ooldea for sometimes there were as many as 150 natives near the Sidings, poor, derelict, lost souls suffering from venereal disease, ophthalmia, measles, ring-worm and just senility. They

[185]

found their way across the desert, shouting and spear-rattling as they saw the trains and the white women, who threw them biscuits and cake from the carriage windows; they sold boomerangs and posed for photographs as they ventured into the twentieth century. 'The train was their undoing', Daisy wrote, 'amongst the hundreds that "sat down" with me at Ooldea, there was not one that ever returned to his own waters and the natural bush life.' Food was always a problem, there was no government hand-out whilst Daisy was at Ooldea and soon she had to depend for money on selling articles to Australian magazines in order to obtain the tea, flour, and porridge so necessary for them. Friends and visitors supplemented the meagre rations by sending flour and sugar and tea, two loaves of bread, one tin of powdered milk, pound of rice or sago which Daisy got each week from the fettlers' stores had to last out.

There was much contentment at Ooldea, in spite of the unhappiness and heart-rending sorrow of her natives; Daisy rose at sunrise and dressed in full view of an awakening world of beauty. 'It was a fastidious toilet, for throughout my life I have adhered to the simple but exact dictates of fashion as I left it, when Victoria was Queen – a neat white blouse, stiff collar and ribbon tie, a dark skirt and coat, stout, and serviceable trim shoes and neat black stockings, a sailor hat and a fly-veil, and, for my excursions to the camps, always a dust-coat and a sunshade. Not until I was in meticulous order would I emerge from my tent, dressed for the day. My first greeting was for the birds.'

Daisy did her best to arrest the onward march of civilization, but death claimed many of the young people. Life became increasingly difficult. There was drought and, for Daisy, an attack of sandy blight which blinded her. 'So grave and so prolonged was this first attack that I believed I was threatened with permanent blindness, and early in 1922 made the thousand-mile journey to Perth to consult an oculist. That was to be the last holiday – if holiday it can be called – for twelve years of so much increasing difficulty and disheartenment that, had it not been for the guiding light of my ideals of service, and my deep love and sympathy for the natives, I could never have lived them through.'

In 1922, salt water gushed out of two bores sunk at Ooldea and in October 1926 Ooldea Soak was closed down, as the blue clay-bed had apparently been pierced. Daisy had to carry her supplies a little over a mile in two four-gallon kerosene tins twice and sometimes three times a day, stumbling and hurting her feet. Water-carrying became more and more arduous, until she could no longer tramp in the blistering heat to the water tanks and asked that a small cart be sent to her. It was sent, but the weight of water broke the wheels and iron wheels three inches wide were fitted. 'The empty cart was heavier than the full', she wrote, 'a matter I have never been able to explain.' An eight-year's drought followed the failure of the water supply and native foods of roots and berries vanished. In *The Passing of the Aborigines* Daisy Bates wrote; 'Sand-storms raged for hours at a time, and the world was darkened. When the heavier gusts threatened to rob me of house and home, I clung frantically to the ridge-pole of my tent, pitting my slender weight against the strength of the elements, and when they abated crept in exhausted to find my stretcher, my table and everything else within covered in nearly a foot of sand.' Her typewriter was precious. She wrote; 'To write the newspaper articles that meant the sustenance of so many under such conditions was at times impossible. My first typewriter became a ruin. The second baffled me in that my hands were so painfully burnt and blistered with the heat and dryness, the wear and tear of constant water-carrying, and my years of attendance on the sick that at one time I essayed the art of type-writing in seven finger-stalls and failed dismally.'

Added to all this was the lack of food for herself and her natives. She kept religiously to their taboos and tribal restrictions, keeping their totem boards hidden in her tent – away from the women. The headaches, the diarrhoea, the tuberculosis, she carefully and lovingly nursed for her blacks; as the only woman to have been allowed to witness their initiation ceremonies they trusted her – their *Kabbarli*. The drought continued until 1929 but food was still scarce and the natives travelled miles in their search for lizards and grubs. Even the rabbits which had scourged the sand-hills were hardly to be seen.

After the drought came the Bush fire, and after a scorching day of 106 degrees, a whirling mass of sand and rain and wind with Daisy 'clinging to the ridge-pole' and shutting her eyes 'in a tornado of blowing canvas and lashing branches'.

Empire Day, which they always celebrated, came and went. Daisy saved up supplies of sugar and tea and jam and told them; 'A long time ago, when the white men first came over the sea to his country the King said to them: "look out for all the *waddi*, *koong-ga* and *gijjara* (men, women and children) and tell them the King's law; they are not to kill the white men and the white men must not kill them" and the King said; "Give food and clothing to all the black people when they are hungry, and old, and sick!" By and by the King's people said: "We will have one Empire Day every winter-time, and on that day every man, woman and child must have bread and meat as much as they can eat, so that they will always speak of that day as the King's day, and a day of happy feasting." '

In 1932 a woman journalist, searching for the 'last of the first, the forgotten pioneers' of Australia, called on Daisy Bates at Ooldea. Ernestine Hill, fearful that Daisy Bates's collection of data and notes on the aboriginal tribes should be destroyed or lost forever, wrote to the managing director of the *Advertiser*, Sir Lloyd Dumas, informing him of Daisy's plight. Her blindness was frightening. 'I am so blind', she wrote, 'that I can only smell the burning when my clothes are on fire.' Daisy ultimately accepted the offer of syndication rights in a newspaper serial of her life story, with transport arranged to Adelaide. It had been a struggle to get her away from Ooldea; the Prime Minister, who had arranged to meet her at the Sidings, had fallen asleep in the train and Daisy had waited in embarrassment as the coaches had passed by. 'I felt such a fool standing there speechless, not knowing which way to turn, till I begged the guard to leave me the key of the lamp room, and there I hid till it was dark. My brightest hopes are gone, my own resources completely exhausted, my allowance too small for me to do anything at all . . .'

She came to Adelaide and an office for her was rented in the Commonwealth Bank, where she could continue her writing. The tent, blankets, and billy-cans were given to the natives and the trunks, battered and worn, were sent off to Adelaide. The natives assembled to say good-bye to *Kabbarli* and each one was given a shilling; back in the sand-hills the old women wailed their sad cries. The Soak had dried up.

She recovered her zest in Adelaide; the easy living, the baths, the rich food, the adulation, and the stories which had circulated about her had lost a good deal of their sting. There was wrangling about money matters, about the idea of a collaborator, but it was out of the question so far as Daisy was concerned. She was, however, given an excellent secretary, and soon her files assumed a neat and business-like appearance. Three events cut across her life at this time; she was awarded the C.B.E. (which made her happy and proud) and she learnt of the death of George V and the abdication of Edward VIII, which saddened her beyond measure. She had tried to find Arnold, her son, whom she had not heard of for many years; she thought that he had been invalided home after World War I and Ernestine Hill, good friend that she was, wrote to Repatriation Departments, Army Pensions' Lists, Anzac Records – but Daisy never found him. The only representative at her graveside was a grandson, Arnold's son.

From 1912 onwards, it had not been possible to turn to Jack for help, for both he and her son, Arnold, had left the Western Territory, Jack in a position as overseer stockman near Darwin and Arnold to be married. Their marriage had broken up in 1903, Daisy referring to him as her 'late' husband who had left her the property known as Glen Carrick, a name which Daisy had always envisaged for a property of her own. Jack had 'done his best', but he and Daisy were of two very different temperaments.

He died at Mullewa in 1935 at the age of seventy-eight, having returned to the west to live a life of retirement, visiting family and friends and reminiscing about his early days: he seldom spoke of Daisy. He died as he had lived, ending his days in a hotel room which belonged to a drover friend, thus maintaining his link with his droving days.

After the compilation of ninety-four volumes of her notes, she returned once again to the Bush to find her natives, but they were all gone. From the shores of the Bight, eastwards along the Murray River she searched for them, setting up her little tent, as she once did, and waiting patiently for them to come to her – their *Kabbarli*. But not one of the old people came; many of them were now dead and the descendants of the ones she had known now worked in vineyards and orange groves. During World War II the tribes were moved to missions and compounds, catapulted into the twentieth century with the speed of their own boomerangs; after the war they became dependants of the State, well-fed and clothed, with their children looked after and educated. The missions had given them Christian names, such as Peter and Billie, for the old tribal names were fast disappearing.

After all her wanderings, she found her rest in a private hospital in the Adelaide suburb of Prospect. On 18 April 1951 she passed away at the age of ninety-one or ninety-two. She wrote;

It seemed a dream that the old was over, the old life of eternal wind and sand, the long, long, droughts that take ten years to come and go, the so meagre yet so crowded years that I had spent in such strange company. There was not an hour of my time wasted in all those years. I did what I set out to do – to make their passing easier and to keep the dreaded half-caste menace from our great continent. I know that I hold a place in their hearts, and that my memory and my magic will keep them *Balya*, lest *Kabbarli* should know, and be *Koordudu yooril* (heart crying).

I have tried to tell of their being and their ending, and the cause of their decline. Nothing is ever lost in this world, and if the slightest impression of anything I have said or done, by example or in devotion, remains with them in comfort for the past or hope for the future, I shall be content.

CHAPTER SEVEN

Mildred Cable and Evangeline and Francesca French

The large official envelope marked 'On His Majesty's Service' lay on the table, and the whole projected campaign seemed a stage nearer as we opened it, and read its announcement to the effect that 'In virtue of these Passports issued to Evangeline French, Francesca French and Mildred Cable, of the China Inland Mission, it was requested and required that they should be allowed to pass without let or hindrance, and be afforded any help of which they might stand in need in travelling through the Provinces of Shansi, Kansu, Mongolia and Sinkiang'.

THE THREE LADIES were members of the China Inland Mission stationed in Shansi Province, China. Miss Alice Mildred Cable went to China in 1901, aged twenty-three; her home address was given as Guildford and her occupation as student, although there is a note that M.P.S. was placed after her name. Miss Evangeline Frances French joined the Mission in 1893 at the age of twenty-two and does not appear to have had any occupation at that time. Her sister, Francesca Law French, went to China in 1909 when she was thirty-five years of age. All three ladies retired in 1941. For twenty-one years they had worked to build up the large teaching complex of the Hwochow compound; the Training School for Women and the Higher Grade Girls' Schools were the culmination of the loving care and strenuous efforts they had put into all aspects of their service. Most middle-aged women would have been appalled at the prospect of hazardous and gruelling travel into 'The Great North West', breaking all the 'dear, familiar ties' that bound them to those they loved.

It had been assumed by their friends that they would end their days in the spot which had been a centre for thirty years after its foundation by Pastor Hsi; a plot of land had been suggested for purchase by Pastor Wang so that 'their beloved teachers' could rest at the end of their days. Instead, however, the sealed orders of the Commander-in-Chief commanded them as missionaries, 'To proceed to the Great North-West to a place at present unknown', and so they attended the last Sunday Meetings and the last Communion Service, gathered up only those personal effects which were absolutely necessary and, on the morning of 11 June, 1923, waited for their rickshaws on the edge of the motor-road at Hwochow. They were no hick travellers, venturing timidly out into the Province of Kansu, painted black on the Missionary Survey Map; they knew all the difficulties, all the prejudice that they would encounter in their evangelism amongst tribes long innured to their own customs and religions. They had studied maps and routes which were available at that time and had no doubt about the hardships and rough travel which awaited them in the crossing of the Gobi Desert, an area measuring nearly 1,200 miles from north to south and 2,000 along the 44 parallel. Wilderness and wastes of incredible perversity would tax all their strength and faith. But they had plenty of that; their accurate observations and detailed analysis of things seen added greatly to geographical knowledge and ethnographical concepts. They belonged, as the Rev. J. Stuart Holden wrote in the preface to their book *Through Jade Gate and Central Asia* to the 'Order of the Steadfastly Set Face'.

The members of the 'Order of the Steadfastly Set Face', having acquired their rickshaws 'passed out of sight of the City which had given us our loved work and home for so many, many years', and trundled off on the road running straight as the flight of an arrow from north to south of Shansi Province. They soon found that the province of Honan was quite different from that of Shansi; brigandage had not been effectively checked and robbers were everywhere, terrorizing the countryside and holding travellers to ransom. They were forced to travel under military escort but the escort took them less and less distance for the money they had to pay and, in the end, the three ladies had to be firm, 'not one cash would we pay until we reached our destination'. For the eighteen stages which lay between Sian and Lanchow, the provincial capital of Kansu, the three ladies rode in litters; they were well acquainted with this mode of uneasy travel, but were apprehensive about the high setting of the body of the litter. 'It is for greater safety in the bad mountain roads', they were told, but undoubtedly they would have further to fall if overturned. Everything was thrown in the well of the litter; cushions, lunch baskets, bed bags, wadded quilts and all the paraphernalia of a travelling home, until it became an amalgate of solidity for their weary bodies.

Into the tunnel-like aperture we finally crept, while with a sickening heave, first the back shafts, then the front were lifted into position on the creaking wooden saddle, whereupon the restive mule dashed for the narrow gate of the courtyard, while the yelling bystanders rushed to its head, to stop the seemingly inevitable smash. Thus through the West Gate of Sian we plunged, past the great well which supplied the city with water, and into the open country where the roads were inches deep in mud.

There was time enough, as they joggled along, to ruminate on their life of service and dedication to Christ. The China Inland Mission was formed in 1865. For thirty-three years its members carried on their work for God, crossing and re-crossing the whole country until fourteen provinces were settled and built up. In all that time, no member of the Mission suffered a violent death; the first to do so was Mr Fleming, who was murdered in November 1898 in the Province of Kuei-chau. The crisis of 1900 saw the deaths of fifty-two adults and sixteen children, while six more adults and four children were feared to be lost due to inability to escape. The loss was greatest in Shansi Province, where forty-one missionaries were feared to have been killed. The Boxer uprising of 1900 followed on the heels of the Empress Dowager's apprehension of reformers and the annulment of reform decrees was soon put in hand. There was great fear of foreign aggression and the government of the day revived the trained bands, which included local hooligans, proud of their name 'Boxers' – a rough translation of the Chinese name for the bands, meaning 'Righteous Harmony Bands' or 'Righteous Harmony Fists'. 'Protect the country, destroy the foreigner', was their cry, and in 1899 Christians and Missionaries were being persecuted and done to death. In June, 1900, the Empress Dowager ordered all foreigners to be killed; Shansi suffered indescribable horror, with Catholic and Protestant Missions and native Christians losing their lives.

The China Inland Mission began its work in Shansi in 1876 and due to a number of factors this province was particularly vulnerable to the influence of the Boxers; the 'Patriotic Harmony Fists' roamed the countryside stirring up anger against the foreigners who had brought bad luck by violating the *feng-shui* by introducing machinery into the coal and iron mines. Their motto was 'By Imperial Command exterminate the Church' and the missionaries were singled out for martyrdom. Evangeline (Eva) French was one of those

Marianne North

Marianne North - photo taken by Julia Cameron

Marianne North at home. Mount House, Alderly

Daisy Bates

Daisy Bates with aboriginal skull

Black friends

'Kabbarli'

'Kabbarli'

Daisy Bates

Camp at Ooldea

Black friends

On tribal ground

Daisy Bates in her tent

Native Camp.
Ooldea.
16/9/28.

Dear Mrs Macdonald.

I received your letter of 5th ult-imo, yesterday (15th) so it has taken ten days to come from Perth to Ooldea. I have a private mail bag from Port Augusta & all my mail matter is supposed to be sent on there (also my mail matter from W.A.) & then sent back to Ooldea in my bag. You will be passing through Ooldea tomorrow (Monday 17th) but I regret that I shall be unable to give myself the pleasure of meeting you at the train. It is 100° in my camp as I write & I am prostrated by the heat & the fierce north wind that is blowing. I have not been able to meet any friends for some considerable time. My camp is a mile from the Siding, & the journey to & fro, carrying my water, mails or weekly stores, is becoming increasingly arduous. You will see the natives - those cannibal mobs that came down in November - at the train. They have returned from Tarcoola & other places along the line, & may be called "civilized" now, so the line & its occupants "civilizes." Only a few weeks ago I had made new dresses for every woman & child amongst them - boys & girls. & you will never think when you see them tomorrow that their rags were so recently his new frocks. I tried to keep them from Siding & Railway line, but altho. I am Hon. Protector for the whole State of W.A. - & I think you know that my W.A. work was amongst them - I have no official standing & no official position in S.A. beyond my J.P.ship for this State. I have no recognition. The Settlers & Gangers control all Sidings

Letter to Mrs Macdonald (and overleaf)

2

& the S.A. Government. gives these natives in the
charge of the employes. But I want you to know that
in spite of this - my very presence here has kept down
immorality at this Siding. So much so. that in the nine
years of my work & service amongst these natives
there have been but three halfcastes begotten in
oodea. That is my greatest pride, that I have kept down
this dreadful immorality, & without friction with the
railway employes. You will see the one living one of these three
halfcastes at the siding tomorrow - a little boy.
If I am spoken of in Adelaide, by those whom you
may meet it will be very pleasing to me to know
that you can set right the ideas of those who neither
know me or my work, or understand the ideas lying
behind that work. I think Adelaide does not like
me - but that dislike comes from Adelaide's German
& pro-German element. & so I am rather glad to
be disliked by that element.
I am giving myself the pleasure of making a little
parcel of curios for you. of some things that are worth
having, & I also keep in view your luggage space.
The articles include the wee-rra - a wooden scoop
which the women use for all sorts of things, from digging
out burrows, & fire shovelling - & carrying the baby. I
women call them the women's "hold all" - really. They are
made from a "knob" off a mallee trunk, & mostly the
women's husbands. This was brought down with
them, so it is a truly genuine native utensil.
The muldharra (Murderers Slippers) are also interesting
as they have been worn by those very men you will see
at the siding tomorrow. These men women & children
ate their last cannibal meal about may or june this
year! so you see they are quite recent cannibals, but
do not scalp. The

creatures because they 3 have been so recently cannibals they drop that practice as soon as they enter civilization, & as they never go back to their native waters again, they never resume cannibalism.

The few little meteorites are interesting. They used to be bartered by the natives of Boolcoo water (all dead) to tribes north of them. I'm sorry they are such poor specimens, but the employees at the Siding get all the bigger & better ones. I call them "jewellers." They take a fine polish & the young railwaymen often have them set in bracelets & brooches & tie pins, etc. & their womenkin wear them. Science has not yet decided whether these are volcanic or extra terrestrial objects, but the native always says they are sky stones, & I believe the native. They call them Nyooloo.

The hair string which they spin so cleverly is called boordsaroo, & with this hair string (or fur string) they attach the emu feather 'slippers' to the sole of the foot, by winding the string round slipper & instep. This hides the track of the slipper wearer & that is why he is called jinna-arbil - from jinna-foot & arbie-hidden or covered.

The deelurn is the nose bone worn in the hole made through the septum of the nose. It is part of their full dress.

I have only one sick woman amongst them, with a stiffening arm & shoulder due to spear wounds.

The wind is bashing my tents so dreadfully. My book tent is already much torn, but it is impossible to mend it today.

Already these poor creatures are feeling the effects of the new foods & new environment & I could almost point out to you those who will pass on early. That is why I stick to them - to make them feel that there are two different white peoples - that not all white people are lustful & blatant & coarse

4.

I should have been so pleased to have a chat with you. I think the last time I saw you was at the Club. And by the way, that is one thing I am always astonished at! The Club comes have so easily done what you, you kindly fellow women Justices have done in honouring me with a life membership. I wonder why the Club has not given me that kindly little "pat on the back". I keep up my membership as I've always loved my Club since Lady Onslow & Mrs Cumming had me elected in 1899. Actually in this month too! I hope the little parcel will not inconvenience you. I wanted you to have some little mementos — & genuine of these poor natives where our 'homes' are hundreds of miles nor' west of here.

If I do not encourage visits from the living women I have only the most necessary intercourse with them in my journeys to & from the living, but I must go up early tomorrow before the heat comes, & find someone to give you this letter & the little parcel. With my very kindest regards — & the hope that your holiday will be a very pleasant one. I was unable to meet Phoebe Holmes, & Muriel Chase & Dolly Ferguson, but my strength all goes in these hot days. I have always felt the heat of this area, & as my years increase my strength lessens, but my spirit will always respond to a call for service from my poor natives.

Ask them about "Kabbarli" — that is their name for me. Ask the women & children! & I do hope you will see their poor faces brighten!

Yours very sincerely
Daisy M. Bates.

Kindly remember me to inquiring friends.

MILDRED CABLE AND EVANGELINE AND FRANCESCA FRENCH

Miss Mildred Cable

Miss Francesca French

Party IV, which escaped from Shan-Si. Miss
French far right, second row

The Inn courtyard, Ansi

Their tent in the Gobi

Caves of 1,000 Buddhas

Fresco compositions in large cave temple,
1,000 Buddhas site

MILDRED CABLE AND EVANGELINE AND
FRANCESCA FRENCH

The City Gate Tunhwang

Temple near the station of Hsing-Hsing-Hsia on
the road to Hami

Gorge on the road from Turfan

Pavilion over the inner west gate of
Chia-yü-kwan (Great Wall)

Bundles of old manuscripts, mainly Chinese,
in original wrappers. Cave of 1,000 Buddhas

Rows of Cave Temples

Cella and porch of Wang Tao-Shih's cave
Temple. 1,000 Buddhas site

The empty throne of Maksud Shah

MILDRED CABLE AND EVANGELINE AND
FRANCESCA FRENCH

Our caravan near Starry Gorge

A Qazaq woman

Isabella Bird Bishop

Isabella Bird Bishop

ISABELLA BIRD BISHOP

Isabella Bird Bishop

May Bird

Robert Bird of Barton House, Warwick,
Grandfather of Mr Bishop

Dr John Bishop

Mrs Bishop in her travelling dress

The Nestonian monument at Chingchiaopei

ISABELLA BIRD BISHOP

Mrs Bishop's travelling party in Korea,
from 'Views in the Far East'

Barrowmen, Chengtu Plain, China

Ichang Gorge, Yangtze, China

Mrs Bishop's boat on the Yangtze

John Bishop Orphanage, Tokyo, Japan

who escaped from Shansi. Of her journey with Party IV from Kie-Hiu to Ping-Yang-Fu she gave a detailed and very touching account in Marshall Broomhall's book and her escape from P'ing-Yang in a party of sixteen missionaries makes horrific reading. At the end of her concise account she wrote; 'On Tuesday, August 28, after having been on the road for forty-five days, our hearts were filled with joy and thanksgiving as we sighted Han-kow, our haven of rest. This series of trials and difficulties had come to an end, and many prayers and hopes had found their fulfilment.' Eva French was just and impartial in her assessment of the situation; 'It is not to be supposed that we received nothing but unkindness from the hands of the Chinese not connected with us by the bonds of Christian brotherhood. Several of the Mandarins showed an honest desire to advise us of the safest route, and provided us with good escorts.' Nevertheless, if Miss French and the four other ladies who went with her to spend the summer months at Kie-hiu had gone to either Fen-chau or T'ai-yuan they would most certainly have been done to death.

When Mildred Cable and the two ladies set out for Kansu in June 1923, the Boxer Rebellion was long gone, but there remained many dangers for women travelling alone, although a letter, written on 3 October, 1899 to the *North China Daily News*, and signed 'An Anglo-German woman', doubted whether the presence of men had much safety value. 'Is there not,' she asked, 'even a possibility that in some cases they are all the safer for being women?' It was a point. There were interesting things to be seen on the way to Kansu; one of the most famous was the Nestorian Monument or *Chingchiaopei*. It stood neglected and abandoned to the wind and the weather, an archaeological treasure of antiquity outside the west gate of Sian-fu. The stone itself, the 'Luminous Teaching Stela' is dated AD 781 and its inscriptions have been translated and photographed in modern times. Nestorian Christianity came to China in the sixth or probably the first half of the seventh century and Nestorians were encountered by Marco Polo towards the end of the thirteenth century. Isabella Bird Bishop was also interested in the Nestorians and visited them in Turkish Kurdistan, where they lived persecuted lives.

The stone was accidentally excavated in 1625 and placed on a pedestal by the then Governor of Shensi, where it was visited by many Chinese, but it later fell into neglect and in 1891 a small roof was erected over the stone to protect it. A sum of one hundred taels, sent from Peking to maintain it, was never received, having lost its way on the long journey; the five taels which did arrive were quite insufficient! The inscriptions are in Syro-Chinese characters and are in upwards of two thousand Chinese ideographs, carved with consummate skill. On the premises of an old Buddhist temple, the Nestorian monument stands on the back of a stone tortoise in a row of five upright stones. On 16 June, 1908, a replica of the Nestorian Monument was deposited in the Metropolitan Museum of Art in New York City as a loan and on 21 September 1911 another replica was placed on the top of Mount Royal, the Holy Land of Japan.

Nestorius was the Bishop of Constantinople in AD 428 but was banished to Arabia in 431 on account of his heretical teachings; i.e. Mary, the mother of Jesus, was not the mother of God but only the mother of his human nature. They were great missionaries and came to north-west China in AD 635, securing many converts, a proof that Christianity was taught in China as early as the seventh century. From the Nestorian Monument we learn that the Nestorians practised baptism; shaved their heads; recognized no distinction of persons; kept no slaves; amassed no riches; and prayed and watched in silence. Roman Catholic missionaries who went to China in the thirteenth and fourteenth centuries spoke of meeting the Nestorian Christians but they quarrelled with them over points of doctrine. Whatever were the virtues or defects of Nestorianism, it prepared the way for Catholicism and the Jesuit influx.

They saw and wondered at the three colossal images of the Buddha, in a temple backed by a plantation; the chief one, with foot thrust forward, waits for the appointed hour when he can awaken his brother, sleeping in distant Kansu Province and when that hour comes they will then join the Buddha at Shensi who will awaken; mankind will then have been raised.

The Kansu border was reached at nightfall, where they stayed in a wretched cave, where the walls were black with grime and the floor damp with stable manure. It was a great relief to arrive at the Mission Compound and receive their 'sealed orders' from the Swedish Missionary. He laid a finger on a spot in the extreme north-western boundary of Kansu; 'Here stands the Great City of Suchow. You who care so much for Kansu, this is the town which awaits your coming!' They soldiered on, drawing nearer and nearer to the area devastated by the earthquake of January 1921, and passed over the waterway of the great Yellow River and into the city of Lanchow, where the officials lived in the grand style of Manchu opulence and green sedan-chairs, oblivious of the new age of the Republic. They noted the brown or even red hair of the people of Piagfan and were astonished to discover that Père Huc had noted the same characteristics over a hundred years ago. They were also visited by a group of fortune-tellers, anxious to be shown a method of obtaining remission of sins and one old lady of seventy told them; 'My son ha s been reading to me the book you sent, and I want some more of the same kind.'

They came to Lanchow, the last place held by the foreign missionaries in north-west China and occupied by the China Inland Mission for forty years. Yungchang was 'a wretched place' and a place of sorrow, for the refugees from the Russian Revolution found their way there following the road to Peking and points east, north or south. It was March before they reached Kanchow City, after 1,500 miles of weary travel by litter and cart, bumping over boulders, snaking down sandhills and squelching through mud, losing axles and breaking wheels. Once they sat for hours with their backs to the Great Wall of China as darkness closed in, helpless to proceed as the cart was deep in mud; help came in the form of a man on a donkey who admired their Amazonian qualities which, according to the Chinese, are inherent in all women who come from 'Woman's land', where they are provided for by the Heavenly Father. Kanchow had a thriving Christian community, cared for by Dr Kao and his band of devoted helpers. It was soon apparent to the three ladies that their ardent wish to advance into unevangelized land beyond the Great Wall was in line with the 'sealed orders' which Dr Kao was now interpreting at a rally at morning service, it being Sunday.

As you know, brethren it was not young women that we were needing, but those seasoned by experience, trouble and hard work. Therefore I would have you remember that when we prayed it was for two elderly women, who yet must have retained all the vigour of youth, as, I need not remind you, Kansu is no place for the feeble! All these things were in our minds, nor did we see for ourselves where those could be found to present such a combination of qualities, yet, behold! God has supplied us, not with two of this unusual type, but with three!

The three were to be responsible for the training of a class of Christian men and women to venture out as preachers into territory beyond Suchow; the summer months were to be spent at Kanchow preparing them to face the unknown. Dr Kao had received the help he had prayed for.

Kin Cheng Kao became a Christian at the age of sixteen. Poverty in boyhood was a stern disciplinarian and Kao saw his future as 'a vendor of peanuts'. His chance came when the Medical Mission offered him work in the hospital; he received his medical degree and became a missionary in Kansu. Kanchow became his home and a fine Mission compound grew out of the shabby vacant lot and a dispensary, guest-hall, school-court and class-rooms remained a living tribute to his selfless work and ardent pioneering spirit. Later, a library, a playground, and a garden planted with trees graced the compound.

[195]

The summer days came and went, while Mildred and Francesca served the Mission and made contact with 'an unusual group of men and women' from six of the eighteen provinces of China. Their most ignorant student was a woman whose husband had been a devoted idol-worshipper. She came to classes and remained a steadfast Christian. 'I am going to have a week's Bible-study here. Bring the donkey with my week's provisions next Sunday, and then see if I want to go home or stay longer', she told her husband. They each stayed – to enjoy the community singing, the graded classes, the lectures on hygiene and the spirit of comradeship dedicated to the 'power of God unto salvation'.

By June it had become unbearably hot and it was arranged that they should spend July among the snow-capped peaks in Tibet. A visit to the Kang Lung lamasery was contemplated and so they set off once again, carrying a load of books, a tent, and a folding organ, on a journey which had little ease or comfort for the river outside Kanchow was swollen and mules and carts eddied round and round relying on the muleteer who knew 'how to look at water'. At midday the next day they reached the watch-tower marking the frontier and knew that they were in Tibet; they passed a *chörten* with a spire (and gained good luck) watched innumerable flags flying down the valley and the carved prayer-wheel revolving methodically in the stream flowing down the centre and gloried in the orchids and golden moss carpeting the ground and the fir trees covering the hill slopes. Their arrival brought out the red-robed lamas and soon their tent was erected and a fire made; the Tibetan women were full of curiosity, touching the hair of the missionaries, examining their fingers and hands, and trying on their cotton hats. It was all quite informal, with much chatter and peals of laughter as the Tibetan ladies tried on the luminous wrist-watches and ran into darkened rooms to see the dials – these Christian men and women were such fun to be with! Seven living Buddhas were in residence at Kang Lung. They were spiritual beings who had voluntarily remained outside Nirvana to help mankind on the upward path. The eighth lama had recently died and the lamas were hoping to find his spiritual successor in the form of a new-born baby who had entered the physical world at the moment of the lama's leave-taking. Buddhism, however, awakened little response in the hearts of the three missionaries. In their book *Through Jade Gate and Central Asia* they wrote;

Buddhism adopts many guises, but in watching these rituals one felt in the presence of very old and very evil influences. From the faces of most of the child lamas all boyishness had fled, leaving only lack-lustre eyes and a dull apathy, while on the features of the greater number of the older men, nameless, convulsive passions had left their hideous traces, showing unmistakably the disintegrating nature of the Power at work. In a country where personal cleanliness is practically impossible during nearly three quarters of the year owing to climatic causes; where women are the common property of a plurality of possessors; where one-sixth of the population is segregated in a so-called celibacy given over to idleness, and where such family life as exists is destitute of the very rudiments of decency or sanitation, nothing short of the deliverance of the individual – body, soul, and spirit – from the grasp of the stultifying Power can effect anything radical. We are dealing here with a fundamental problem of human existence, for which there is but one Master-Key. Only one, Who is the Giver of Life Eternal, can overcome this darkness.

The year 1923 not only saw three lady missionaries battling their way to Kanchow City after miles of tortuous travel by cart and litter, it also witnessed the departure of another traveller, Alexandra David-Neel from a Mission Home up the Mekong river to the Kha Karpo mountains on the threshold of Tibet. The three ladies were professed Christians; the woman determined to reach Lhasa was an oriental scholar, a 'lady lama', and a serious student of Buddhist scriptures.

Kanchow's wheat harvest was almost over when the three returned and there was now work to be done in another sphere. The greatest stumbling block to education was illiteracy; classes in the village centres were well attended but it was vital that the pupils master the Government Phonetic Script, by means of which an illiterate could be taught to read in twenty days and in three years 523 students mastered the Script in the time the three missionaries were in Kansu Province. The city of Suchow had been fixed on as the campaigning place for the Pioneer Band and so Dr Kao, with a few leaders and the three devoted ladies, set out with an old and faithful servant of ten years' service, travelling in a 'Peking cart', with the ubiquitous food-box, bedding, and one valise, one white mule, one brown mule, and a second servant known as 'Welcome Home', a name given to him at birth by his father.

Before they left they made good use of their time, seeing the sights and visiting the many temples, for Kanchow was a city of temples. The most highly-prized one was that of the Hall of the Sleeping Buddha. It was a colossal figure, one hundred and twenty feet in length and was believed by the Kanchow populace to be the largest image of Buddha in the world. It was made of earth and plastered with a composition of lime and paper pulp and had no artistic merit whatsoever. There was also a *chörten* (relic tomb) about one hundred and fifty feet high: the *chörten* is considered to symbolize the five elements into which the body is resolved at death – earth, water, fire, air, and ether. In her book *A Desert Journal* Mildred Cable wrote;

We are witnessing a social revolution in the course of which China must slough the dead skin of age-long repressions ... it is evident that both missionaries and Chinese Christians are being called upon to manifest a spirit of meekness and humility, and to prove by action that the doctrine professed is no mere form of words, but a transforming power for life and conduct. The attitude in the Epistle of St. James 'What doth it profit if a man say he have faith, but have not works?'

They left Kanchow on the next step of their journey to Suchow 'The Spring of Wine', a distance of seven days by cart. The ancient city was destroyed by the Mohammedan uprising of 1862 and a decree was enacted that no Muslim should hereafter reside within the city walls. In this city the three ladies made a home, after various inspections of rat-infested dwellings, dark and dismal lumps of 'desolate earth', and a poor-house with a ghost which refused to be laid. A leading gentleman of Suchow offered to Dr Kao and the missionary ladies the use of his vacant house and they were only too delighted to accept for not only was there room for two Bible-study court-yards, but a spacious hall and a waste ground which could be planted with trees and vegetables. There was also a sitting room and a verandah with a chair upon which no local would sit, it having received at one time the body of a young man who disported himself at a party by pretending to be a Mandarin. He had adopted a stupid sideways grin to amuse the guests, but when he arose from the chair the grin had become fixed on one side and remained there ever afterwards.

Suchow was a delight and a challenge; the delight lay in their home in the best residential quarter, and the challenge came from the confrontation between the minds 'blinded by Heathenism' and the gifts of Christianity in the form of education and brotherly love and the ability to understand and to persevere in spite of all difficulties. Twenty miles away was the frontier fortress of Kiayükwan which guarded the end of the Great Wall. The news soon spread that 'the Christians have come!' and the three ladies set about their mission, distributing books and tracts and arranging the students' work in a town *en fête*. At noon the men left for a two-hour stint of street preaching, which could be arduous and sometimes dangerous; the Muslim visitation in the eastern suburb was reserved for the most experienced of the men Evangelists and insults and abuse were nearly always their lot. The work was uphill and frustrating and little break-through could be effected, especially as minds were so perniciously hostile and closed to all liberal thought. But it was the plight of the children which tore at their hearts; 'The sight of naked, starving bairns, huddled at street corners on a little heap of straw which is their only bed, is once more forced upon us, and our helplessness in view of such suffering, is the hardest thing to bear.' The children adopted a policy of 'wait and see', only half-believing the superstitious tales of their parents, and quite ready to examine for themselves the teachings of the Pioneer Band. The Pioneer Band saw to their bodies as well as to their souls and looked after the sick and the starving little derelicts in danger of being frozen to death in the bitter winters. When the Mission announced a Children's Service, there was a huge response and hymns were sung in the great tent telling of 'the one God, the only Saviour, and the renewing spirit'.

At the end of March they visited Kinta, the city of the Golden Tower, which was no longer gold but white-washed, for the Muslims had stripped off the gold and replaced it by brass, which was stolen. Kinta was only thirty miles distant and as it was the only city between Suchow and Mongolia it was hoped to reach it in one day but the ladies reckoned without the wily carter with the usual plausible tongue. A Chinese proverb declared; 'Every carter is a scoundrel', and this was evident on the road for every conceivable hazard was thrown in their path, including a snowstorm of immense proportions, which could not have been attributable to the carter. It was now late August; they returned to Kanchow, and passed fields of poppies whose heads were now naked and dry, while the juice from the poppy filled the bowls of the farmers with thick, brown liquid. There had been some persecution of the Christians during the year, but a big crowd met them at the City Gate, many of the persons desiring baptism.

They were now planning an extensive journey beyond the Great Wall and on 24 August they reached Suchow, well-remembered for the visit of a member of the Sven Hedin Archaeological Expedition who announced his presence;

We came forward to find ourselves facing a burly Mongolian, over six feet high, clad in sheepskins and heavy leather overboots, with the typical maroon cloth sash tied round his waist. His shaggy hair stood out in a fringe from under the sheepskin cap, but from beneath this furry mass we discerned the mild blue Scandinavian eyes and the fair skin of the Nordic race.

They were a party of eight, including a little boy, son of Mr and Mrs Liu and they were to travel in a 'Kansu' cart with high wooden wheels and a shaft-horse instead of a mule. It was a familiar way as far as Kiayükwan (barrier of the Pleasant Valley), but one traditional custom had to be complied with before they turned their backs on China; it was incumbent on them to throw pebbles against the outer side of the Great Wall to determine whether or not they would return in safety; if the stones rebounded towards the thrower, safety was guaranteed, but if the stones fell in the already high heap, then there was no doubt that the traveller would live out his life, or lose it, in the vast wastes of Central Asia. The pebbles having been returned to everyone's relief, the little entourage passed beyond the barrier and into unknown land.

Kiayükwan marks the western end of the Great Wall of China, built as a protection against Tatr hordes in 214 BC. A single door of great beauty controlled the fortification which was known to the Chinese as her 'mouth'; those who have passed beyond it are 'outside the mouth' and those who are still inside are 'inside the mouth'. There were three gates in the old citadel; one was the low door of Necessity, through which the older residents passed to obtain water from the spring in the hill; another was larger, made of heavy wood studded with nails which saw each day the passage of the soldiers to the plains beyond to fetch luxury food for the Governor and his ladies and friends; the Travellers' Gate was the third one, a true 'Gate of Sighs' for many travellers had passed through the deep archway leading to the vast inhospitable wastes of the Gobi Desert. The long archway was covered with calligraphy, the outpourings in verse of men of learning whose hearts and souls were heavy with the despair of exile. 'It is terrifying indeed when the traveller hears the bolt being shot and the great gate being closed behind him and he faces the demonic blizzards and the furnace of the desert.'

All stages were taken at night, for the heat of the desert was unendurable. They took the journey easily and slowly; carts from Turkestan passed them in the night and the courier carrying mail dashed past in a high lick to the next stage; he was cheerful but not enthusiastic about his heavy loads; 'If it were not for those Christians my load would be light! If I am not carrying books for them, then it is letters; and if they have no letters, then it is books!' They pushed on to Yümen, the site of the ancient 'Jade Gate', the barrier ending the line of guard-houses from ancient Suchow in a north-westerly direction on the Kansu border. Then to Pulungki, thirty five miles distant, a ruined city encircled by an immense wall and strangled by the encroaching sands of the Gobi. Pulungki was believed to be the original Garden of Eden; fantastic tales had been circulated of buried treasure, beautiful and priceless vases buried deep in the sand, and a deep, subterranean shaft where a tiny oil-lamp burnt, fed from an enormous vat of vegetable oil which kept the lamp alive and had done for centuries. At an inn the next midnight, they received gifts of small cabbages and turnips from a very old woman who was anxious to be taught the 'way of Life'. 'There was something inexpressibly pathetic and moving in the way in which she drank deeply of the truth as it is in Jesus, memorising with the utmost reverence the brief prayer we taught her.'

From the inn at Ansi they went to the oasis of Tunhwang, a weary trek of four day's hard, gruelling travelling, almost frozen by the biting wind and only half alive for want of sleep, cruelly disappointed by the inn which turned out to be a rude shelter with a well of brackish water. In the bitter cold before sunrise they camped outside the gates, their only warmth a bundle of straw which they set alight to keep warm, but the fourteenth day of the eighth moon (1 October) was the eve of the Moon Festival and the time was right to missionize amongst the populace. 'They gathered round the organ, some sat on the shafts of the cart and others stood at ease listening to the preaching. They heard a few straight things based on the Ten Commandments, which poster was in our hands at the time.'

Tunhwang was an important centre; roads from Lhasa, Mongolia, India and South Siberia converged here and merchants from far-away Kashmir travelled with merchandise packed on the backs of sixty or more donkeys and mules. In Tunhwang the three ladies settled down to constructive work by organizing their Children's Band and holding Sunday and weekday services, attended by the monks, lamas, and pilgrims who cluttered up the streets of the town. They planned their campaign carefully each day after morning prayers and had their own method of gaining admittance to the distant farm-houses.

Our method of gaining an entrance into the distant farm-houses was to carry an English book, and after walking a suitable distance, sit down and read aloud in the foreign tongue. On not one single occasion did we get through a page before some woman came out, greatly interested by what was taking place, and invited us into her home.

Sometimes there was humour tossed into the raw salad which was their daily life in Tunhwang. One day, the ladies found about fifty men listening intently to an old man dressed in a purple silk gown which had seen better days. In the courtyard he addressed them from his little rostrum, peering at them through his large horn-rimmed spectacles and extending a long finger. 'You know nothing about it', he said, 'I have read all their books, and I understand their religion thoroughly. They are good people, I tell you, and the reason for their coming here is this – *The King of Europe* has sent them! It is he who meets all their expenses! Ever since the War, girls are scarce over there, and so he appointed these persons to select brides for the young men of his household!'

A question frequently asked the missionary ladies was; 'Have you ever heard of the "Caves of the Thousand Buddhas", eighteen miles from here?' They were famous for their art treasures and had been visited by a team from Harvard. The caves lay in a south-easterly direction across a way which was hard going, being composed of sand, mica, and pebbles. This did not deter the ladies; even a lonely trek on a hard road where they did not see a single, solitary traveller failed to dampen their enthusiasm, for they were sightseers, collectors of curios and rarities, seekers after archaeological treasures and ancient places lost in the mists of oblivious time. At the back of sandhills was a green oasis and here were the rock temples.

Four hundred years after the birth of Christ, Buddhism had become the religion of the merchants who crossed the great caravan routes leading out from Tunhwang; life was hard, travelling dangerous, and in a narrow gorge between the mountains Buddhist monks established a temple in a great cave, one amongst hundreds hollowed out from the rock-face, sometimes as many as four set one over the other. Here the devout travellers could pray for a safe journey and, in the quiet of the caves, meditate, listen to the ancient litanies and make their sacrifices before setting out. Over the long centuries, the caves were filled with paintings and frescoes and their fame spread far and wide across the vast deserts; one month nearly 50,000 made their journey across the wilderness of sand and pebbles. Unfortunately, the caves suffered from the grasping hands of western explorers and Chinese looters and now only farmers and nomadic Mongols lived in the surrounding wastelands. Twenty eight years before the visit of the missionaries, a Taoist priest from Hupeh Province came on a begging pilgrimage to Chienfutung, walking through the desolate country, watered by only a small brook. He stayed, to bring life and beauty to a scene of utter desolation; he planted whole plantations of trees; he sowed crops for himself and his acolytes; he erected a commodious rest-house and, in order to maintain the caves, he went on a begging expedition to raise money. When the three ladies arrived on their later visit in 1931 they were met with the sad news of the death of Wang tao-si, whose grave was shown to them, standing in sight of the caves he loved so well. They knew the old man well and had often spoken to him of 'Him who is the Way' and he had read with much interest a copy of *The Pilgrim's Progress* which they had lent to him.

The Hall of the Great Buddha, set almost in the middle of the long cliff, contained an enormous seated Buddha surrounded by thousands of smaller Buddhas. The giant Buddha, however, was not ancient, but comparatively modern. It was the smaller caves which were more interesting and contained particular representations of the Buddha; 'The Temple of the Precious Three'; 'The Hall of the Solitary Buddha'; 'The Shrine of Sakimuni'. At the southern end of the cliff were the twenty-two Wei Caves, where the paintings, in their rich colours, were representative of the primitive period of Chinese Buddhist painting. The paintings covered a long period of time, from the Han dynasty to the Sung and there were 177 Tang caves at Tunhwang. In the Sui and Tang caves a group of small images represent those Bodhisattvas who had not attained Buddhahood and it was quite a point of interest to the ladies to note that the posture and draperies were reminiscent of the Greek influence which came from the Graeco-Indian school at Gandhara. There were more than 500 caves to explore, some just tiny areas with a single Buddha, others larger with more figures. The paintings and frescoes depicted varied scenes of grace and charm showing the blessed reclining in pavilions and celestial beings dancing for their souls. Animals, too, were not left out, for rabbits and foxes stared in wonder and fawns, Bambi-like, sprang through the air in the unbounded joy of life. There were idols in raised alcoves and colossal figures, one of which represented the Buddha reclining in the final state of Nirvana. There was also a grotesque representation of 'The Pitiless One' in a shrine at the southern end of the caves; on either side stood attendants who surely must have gathered to themselves all the powers of evil for they induced the beholder to take his own life, either by taking opium or cutting his throat. The 'consummate horror' of the scene impressed itself forcibly on Mildred Cable and her two colleagues. Many of the shrines had no façade and so the upper shrines could be seen from below; it was possible to visit the whole length of grottoes through small doors of communication and so wander through the great galleries of beauty and horror from one end to the other.

Sir Aurel Stein visited the caves in 1907 and gives a detailed account in his book *Ruins of Desert Cathay*. In company with Wang tao-si, a temple was opened up which contained a mass of ancient manuscripts written in Chinese, Tibetan and Sanskrit and a peculiar form of Syriac script used in Manichaean writing. There are many records of ancient Tunhwang in the

King's Library of the British Museum and among some 15,000 Tunhwang manuscripts discovered by a Chinese priest in 1899 was the world's oldest printed book, now in the British Museum. A scroll from the Buddhist scriptures is preserved in Washington, D.C.

The three ladies paid another visit to the caves, seeing once again the 'cherubs with folded wings, the virgin-like goddess holding an infant on her knee and the striking figure of the man who stands by a tree but the grotesque and hideous idols of the lower shrines seem to get more than their share of worship and incense. What a mixture it all is!'

After visiting the Caves of the Thousand Buddhas, they were urged to visit 'The Lake of the Crescent Moon', three miles from Chienfutung. Here they encountered the phenomenon of the 'door of Thunder' for the sand, moved by vibration, rolls for hours on end, echoing through the valley like a mighty drum. They also met a lama, who had travelled barefoot all the way from Shansi who was on his way to Lhasa to fulfil a vow made 'many years ago'. They handed him a copy of St John's Gospel and spoke to him of Jesus. 'I know about this', he said. 'This Jesus, of whom you speak, has been greatly troubling me lately in my dreams. I know I shall *have* to believe in him!'

Back in Kiayükwan, 'within the mouth', it was evident that the work of Mildred Cable and her colleagues had borne fruit for there had been many who had professed Christ. The winter term of the Bible School commenced auspiciously and everyone praised the Christian Community for its devotion to the sick and the poor. But the bitter winds and cold were now upon them and the plight of the children could never be overlooked. Due to the thoughtfulness of one of Marshal Feng's magistrates, a shelter was built about this time in which the poor, pitiable dregs of humanity could obtain some degree of warmth, but there was no money for clothing and the children remained naked in the freezing temperatures.

In *The Desert Journal*, published in 1934, Mildred Cable wrote;

Such sights are not to be borne by those who put themselves in a position to witness them, and they who would not be involved in exacting works of philanthropy must take care to live in their own ceiled [*sic*] houses and remain unaware of poverty's woe, else that's the end of their own peace of mind.

Their own 'peace of mind' was to be shattered only too quickly after their return, for there were signs of a gathering storm of hostility against the Christian Missions. Kanchow, particularly, was the scene of much intimidation, due to economic difficulties over the opium tax and the Christian farmers' refusal to sow the seed. Armed thugs were secretly employed to waylay Christians and Dr Kao himself underwent the embarrassment of arrest, due to a misunderstanding which led him into prison 'a veritable Black Hole of Calcutta', a filthy place, full of rats. He was eventually released as the District Judge refused to ratify the sentence and the Commissioner of Lanchow insisted upon his removal to a 'House of Detention', where he had a decent room surrounded by pleasant gardens. Kansu gradually quietened down, although it was still a time of great political unrest. Suchow became transformed under an officer sent by Marshal Feng; streets were widened; a market place was built; the poor children were adequately cared for, and public works were ordered for the unemployed.

It was now time to leave Suchow. 'We bade Dr. Kao "farewell and God-speed" at the Temple of the Spring of Wine, and we stood for a few moments in silence watching as he and his mounted guard disappeared in a cloud of dust on the Lanchow road, and then turned back to face an important question.' The 'important question' was that of leave. It was imperative that the little band of three should now return home; there was illness in the home of one of them and a growing strain due to political pressure against the Christians on the part of the Mandarin clique. Letters were censored and it was only with the greatest difficulty that they could communicate with the outer world by telegram. Now that their beloved Dr Kao was released and safe, it was necessary to plan their way out of China as quickly as possible.

There were various routes to choose from; the one through Central China was discounted as the War Lords were on the move and the advice from Chinese and Turki travellers was contrary and often unacceptable. One of their students recommended his journey across the Gobi Desert; 'I joined the camel drivers and took it slowly.' A wiseacre pointed out, 'The best way to travel is with a string of small donkeys. They eat little, are quick on their feet, and if some die the loss is insignificant.' Even the hardened Chinese and Turki travellers differed in their views on getting across Central Asia. Lady friends, too, were importuned for specific views of travel; 'We get into the carts at sunset, and know nothing until we reach our inn the next day', (the opium tray, served to officals as the mules were harnessed, accounted for the beatific rest enjoyed by the officials and their wives).

In the end, they opted for a route via Kiayükwan, Yümen and Ansi to the Turkestan border, then to Hami and through the Tian Shan Mountains and on to Urumchi. From there, they would proceed through Manas and cross the Russian border at Kuswan, going from there by river steamer to Omsk, where they could join the Trans-Siberian railway. The time of preparation was very short and it was vital that suitable animals be found to pull the carts laden with provisions, kitchen utensils, coins, and books. So many poor, aged and sick animals were paraded in front of them that it became a matter of routine to overlook the beautiful saddles and fine harnesses and cast professional eyes on the pitiful creatures staggering beneath their weight. In the end, nine mules were selected to pull two large, strong carts; their own little Peking cart would carry them and their bedding. Clothes were no problem for the Chinese dress was adequate for the summer and the stout velvet shoes made by local women would suffice for all the rough walking they would be required to undertake. Lambskin coats were purchased for cold nights. Their most treasured possessions were two saucepans, a cake-tin, a couple of jugs and a small cooking-stove on four legs. Another missionary, Miss Annie Taylor, had used the same stove for many years before and it was no doubt pleased to be journeying home at last. Food had to be taken with them; flour, beans, dried peas, dried apricots, celery, radishes, green celery leaves – all were added to the carts.

The caravan numbered eleven persons and it was intended that they should stop at important oaises *en route*, setting up their large tent for preaching purposes and gathering in their flocks to hear the Gospel. It was such an important campaign and one to which they had all looked forward during their sojourn at Suchow and, besides, it would be a chance to practise the Turki language, which they had been studying so assiduously whilst at Suchow, having commenced at the School of Oriental Studies with Sir Denison Ross.

11 June, 1926 was the day decided on for the start of the long, long journey. There had been the usual leave-takings and teas with various Chinese friends and a 'farewell' with 'Welcome Home', who had enlisted in Marshal Feng's Army, and had been promised a military career and a fine education and who looked as bright as fresh paint in his clean cotton suit. They arose at 4 a.m., drank a single cup of tea, and made their way to the North Gate in the heavily-loaded carts. The whole city turned out to say 'goodbye' and friends escorted them for the first few miles. In their book *Through Jade Gate and Central Asia*, Mildred Cable wrote;

None perhaps so well as the Missionary is able to realise the strength of the spiritual ties which bind men and women together irrespective of race, class or nationality. Great as are the joys which arise from such supernatural relationships, they help to create also for the Missionary, circumstances which constitute a constant strain upon the emotions and sympathies. Whichever way he moves, some torn root is bleeding, whether it be in leaving spiritual children in the land of his adoption, or in parting from parents, friends or children in the homeland.

The Missionary life was a pilgrim life, the security of a normal environment being denied to him until he found it in the 'City that hath the foundations, whose Builder and Maker is God'. It was easy to fall victim to the illusion that the Church was held together by man and to miss the basic fact that it is the Holy Spirit which is the Life-Source. Thus the philosophy of the three lady missionaries as they contemplated the long journey back to the source.

So they trundled off to Kow Wai – 'without the mouth', to them, an unknown land, to the Chinese a dreaded place of howling winds and powerful demons ready to inflict untold agonies of torture. They came to Ansi from the town of Yümen (Jade Gate), where they had been three times before, to find friends to greet them. Their direct route lay from south-east to north-west, but they ventured off the main road to visit important oases and set up their preaching tent which was crowded from morn till night, with the populace eagerly searching for books. The grinning face of an old carter they had known was one of the first to greet them. 'Why! Miss French and Miss Cable! Who would have thought of seeing *you* here? Where *do* you not go with your tent! You must listen to their preaching', he told the crowd, 'it is all true.'

The journey, on the whole, had been pleasant, for they were known to the Chinese and so fruit and fresh vegetables were brought to them and the Gospel propounded to eager listeners in the preaching tent. In spite of the difficulties which had arisen over the Governor of Sinkiang's regulation that no man from Sinkiang could enter China and no man from Kansu could enter Sinkiang, they considered their days well spent, although the fact that their students would probably be impressed into the Turkestan Army of Defence if they crossed the border caused some apprehension. At 5.30 p.m. they left the inn at Ansi, to enter on a completely new stage of their journey 'and which we were warned held difficulties greater than any which we had already faced'. From the little bridge which spanned the irrigation canal at the North Gate 'Black Gobi' stretched out in an endless waste of grey grit and small, black pebbles, its feathery sand blown to the four winds. 'The word "Gobi" is not the proper name of a geographical area, but a common expression used by Mongols to designate a definite order of geographical features', wrote Vidal de la Blache and L. Gallois in their *Géographie Universelle*.

The very name was a literal translation of the Chinese ideograph meaning 'a wall of spears' and this it certainly was, for the traveller faced hunger, thirst, robbers, and death as he attempted to cross it. In her address to the Royal Geographical Society in 1942 Mildred Cable spoke of the variety of the Gobi; of the old towns long buried in the sand where treasures lay near the surface and the desert *Wutung* tree which grew among the mounds of silver sand, a tree of sadness to Chinese and Mongolians alike. The 'Curse of Allah' lay on the hot, barren hills, but the bare, stony ground of the ranges was shot with vivid colours of green and tender pink, making a garden of stone in a wilderness. Gobi was for several million years extremely favourable to the evolution of mammals, reptiles and plants and there is evidence that the desert region of Gobi abounded with life in past geological ages; anthropological evidence, too, points to the presence of stone-age tribes spread over the borders of the desert region during the Ice Age to the large lakes of the Altai Mountains. 'Gobi takes the place of the mythical Atlantis and other imagined continents, as the source of most of the animal civilizations and probably also of most of the vegetal civilizations of the northern hemisphere', wrote Professor Osborn in *Discovery*. 'The Gobi lured me from place to place, disciplining me by its spirit of austerity, strengthening me to endure its hardships, and then, as if in compensation for its rigours, it took me to see some of its hidden treasures.' Mildred Cable spoke lovingly of the Gobi in her address, but she never forgot the purpose of her journey across its vast wastes;

I tramped the desert highways for one purpose only; that as a missionary I might reach its surprisingly varied people. These people are my comrades and I learnt to know and to love, and to find ourselves equally at home within the Palace of the Khan, the *isba* of the Russian, the tent of the nomad, the court-yard of the Chinese and the *oy* of the Turki. I talked with veiled moslem women, the Turki Mullahs, the Mongol herdswomen at their tent doors, the inn-keepers of the main road, such as the inn-keeper of Pichan who would never let me pay for my lodgings. I met priests in wayside temples, Kirghiz who rode down from the hills, and Qazaq women, who, while still living in tents, had children in Siberian colleges.

But all this was the fruit of her recollections; the journey upon which they were now setting out was the seed to be sown before the advent of the Second World War which changed the map of Europe and altered the political face of the China they knew.

Three hours before sunset the carts rolled out on the black, gritty surface of the Gobi, but it was not long before the animals showed signs of fatigue; negotiating loose grit under a burning sun was torture for the poor beasts and it was with neighs of relief that they pulled in to the oasis of Petuntz – 'White Tower' – to leave at sunset for the next stage, trundling over alkali deposits which looked like snowfields and curving round spiked ranges of granite-bearing hills and ground covered with small pieces of white porphyry, pulling in from time to time into oases reminiscent of old-time western movies – Bitter Well Halt; Iris Well; Eyelash Oasis; Gates of Sand; Mud Pit Hollow; the Robbers' Den. Fortunately, they had food with them; soap and bread and a slab of brick tea; water bottles with tubes at one end to limit drinking; a new set of horseshoes and a bag of nails. In the carts it was all a question of balance; the clever carters placed the books of scripture on an outside board attached to the sides of the carts; they were in many languages besides English, all carefully wrapped in parcels which could be easily got at in case enquirers of the wilderness should profess an interest in the Christian Gospel.

If the Gobi was a burning expanse of sand and grit during the day, by night it was a place of quickening life. Criss-crossing the desert were the usual camel caravans, long trains of many beasts, laden with merchandise, halting half-way through the night to exchange news and pleasantries with the carts and caravans within hailing distance. The stars were brilliant; the moon a golden lamp lighting up an enchanted land; the magnetic lights flickering on the horizon – the Mongol's 'Rosary of Heaven'. The small insects and animals, securely tunnelled in day time, scurried about ceaselessly until morning, when the desert resumed its relentless hold on man and beast.

There were compensations for the hard journey for they met many people of the wastelands and visited them in the settlements.

Here, as in every other place, we visited each family, sat with them, talked with them, proclaimed Christ as Saviour and King, and on leaving saw to it that each family had now some Christian literature, which we hoped would be read during the long and dreary Gobi winter days and nights.

They talked, too, with the Buddhist priests who guarded and looked after the wayside shrines and temples and provided a resting-place for pilgrims to and from the holy mountain of Shansi. They had fantastic stories to tell of their birth and their desire to shut themselves away from the world, in a region far removed from their homeland, where they could pursue a life of asceticism which was, perhaps, at variance with their own natures, but which, for many reasons, was the only one which they could contemplate. They talked with such a man who told them he had heard about 'your Jesus' in a monastery in Kansu Province. He told them of *Tao* (the way), the principle of nothingness and they spoke with him of *Tao*, the Christian way of completeness in Christ. They handed him a book in which was the sentence; 'In the beginning was the Word [the Chinese translated this as *Tao*] and the Word was with God and the Word was God.' He read this with 'profound attention'.

From Iris Well they journeyed on to Hsinghsinghia, a distance of thirty miles. Hsinghsinghia was an important military frontier station of Turkestan and they were anxious to arrive by daylight and have plenty of time to see to permits and passports. At the entrance to the ravine known as the 'Ravine of Baboons', the soldiers and the N.C.O. were in full command, scrutinizing their permits and informing them that a telegram from the Governor was awaited. A room in a wretched inn was their resting-place for the night and a basin full of cold water their only chance of a wash. The soldiers left them no privacy. 'They are extraordinarily clean, always washing!' was their comment on the Christian missionaries. Soon the travelling harmonium and the books were unpacked and the hymn-sheets handed round to the crowd of listeners who not only sang 'vigorously', but bought the gaily-covered book as well. They heard many tales of woe from groups of 'poor-travellers and it was impossible not to feel the heartbreak of the young man detained at Hsinghsinghia on his way home and impressed into the army; the frustration of an elderly man wishing to transact business in Kansu and kicking his heels for over a year as a clerk in the garrison; the pain suffered by a youth whose legs were a terrible sight from flogging.

In their book *Through Jade Gate and Central Asia* Mildred Cable writes for the three missionaries;

The Chinese are a long-suffering people; they bear the tyrannies of their oppressors, and the dominion of rapacious officialdom, with a pathetic resignation, but the hour is at hand when they will rise and avenge the wrongs of generations. In such an hour no violence is regarded as an excess, and they will deal with their oppressors in their own way.

Four long days passed in the garrison town before the permits came through, but come they did and the officer flatteringly read the contents of the telegram; 'The Governor declares that the three ladies, Feng Precious Pearl, Feng Polished Jade, and Kai All Brave, are people of the highest reputation, and therefore they, their escort and baggage, are permitted to enter Turkestan without delay.' They entered Turkestan 'without delay', only too anxious to leave the garrison town and pass through the Ravine of Baboons, with its grey granite rocks covered with invisible soldiers, into more pacific country. The twelve hard and gruelling stages between Ansi and Hami were traversed through the hours of darkness; their lives devolving into a pattern of tranquil meditation as they settled down into the carts under the brightest of stars, with the camel bell swinging from the axle with a rhythmic clang. Water was a problem for it was always objectionable to drink, often foul, sometimes brackish, and invariably tasting of magnesium sulphate. But they jolted along in the Gobi nights until they passed the three oases; the Spring of the Sands, the Spring of Bitter Waters, and the Dove Tower, where they passed the Inexhaustible Spring, where the poor tired mules lifted their heads and smelt the sweet water and where fresh vegetables and a melon were purchased from the peasants' carts from Hami. It was a Mr Hunter who rode out to meet them in a small ammunition-wagon which he had bought from the Russians in Urumchi during the war.

This was the man from the Scotch Highlands who a quarter of a century ago had made his way to Central Asia, and establishing his base at Urumchi had lived there ever since, often travelling, however, over great distances driving from Chuguchak on the Siberian border to the Ili Valley, Barkul and Hami, Turfan and Kashgar

They were delighted with Hami; the city was spacious and the surroundings fertile and bright with colour; the landlord of the well-kept inn had allotted them a suite of rooms and the exclusive use of a kitchen where a repast was prepared of 'rice, good Chantow bread, a dish of chopped mutton and egg-plant fried together, a plate of French beans *sautéd* in mutton fat with sliced cucumber, and the whole accompanied by unlimited sweet water tea followed by slices of cantaloupe melon – truly a feast for the gods!' A hot sponge-bath followed and completed the rest-cure, the first one since leaving Suchow!

The Gobi had its hereditary king, ruling over a vast area to the frontiers of Mongolia and holding his Khanate under the suzerainty of China. When the Mongols were supreme in the time of Genghis Khan, the area of the oasis of Hami was part of the great empire of his third son; since that time the sovereignty of the Khan had always been recognized. Marco Polo wrote;

The Province lies between two great deserts. The people are all idolaters and have a peculiar language. They live by the fruits of the earth which they have in plenty, and dispose of to travellers. They are a people who take things very easily for they mind nothing but playing, singing, dancing and enjoying themselves.

The King of the Gobi lived in Hami, in a palace containing the bulk of his wealth. His nephew, the Khan of Lukchum, had been his representative but had lost his reason and was kept in rooms at the top of the palace. The women of the harem were many; they were dressed in emerald silk and had their own retinue of servants and lived indolent lives of luxury. As a young man, the Khan was required to go to Peking every sixth year and act as a personal servant to the Emperor for forty days. He also took with him gifts of the famous Hami melons, very much liked in Peking.

When a western visitor once asked the Khan to show him the extent of his dominion he did so by a sweep of his arm; 'All that you see is mine', he said, 'and more that you cannot see.' Writing from Suchow on 1 September 1930, Mildred Cable and Francesca French described a visit to the Khan's Summer Palace. It had been a summer of stifling heat and stinging flies and the town itself became a furnace from which they longed to escape. It was by the kindness of their landlord that they were able to do so. 'How would you like to spend a few days at the Khan's Summer Palace? It is thirty miles across Gobi, but cool, shady and well watered.' The family were not in residence at the time and so they left joyously for the Gobi with a devoted Turki escort who watched over them all the way and handed them over to the graceful women of the Royal Household who served them with cold salted tea and baked loaves in a thickly-carpeted apartment. Unfortunately, they were not left alone for the night; by Royal Command, a fussy lady-in-waiting insisted on attending to their every want and remained within earshot at night – luckily they slept soundly. Their equerry escorted them on every expedition on the estate; it was apparent that they were not going to be left alone and that the Khan's royal orders were to be carried out punctiliously.

The estate was divided into large enclosures which contained parks and gardens of walnut, peach, mulberry and apple trees, watered by a single rushing torrent from the snow hills – water which was temptingly inviting to the ladies whose only thought was to get rid of the conscientious escort. They had brought with them their books, which they now proceeded to read, apparently totally oblivious to everything around them. The escort became bored and, by the third day, decided to stay at home. The cool waters now had their grateful devotees! It was a time of great luxury and refreshment for the three wanderers of the desert. In the beautiful apartments of the Khan's wives, they received the hospitality for which Hami was famous and discussed the matters of the day with the son of the Khan who came to talk with them in the apartment of the harem's immediate favourite. The apartments were certainly unlike the filthy inns they had slept in during their travels; they were carpeted with silk rugs from Khotan, embroidered silk cushions, a low table spread with sweetmeats, polished brass candlesticks, and bowls and teapots on every shelf. There were exquisite gardens and beyond them a road leading across to sandstone cliff where there were caves with traces of frescoes and stately figures of the Buddha. Sir Aurel Stein visited the caves in 1891 and was greatly impressed by the approach to the gardens of the Khan; 'No landscape gardener in far-away England', he wrote, 'could have laid out his drive with more cunning, nor could any gardener's art produce such strangely varied, fantastic shapes of trees. Not since I made my way through the terminal jungles of the Niya River had my eyes been treated to such a feast.'

But the days were fast approaching when the old Khan, the Maksud Shah could no longer hold on to his former glory and retain control of his enormous flocks of cattle and sheep grazing peacefully at Bardsah in the mountains. Even Yolbas, his dynamic chancellor, known as the Tiger Prince, was quite aware of the Chinese attempt to abolish the age-old Khanate and bring Hami under Chinese suzerainty. At midnight, on the eighth day of their stay at the Summer Palace, the old Khan died and everyone who could sped to Hami to witness the last obsequies paid to a descendant of Genghis Khan. Maksud Khan was the last King of the Gobi, a supreme Khan who ruled wisely over his Turki subjects and who made Hami into a beautiful Muslim city, famous for its hospitality and its melons The Khan's heir, Nazir, was taken to Urumchi by order of the Provincial Government and deprived of his liberty; insurgents vandalized the gardens and burnt down the summer palaces, and the fruit trees, so lovingly tended by the gardeners, were chopped down for firewood. Even the luscious melons were no longer the same, for the growers had vied with each other to produce gifts for the Royal Household; now the incentive had gone. The 'Hami' melon, so much prized by the Chinese, was no more.

The three ladies did not neglect their work for evangelism; the parcels of books were duly opened as they sat on their cart surrounded by eager buyers, many of them cheeky Muslim schoolboys, only too willing to treat the volumes with a certain amount of disrespect. This was evaded by the simple ruse of writing on every page the sacred name of *Huda* (God) and explaining that this name must never be treated with derision. In the Chinese city the crowd were respectful and quiet and when the ladies went on a shopping expedition much courtesy was shown. They partook of the tea brought to them and were entertained by good conversation and the solicitations of apprentices who flittered around with bales of material for inspection. They came from England? 'Ah! yes, the capital, London! A bigger city than Peking. This is a good piece of silk. Is England a republic? I have heard you are ruled by Upper and Lower Houses.' It was difficult to bargain; there was a sign hanging on the outside of the shop; 'No prices discussed here', but the Chinese shop-keeper met them half-way with a wave of the hand; 'You are guests from a far country. Have a little more tea!' Thus was the bargain sealed.

The time of the great heat was approaching and it was imperative that they continue on their way; with great reluctance they left Hami, the city of peace and comfort and luscious melons and travelled out in their cart fitted with new wheels, taking the north road through the Tian Shan range. Hami had been such a fascinating city, so full of links with the past; Marco Polo had written;

Camul (Hami) has customs of the husbands giving up not only their house but their wives also for the entertainment of strangers. The women are, in truth, very handsome, very sensual, and fully disposed to conform in this respect to the injunctions of their husbands.

The mules were rested and refreshed for the long journey to the first stop and pulled merrily away along the north road. There were many methods of travel over the Gobi, the great transport agent being the camel-caravan with its leader – the *bash*, pulled by the bulky Bactrian camels, trained to a slow, steady pace. By the wayside the baby camels are born, and carried in a little cradle on the mother's back; by the time they are a week old they run haltingly and erratically alongside the caravan, developing rapidly as the days go by until they, too, can carry a very lightweight load of spare clothes, cooking equipment and so forth. The drivers, (the best were the Chinese and some northern Mongols) were thoughtful and considerate of their animals and the more aware of them judged their moods very accurately. The camel driver knows instinctively when the camel is overloaded; when it kneels to be laden it always grumbles and is surly, often throwing into the face of the *bash* a filthy load of regurgitated cud; when the beast is silent, then the driver knows that it is overloaded. It is a slow beast, with little cleverness, easily discouraged and liable to hair off across the desert with those aggressive camels who make a periodic flight to freedom, their harnesses pounding against their sides. The little donkey, by comparison, is a poor, wretched, unhappy animal, driven in droves by its Turki masters to supply the markets with fresh produce, bales of cloth and undyed cotton.

Speed is of the essence and so the donkeys, being cheap, are flayed all along the route and often driven at break-neck speed over by-ways used as short-cuts. The Chinese used great carts, with wheels which could be adjusted according to the differing gauges of the tracks. They were 'organization and methods' men, carefully calculating the distance and possessing the ability to think ahead and organize, using the Chinese principles of *ta-suan*. Their transport system had been built up on this principle and had enabled the carters to amass money from good exchanges and investment in each area through which they passed. Women and children often travelled in camel-litters, narrow wooden boxes with seats which allowed for no change of position, as they were balanced by boxes fitted on the other side of the camel. This mode of travel, however, did not appeal to the three ladies who did not fancy being cooped up in a box on a camel which, at any moment, might join a more cunning fellow-camel opting for liberty at a thunderous pace into nowhere.

They arrived at Urumchi after passing the 'three stages' of resting posts and coming nearer to the foothills of the Barkul Range at an altitude of 5,500 feet, their last stage having been taken in company with Mr Hunter, who shed the mules with his travelling farrier's kit, greatly to the admiration of the Chinese. The Turki inn-keeper was suspicious; 'What have they come for?' he asked Mr Hunter; 'Is it bones, plants or game that they want?' Upon being told that the ladies were missionaries, he said; 'Oh, that's different, but some of those who come, why there's no knowing what they want! There was a man here once upon a time, and his servant told me he came to Chekulu in order to measure the distance to the sun! A likely tale! Couldn't he measure it in his own country? Surely you can *sometimes* see the sun in western lands?'

The road over the watershed dividing Chinese Turkestan from Dzungaria was hard and stony and difficult to see in the dark, but on the northern slopes of the Tian Shan the way was down wooded slopes to Muleiho, they slept in the only rooms available, while bugs dropped from the ceiling and flies plastered the walls like a collage. In the little, unimpressive town they met two elderly men, brothers, who had been converted to Christianity by Pastor Hsi whilst in Shansi. Pastor Hsi was a scholar and a student of Confucius and was the first ordained Chinese minister of the Shansi church. Mildred Cable wrote about him in her book *Fulfilment of a Dream*, and told of their appreciation of the Shansi meal that the Christian community had prepared for them in the back room of the shop kept by the brothers. They came to Kuching, 'Ancient City', and immediately stepped into a town full of surpises – a thriving metropolis with many shops of glittering wares; the bakers piled hot rolls on to their counters, the silversmiths vied with one another to produce the finest silverware, the tailors sat at their shop doors, busy with their Singer's sewing machines. As usual, they had callers and purchasers of books and invitations to private homes. 'We bore witness in Kuching, and then passed on.'

The last stages of their journey to Urumchi were now upon them and it was a question of taking the Express Cart in order to expedite the day of arrival. Natives of Urumchi were enthusiastic about the 'Express Cart'. 'The Governor's Express Cart Service takes you over six stages in one day and a half, that is, by travelling straight through, and only stopping long enough to change the horses.' But the cart proved to be nothing more than long poles lashed together – a terrifying contraption fit only for the carrying of mail and postal parcels, driven by bony horses at a highly dangerous speed, whipped on through a cloud of dust as it entered Kuching. Mr Hunter himself cautioned them against taking the 'Express Cart'; '*I* would not take such a risk if I were you!'

'The City of Everlasting Trust' belied its name. At the Military Gate, passports had to be produced and the whole proceedings which should have passed off pleasantly enough (for their papers were quite in order) aroused the ire of the soldiers. The innkeeper had not informed the Military Guard of the arrival of the 'foreigners' and had thus neglected his duty towards the authorities. 'It is of the greatest importance that travellers' passports should be in strict order and up-to-date', wrote Mildred Cable, 'we were required to produce these documents at the most unlikely places, and sometimes they were examined both on entering and on leaving a city, as well as at the Yamen'. Day followed day in quick succession as Urumchi drew nearer. At a site near Santai, the terrible holocaust of the Muslim rebellion of 1862–77 was sharply brought home to them in the ruined villages and farmsteads sacked by the Tungan rebels as they marched from south Kansu to Turkestan, cruelly exterminating the Chinese population and carrying off the women and boys. In her book *Through Jade Gate and Central Asia* Mildred Cable wrote;

Dawn saw us again on the road, thrilled at the prospect of so soon seeing the great capital of Sinkiang, on which our thoughts have so often centred as we pictured the base from which Mr. Hunter and Mr. Mather had carried on their missionary operations for so many years. Mr. Mather had now been in China for sixteen years without taking any furlough, and considerable pressure had been brought to bear upon him to return for a short period to England. This, however, he could not consider, unless a companion were forthcoming who would stay with Mr. Hunter during his absence. A volunteer was found in Mr. Ridley of Sining, in Kansu, who had, we knew, recently arrived in Urumchi to take over Mr. Mather's work, and thus release him for furlough; and this being so, we had mutually agreed to travel together from Urumchi to Europe.

Mr Mather welcomed them as the first fellow-countrymen he had seen for twelve years!

They were not impressed with Urumchi, but they were delighted with the Mission House; 'there were fine stabling and spacious hay lofts; the flat mud roof was accessible and enabled one to get a good view of the city, a new, roomy church was entered from the street, and a row of Chinese guest-rooms completed the buildings. Here was luxury indeed!' There was good conversation in Urumchi and they asked innumerable questions about Turkestan and its language and sociology; Mr Mather was only too happy to oblige for he was a scholar who had acquired his knowledge of the Mongolian tongue from a bi-lingual prisoner who had given him lessons inside his prison cage, and he was ready to embark on a Manchurian-Russian grammar 'when he had the time'. By means of a small mimeograph he had printed the early copies of the Gospels in the Turki language and had introduced Turki readers to *The Pilgrim's Progress*. So time passed quickly and very happily in Urumchi but seven hundred miles still lay between them and Chuguchak, the last city in China before the Russian frontier. They were the first British women to visit Urumchi and their application for passports to cross the Russian frontier created a precedent. Their original British passports had been stolen and their papers were passports printed in Chinese and issued by the Chinese Foreign Office and the British Consul in Hankow; even their names were in Chinese. However, permits arrived in time from Moscow and preparations were made for their departure. Urumchi had been such a fascinating town that they were almost loath to leave. Mongol, Tibetan, Tungan, Qazaq tribes galloped down the streets, each handling his horse in his own inimitable way. The heat was intense, the flies innumerable and abominable and the piles of discarded melon rinds reached up to the eaves of the houses. It was a colonial city, 'without the mouth', segregated from the rest of the unsettled nations by a system of strict censorship instituted by the Governor, who controlled the newspapers and the postal and telegraph offices. To ensure complete placidity, all restaurants were posted with the announcement; 'No political discussions allowed'. It worked.

Following on the receipt of their passports, they bought Russian roubles

and made preparations to travel the last stage of their journey in a *tarantass* –
a long, four-wheeled, springless cart, harnessed to three horses abreast,
with a painted wooden hoop fastened to the shafts which stood high above
the horses' heads and from which several bells tinkled as they sped along. It
was a sad moment when they sold their mules, but the patient animals were
duly trotted off to the horse fair. On Friday, 27 August, they were off,
speeding away to the Russian frontier, having wisely skimmed off all surplus
luggage in order to lighten the *tarantass* and avoid any 'incidents' due to the
importation into Russia of cameras, books, papers, letters or photographs;
their small harmonium, too, became a victim of pruning.

Their food was plentiful and luxurious; Russian friends had supplied
them with the staple diet and with delicacies, such as the delicious conserve
made from mountain strawberries. With packets of tracts, gospels and a
fair-sized cushion, a kettle, saucepan and iron tripod, the *tarantass* became a
tight squeeze for three but the vehicle was far quicker than the lumbering
Chinese cart and they were now able to cover the distance in half the time.
The roads were busy with merchants bringing goods from Russia and the
inns were always full of carts, carrying the ubiquitous galvanized bucket,
popular in Urumchi. On 2 September they were within sight of the important town of Hsihu on the way to the Russian frontier, having come
safely through 'fly-land', aptly named on account of the flies which abounded
to torment, revolt, and demoralize their captive victims. With no telegraph
wire to guide them, and a bog into which three of the carts of merchandise
had sunk, necessitating the whole party sleeping on the ground, Chuguchak
was eventually reached. 'The Town of Seagulls', so-called because of the
many hundreds of birds which followed the course of the river Irtish from
the Arctic, was a populous city made up of Qazaqs, Tatars, Siberians, Chinese
and Mongols, with a Russian Consul in residence. Here they were entertained by Mr Chang, the postmaster, who sent his Russian carriage and
driver to show 'the ladies' the 'Grand Tour', which turned out to be slightly
embarrassing as they went round and round the same circuit, looking elegant
but non-plussed as they sat in the comfortable carriage with the shopkeepers
crying; 'Here they come again!' Mr Mather was to spend some time in
Chuguchak for he was able to obtain the services of *emigrés* who spoke
several Asian tongues and so helped him enormously with his translation
work; the result was a pile of manuscripts which would undoubtedly assist
the labours of Mongol and Manchu scholars.

Now came the final stage of their journey to the frontier town of Kuswan;
thereafter they would be in the land of the Reds, as they put it. They now

had two drivers, one a burly Qazaq, the other a borderland boy. For three miles along the road, they were accompanied by Mr Hunter and their 'farewell' was poignant and sincere;

For twelve years he and Mr. Mather had sustained one another through loneliness and discouragement, strengthened each other's hands in joy and in sorrow, and when the time for parting came it was with poignant grief that the last farewell was said. Once more Mr. Hunter bought ripe melons and handed them into our cart to refresh us by the way, then turned away and we saw him no more.

They were also accompanied by a 'military escort', an old soldier of sixty years who had been deputed by the Russian Authorities to look after their safety on the road. He was disgruntled at having to turn out again. 'I am always on the go. In one night and off again the next morning!'

The road was tortuous and the *tarantass* negotiated the twists and turns with difficulty; the higher they drove the greater was the danger of overturning. On the topmost ridge of the great watershed dividing China from Russia they stood where the water flowed in two directions – one into China and the other into Russian territory. 'Here we looked back for a last farewell to the land over which we had travelled, then, seeking expression for the deep emotion which the missionary must feel each time he leaves the country to which he gives his life, we worshipped the Lord, rejoicing in confidence that all nations shall yet call him blessed; then, turning away, we slowly walked down the slope to the land of the Reds.'

There was a steamer which called twice a week at the town of Topliefmus which was called *Parahot*. As the missionaries kicked their heels in the desolate little place on the border of Lake Zaisan, waiting for the steamer to come, they were the unwilling spectators of scenes from family life. There was drama, and there was comedy, and there was also a great deal of discomfort. They 'boarded' in a cottage built on the beach at the end of the promontory, where a large family lived, and many visitors came and went. They slept in an inner room, where water melons were kept snugly in rows under the single-bed; often during the night the children sneaked in to carry off a melon which would be divided between them and greedily devoured. Sleep was impossible, for the parents and children slept side by side on the mud floor and father would decide to entertain his offspring by recounting tales and romances for hours at a time – fleas and other insects were not conducive to settled rest. Mr Mather also suffered a great deal for he shared his wooden bench on the porch with a flock of geese, whose cackling became a tortuous nightmare which never stopped.

However, the *Parahot* came at last, gliding past the cottage towards the landing stage. 'We could see through the windows into the brilliantly lighted cabin, and the blaze of electric light held us fascinated. It stood to us for all the amenities of Western life and, emerging as we did from the hard conditions of a toilsome desert journey, which in itself had been but the conclusion of a period of arduous pioneer life, the mere sight thrilled us with inexpressible excitement', wrote Mildred Cable.

They discarded their Chinese dress, and donned blouses and skirts, for they were now in the Western world and conformed to the style of the country in which they found themselves. If their long journey of over three thousand miles from Suchow to Chuguchak had been, at times, one of unspeakable wretchedness, the one on the steamer down the Irtish to Semipalatinsk was one of heavenly delight, consisting as it did of a clean, private cabin and 'admirably contrived' meals, supplemented by luxury à la carte dishes and creamy butter, eggs, curd cakes, tomatoes and fresh bread which they bought from the peasant market at the landing stages. On the fourth day they reached Semipalatinsk and decided to board a second steamer for Omsk, which came in the late afternoon.

The steamer to Omsk was even more interesting than the one down the Irtish; the majority of the passengers were Qazaqs who had liberated themselves from the nomadic tent life of their inheritance and had pulled themselves up by their own bootstraps into a world where they could assimilate the education and culture which they wished for their children. They were intensely curious and extremely knowledgeable about current affairs, especially about the state of British politics and very anxious to know what the missionaries thought of the Labour Party and of Ramsay Macdonald. They had given generously to the British miners in their struggle and had a great admiration for the British people. On a piano in the first-class dining room the strains of 'Onward Christian Soldiers' rang out, accompanied by much hand-clapping.

On the fifth day they came to Omsk, but it was long after dark when the city landing-stage was reached and they were able to find a hotel where they could procure two vacant rooms without board. They found it a busy city with crowded streets and roads filled with motor traffic and endless queues of people patiently waiting for goods and commodities.

Omsk was toured in another mode of travel – the Russian *droshky*. Business was brisk and food abundant, but the dress of the people was poor, in spite of the 'Paris' models on display in the shop windows. However, there was a Post-Office and a German-speaking young lady clerk who stamped and registered their letters, which, incidentally, never arrived at their destinations. Mildred Cable wrote; 'In due time we made our way to the railway station, which was several miles from the hotel, in order to take our tickets for Moscow.' Their enquiries proved fruitless; they spoke no Russian and were informed that there were no travellers' tickets in the Moscow train. This, apparently, was a normal condition on through trains and it must have evoked memories of the one-wheeled Chinese cart which had carried them across Eastern China and Turkestan. They found a friend in a tall, good-looking man who spoke perfect English and lived across the hall from them in the Omsk hotel. He was frankly curious about them and their passports. 'English people do not come to Omsk', he said, 'what are you doing here?' It was explained to him that they were missionaries travelling from Turkestan on their way to London and that no tickets were available on the train. At 10.30 at night they left the hotel, hoping to board the train as it stood in the station and thus surreptitiously gain seats. This was not possible and so they made their way to the heated waiting room, filled with peasants sleeping with their heads on their baskets or passing the time by eating curd cakes. Their friend appeared, waving tickets, 'I have the tickets. I thought it better for you to travel "hard".' He was evidently a man of some authority for the station staff appeared to treat him with respect. During the long wait for the train, conversation led them on to the subject of the cruel years through which Russia had passed and of the starvation and fever which had followed upon the fighting in Odessa, which he had seen for himself. 'When you reach England', he said, 'many will tell you that Russians are wholly bad. Please let them know that *you* did not find this to be the case!'

(In a personal letter home, written from Berlin on 21 September, 1932 the three missionary ladies spoke of the tremendous difficulties they had encountered upon a later occasion when they journeyed home to England from Sergiopol, changing trains at Novosibirsk, capital of Siberia. This time they took with them a little Chinese child, Topsy, who was deaf and dumb and needed a special passport from an efficient and ruthless-looking woman on the Consulate Staff. The visa was acquired and they were all ready and anxious to leave the bureaucratic stronghold when the woman, with tears in her eyes, took Topsy in her arms, explaining that she had once cared for a group of deaf children 'down in the Caucasus'. 'The whole incident was unexpected, touching and revealing', wrote Mildred Cable, 'as we drove back we said to one another: "That just shows how easily we understand each other, when we touch human need and the instinct of pity".')

The train opened up another new vista.

Life on a long-distance Russian train is brimful of interest, whether from the geographical, sociological or psychological side. On previous occasions when travelling either by the International Wagon-Lits or by the daily Post-Train, we had enjoyed the privacy of our own compartment, but the new conditions brought us into the closest proximity with a large number of fellow-travellers; for there is no corridor, and the space which used to be occupied by this is now made to supply extra sleeping accommodation.

The 'new conditions' proved interesting. A jolly little Siberian townsman was their nearest neighbour; he seemed to find everything most amusing and broke into loud laughter continuously without any apparent cause, pausing only to go to sleep, which he did after laughing softly to himself. Men snored, women nursed their babies and the train bell sounded at intervals for thirsty passengers to descend at wayside stations and fill their teapots with hot water from the ever-ready tanks. Hot bread, butter, fish, eggs, tomatoes, could all be purchased at the peasant markets and taken by flying passengers back to the train, there to be eaten with relish and passed to less fortunate folk who had not made it to the platform.

The dark, Siberian forests went on for miles, beautiful with the tints of autumn and it was now only a matter of hours before they reached the outskirts of Moscow, recognizable by the lines of concrete buildings put up to house the workers. Once in the city, they secured a suite of three rooms in a hotel, breakfasted in their bed-room, following the local custom of carrying bread and pats of butter and other delicacies up the marble staircase into their apartments – and paid as much for a slice of melon as they would have done for the whole fruit on the Irtish steamer. Visas, once again, were an irritation and two whole days were spent in obtaining one for each country through which they were to pass before they entered Belgium on the last stage of their long, long journey and boarded the boat for the Channel crossing, which proved to be of utter wretchedness, with huge waves tossing them about on deck and ruining the model hats they had purchased with so much delight in the Brussels *Bon-Marché*.

It was late at night when they arrived in London in 'drenching rain', forced to wander from hotel to hotel to find a room for the night. The landlady of a 'private Hotel' took them in, looking them up and down as they queried the price. 'See 'ere, you can have the beds for six shillings a 'ead, and in the morning, I'll throw in a pot of tea!'

From 11 June to 12 October, they had travelled from Suchow to London, a journey of over 6,000 miles. Months later, they were off again from the self-same Victoria Station, to proceed to Paris, Annecy (where they enjoyed a short holiday) and Marseilles, where they were to embark on the P. and O. Liner *Mantua* for Bombay. At Marseilles they greeted Percy Mather, who was returning to Central Asia and was, once again, to be their fellow-traveller. Their journeys were recounted in the form of letters and published as *A Desert Journal: letters from Central Asia* in 1934.

The book was well received. A reviewer in *The Geographical Journal* called it 'a delightful book' and wrote;

Explorers prepare expeditions with elaborate care, and yet their dumps of supplies are looted by bandit generals; but these three English ladies in the normal course of their missionary duties think little of starting off on a preaching tour of many months with only a light cart and a hired wagon, along the Gobi Road and away off it to visit isolated fortress-farms in distant oases, or up the wild valleys of the Richtofen Mountains to reach Tibetan lamaseries.

They had long looked forward to a holiday in England ('we saw our last countrywoman in the autumn of 1928') and purchased by cablegram a little stone cottage in Stour Row, Shaftesbury, Dorset – a cottage they had never seen.

Until now our furloughs have been spent in sampling the various kinds of London *caravanserais* but we have wearied of them all. Now we have a place of our very own and it is called 'The Willow Cottage'. Our friends will always be welcome there.

All three ladies retired in 1941. On 19 March, 1934, Mildred Cable delivered the Fifth Asia Lecture at the Evening Meeting of the Royal Geographical Society on 'The Bazaars of Tangut and the Trade-Routes of Dzungaria), and at a meeting of the Society on 26 October, 1942 she addressed her audience on 'A New Era in the Gobi'.

Mildred Cable died in 1952. Miss Evangeline French on 8 July, 1960 at the age of ninety-one, and her sister Francesca on 2 August, aged eighty-eight. Evangeline French had worked for fifteen years in north-west China; after their mother's death, Francesca joined her. On retirement from missionary work, Francesca did voluntary work for the British and Foreign Bible Society and became an honorary life governor in 1945. They were younger sisters of Field-Marshal Lord French, first Earl of Ypres, though this fact was not well-known.

Besides their scholarly records and painstaking attention to archaeological and ethnographical work in the wildernesses of north-west China, Turkestan and Tibet, 'the Kingdom of God' claimed their love and attention. The two books, *Grace, Child of the Gobi* and *The Story of Topsy: Little Lonely of Central Asia*, expressed all their great sympathy and concern for the neglected and the downcast of the world. The little 'Topsy', the deaf and dumb, talented Mongol-Tibetan girl for whom they had to obtain a visa when changing trains at Novosibirsk, became a British Subject and changed her name from Ai Lien (Topsy) to that of Miss Eileen Guy; she entered upon a life of devotion and service.

They paid tribute to their colleagues, too, those fellow travellers and dwellers in the wilderness, George Hunter and Percy Mather, in the books *George Hunter: apostle of Turkestan*, and *The Making of a Pioneer: The Life of Percy Mather* (1935).

The 'trio' told of their experiences as they toured Australia, India and New Zealand after the war in the book *Journey with a Purpose*, and in *Miss Brown's Hospital* (1954), Francesca revealed a deeper personality for she wrote the book alone after Miss Cable's death. Mildred Cable also travelled extensively for the Bible Society, where her journeys took her to India and Brazil.

Between them the three ladies gave ninety-eight years to missionary work in China and the Far East. The 'Willow Cottage' was their final oasis.

CHAPTER EIGHT

Isabella Bird Bishop

Switzerland was very nice, but I don't like the Swiss,
and, after the frank, genial manners of the people of
Southern Italy I found them specially ungracious. The
most delightful place we were at was Soglio high up
above the chestnut woods of the lovely Val Breguglia
where we lived in an old palace of the De Salis, built
in 1538, and with furniture of the sixteenth century,
looking across to the glaciers and snow-fields of the Val
Bendasca. That was the kind of place that I like.

ISABELLA BIRD BISHOP was to visit many places that she liked, and a few that she didn't like, in the span of her varied and colourful life. She travelled far and wide over the globe, often in great pain and under the most trying conditions that ever beset a Victorian lady; she rode on horse-back for thousands of miles, stayed on a kicking and rearing yak whilst it almost plunged over a precipice in the Tibetan Highlands, crossed a seven-thousand foot mountain pass in a blinding snow-storm in Persia, while she literally froze to her saddle, penetrated high into the Rockies on a wild two-day ride, and went up the Yangtze river in China over rapids and cataracts on a Chinese junk before floating down stream for 2,000 miles in a flat-bottomed boat to Shanghai. On pony, yak, elephant and mule and by boat and train she pushed doggedly on, a strong-minded Victorian middle-class lady, taking it all in, assessing it all with her logical mind trained in early years to weigh up the balance between freedom and lawlessness. She was often in extreme agony from back pains, but her cast-iron digestive system never let her down and her deep spiritual beliefs and devotion to Christian duty laid a patina over any romantic illusions that she may have entertained in those rare moments of male friendship. Her letters to her sister, Hennie, were the fullest expressions of her keen observations of life and people throughout all her wanderings. She was one of a band of intrepid ladies who left their comfortable and conventional homes to trot off around the world, buoyant and self-assured globetrotters in an age when much of the map was coloured red. Unlike Kate Marsden, who had her goal always in her sights, and Marianne North, who was perfectly happy doing what she liked best ('Did I not paint? – and wander and wonder at everything?') Isabella sought out the unbeaten tracks (twice she rode out to the frontiers of Tibet) and wrote to her publishers that 'Travellers are privileged to do the most improper things with perfect propriety.'

She was short and dumpy, but with a 'tranquility of manner' and a dignity of bearing that made up for her loss of height. Her eyes were large and luminous, her speech slow and deliberate and the sentences measured and well-thought out.

Lady Middleton, talking to Miss Gordon Cumming at Applecross in 1870 relates, in a perfect vignette of concise description, that 'She had very projecting front teeth then, and they may have affected her utterance, but she had the pluck to have them replaced'. Isabella always 'had the pluck'.

She was born at Boroughbridge Hall in Yorkshire on 15 October, 1831. Theirs was a large clan, tracing its descent from a William Bird who died in 1731. Isabella's father, the Rev. Edward Bird, married Dora Lawson of Boroughbridge in 1830 when he was a young curate; she was a relative of William Wilberforce and thus the mantle of evangelism was laid upon the household. Her younger sister, Henrietta (called 'Hennie' to distinguish her from a distant relative of the same name) was born in Cheshire. Isabella rode and walked from a very early age and it was due to the country rides and rambles with her father that she acquired the habit of observation and accuracy in all she saw. Her mental growth was quick; Mrs Bird taught her children herself and implanted in them the arts of reading and writing and encouraged the cultivation of measured judgement and the absorption of 'opinions, standards, tastes, and distastes'. Family prayers began the day. Isabella's two maiden aunts were strict; sitting during the Sunday services was not allowed. This was particularly painful for Isabella for she suffered a great deal from back pains and was unable to stand for long. From Cheshire, the Rev. Bird moved to a living in Birmingham and here Isabella, young as she was, taught in the Sunday School and formed and trained the choir, although she was not very musical. In great pain, and with abcesses on her feet, she rarely failed to put in an appearance.

After the death of her father, the family moved to Edinburgh, where the bracing climate was expected to improve Isabella's health. Here she took up social work and both she and her sister were known as ladies of 'culture and broad sympathies', deeply interested in the Clapham Sect, Free Trade and Protection, and the Chartists. Isabella was very concerned with the question of the poor and a small pamphlet of hers 'Notes on Old Edinburgh' was concerned with the recently established Society for Improving the Condition of the Poor. She received correspondence from John Bright and the problems of the housing of the poverty-stricken working classes greatly affected all the family. For those who saw no hope in their condition, she did her utmost to persuade them to emigrate and, before they did so, provided new clothes for them. Gowns, coats, calico, flannel, shawls – all were lovingly and patiently made up at a series of sewing-bees and 'twelve unhappy Highland Laddies' struggled with twelve kilts which had been hurriedly made. She also founded the Harris cloth manufacture, in conjunction with other equally socially-conscious ladies. Catherine Sinclair, the lady of the monument in St Colme Street, Edinburgh, was thanked in a letter for taking so much trouble with two *protégés* of hers; 'I enclose what will perhaps be sufficient to embark the two emigrants, but if more be absolutely necessary I must not, to use a vulgar phrase, choke upon the tail.' She lashed out at the young of Edinburgh; 'If you knew how degenerate you are, you young people in Edinburgh, you would be ashamed of yourselves. We thought nothing on any wet night of tramping out to the Literary Institute to hear the weekly lectures there.'

On 14 August, 1867, Mrs Bird died; to the sisters it meant departure from Edinburgh for six months, Henrietta to Tobermory and Isabella to London and other places in the south. No. 3, Castle Hill, was sadly given up and Henrietta departed for Mull. Isabella's old back trouble recurred and she was in constant distress from spinal pains, afraid that the habit of late rising and the 'careful protection of her time and strength against intrusion', prescribed by doctors might tend to 'great danger of becoming encrusted with selfishness'. In July, 1872, Isabella left on a voyage to Australia, 'desolate at parting with Henrietta', who was embarking for Mull, but greatly relieved no doubt that the 'encrustations of selfishness' caused by a narrow life of social duties in the Western Isles would gradually drop off as a larger horizon loomed before her. For the first few weeks she was dejected; the loud quarrels and the conversation of her travelling companions made her uncomfortable, but Australia's Bush country appealed to her and on 1 January, 1873 she left New Zealand (which interested her very little) for the Sandwich Islands.

Henrietta settled down in Mull and the West Highlands; during the sojourn in Edinburgh she had longed for the quiet and retiring life like a 'fragrant violet' and, as Isabella gadded about the world, she sat in her cosy four-roomed cottage at Tobermory reading the long, treasured letters that her sister sent. She was unlike Isabella in many respects; they called her 'The Blessed One' in Tobermory and loved her for her spiritual attainments, high moral code and purity of heart. She lived in a world apart, a world of nature, of flowers and sea and sky, fulfilling each moment with some task to be done, some person to be comforted, some study to be undertaken. The Bible was her great love; the Birds were all Bible students and Isabella herself rested all Easter Sunday on the slopes of Mount Sinai reading the story of the Exodus with the thermometer at 110 degrees in the shade. While Isabella disliked the dull, grey skies of Tobermory, Henrietta settled down in a little cottage of her own, loving it for its beauty and its nearness to the sea and the bay; friendships were formed with the poor and the neglected and Henrietta's great soul shed its mantle of spirituality upon all. The books of travel which Isabella was later to publish could never have been written by Henrietta, for the independence, the great physical courage, and the zest for life and far places which prompted Isabella to plant her feet on other shores and leave the 'constant murk of Scottish Skies' were not a part of Henrietta's make-up. The letters from Isabella sufficed – the cottage was the sphere of *An Taon Bheannicht* ('The Blessed One') until her death in 1880. The little four-roomed house, at a rent of £5 per year, at the top of the upper village, filled all 'Hennie's' wants and her flower garden, her literary life and her humble, unassuming village friends sustained her. The letters from Isabella came from all over the world and were travelogues of sparkle, wit, courage and endurance. 'No bad news in this one packet; may be read little by little', she once wrote on the outside of the envelope.

Isabella was not sorry to leave the *Nevada*. It was an old ship with old fittings, 'the mattresses bulge and burst, and cockroaches creep in and out, the deck is so leaky that the water squishes up under the saloon matting as we walk over it, the bread swarms with minute ants, and we have to pick every piece over because of weevils. Existence at night is an unequal fight with rats and cockroaches, and at meals with the stewards for time to eat. The stewards outnumber the passengers, and are the veriest riff-raff I have seen on board ship.' It was with the greatest of pleasure that Isabella watched the approach of the Islands on the morning of 25 January; the blue sea, the coral reef, the white surf, the long line of feathery palms and coconut trees and the 'very perfect extinct crater' of the Punchbowl were a welcome sight after the dried-up browns of Australia 'a prosaic hideous country'. She loved it all; the whites, Kanakas and Chinamen at the mooring, the countless canoes filled with natives in the harbour and the smiling brown men and women wearing wreaths of garlands twined around their necks. The easy contentment of life in Honolulu contrasted with the condition of the Hawaiian horses 'sorry, lean, undersized beasts', standing in the sun with the Mexican saddles and great wooden stirrups the 'only element of the picturesque that these Hawaiian steeds possessed'. The natives were kind and it was possible to travel wherever she wanted, riding side-saddle which did nothing for her old spinal trouble. A change to a Mexican saddle alleviated the 'excrusciating back-ache' and off she went in a specially made riding dress – a short, dumpy Victorian lady in 'full Turkish trousers and jauntily made dresses reaching to the ankles' which modestly covered the voluminous undergarment, riding like the wind to see the Kilauea volcano.

Isabella stayed six months in the Sandwich Islands (now the State of Hawaii) and thoroughly explored them, staying in native huts and making friends. Among her friends was the American Evangelist, Titus Coan, who told her about the Revivalists of the early Victorian century and their efforts to stamp out the amoral and immoral ways of the islanders. Miss Constance Cummings (a friend of Isabella and Hennie) pointed out in her visit; 'Men and women, lads and lasses are all herded together promiscuously with one large sheet of woven grass acting as a household blanket.' For unwanted babies 'a hole was dug in the earthen floor of the house and the wailing baby was therein deposited, a bit of cloth thrust into its mouth to still the cries, the earth and mats replaced and quiet being thus restored, domestic life continued peaceful as before'. Nakedness was no sin to the natives. The missionary wives had their daily assemblies where short shirts and top-hats were hastily donned in order not to offend Christian susceptibilities.

The *Kilauea* took her with a companion, Miss Karpe, around the islands but there were no ladies' cabins and she was much amused, upon coming down in the morning, to hear a gentleman asking her if she knew that 'I was using the Governor of Maui's head for a footstool'. With Mr William Green, the acting British Consul and Shipping Agent, she set out for the crater of Mauna Loa, clad in her red suit, little hat and a long white scarf. She put on all her clothes 'which gave me the squat, padded, look of a puffin or Esquimaux, but all, and more were needed long before we reached the top'. The top lay at upwards of 7,000 feet, its bulk 'one frightful desert' of lava with the mules 'struggling, slipping, tumbling, jumping, ledge after ledge'. After two days they sat on a ledge and watched the fires of Mokauweowee glow in the sunset; she was utterly untroubled by the presence of Mr Green for the achievement of the planned journey was sufficient to occupy her and little did it matter if men, women, or animals accompanied her on the way. 'Travellers are privileged to do the most improper things with perfect propriety, that is one charm of travelling', she declared. The top of the crater was hard and Isabella wrote to Hennie by the firelight with freezing fingers from the cold, unable to sleep a wink for the fleas which had travelled in the blankets.

After the descent from the crater, there was a period of 'sybaritic' comfort in the home of a wealthy rancher where she wrote to Hennie that she read a great deal of *Paradise Lost*; she also dismissed the suit of one Mr Wilson, a bullock-hunter and 'jack-of-all-trades' who, though perfectly respectful towards her, had once been 'what women call very wild'. After an inspection of schools and a visit to the leper colony on Molokai, she began to complain of the 'low American influence' on the island and felt that it was time to pack up her travelling dresses and spurs and travel hopefully on. She had written to Hennie suggesting that she should move to the Islands; it must have been penned in a mood of supreme exuberance of spirit and a temporary withdrawal of those barricades which she had erected around herself. It was a mistake; Hennie wrote to say that 'yes, perhaps she *should* join dear Isa in Hawaii, for it all sounded so wonderful'. Isabella gave no further signs of encouragement; the dream of a life of plenty, with servants, lots of horses and a supply of cheap beef, had vanished and even if she could write to a friend after Hennie's death that she was 'my world', there were other worlds to visit far away from 'murky' Tobermory – Hawaii was beginning to pall.

On 7 August she sailed for San Francisco. 'Farewell for ever, my bright and tropic dream!' Another view was now in Isabella's sights; gone were the coconut palms, the blue seas and white sands, the snow-capped summits of Mauna Kea and Mauna Loa, the dark-skinned swimmers in the surf. The beauty of North America was a 'strictly North American beauty' which contrasted ill with the Sandwich Islands. The rich Sacramento Valley and the Californian townships appeared to make little impression upon her.

The city of San Francisco scarcely gets a mention, except for a few words on leaving it to catch the Oakland Ferry in morning fog. The short dumpy lady who had got off the boat at San Francisco left the dust of the valley behind her and boarded a train for the High Sierras, delighted to sit in a coach pulled by two engines with the charming names of Grizzly Bear and White Fox. Hennie duly received the letters of description; the long train with its four front cars 'clustered over' with Digger Indians, dirty and swarming with vermin, and the wholly masculine crowd in the Western Hotel at Truckee where she stayed the night in a bed and room 'quite tumbled-looking'.

It was her intention to visit Estes Park, Rose Kingsley, had visited Colorado Springs and was full of praise for the 'Little London' under Pike's Peak, so Isabella hired a horse at Truckee and slipped on her Hawaiian riding dress (which she explained to readers was the American Lady's Mountain Dress) and 'rode her own fashion' on a large grey horse with a Mexican saddle. On horseback, and in a 'huge Pacific train, with its heavy bell tolling', she passed through Utah and into Colorado, picking up at the post office in Cheyenne a letter of recommendation from ex-Governor Hunt and one from Mr Bowles, of the *Springfield Republican*. From a rude log cabin where a Mrs Chalmers told her she could stay for five dollars a week, 'if I would make myself agreeable', she wrote, 'Five days here and I am no nearer Estes Park.' The scenery was glorious in the autumn days, but the rude cabin, the broken-down roof, the hard wooden floor for a bed, wolves and snakes for company, not to mention 'all the careworn, struggling settlers within a walk', camped in the canyon disheartened her and filled her with a singular lassitude known in those parts as 'mountain sickness'. With Chalmers as her guide, she set out once more for Estes Park on 'an old iron-grey horse, whose lower lip hung down feebly, showing his few teeth while his fore-legs stuck out forwards, and matter ran from both his nearly-blind eyes.' Isabella was always deeply concerned about the horses; the cruelty shown to them in Hawaii had greatly distressed her for she had, like Marianne North, a deep affection for all dumb animals. They rode for miles into the Rockies, with Chalmers losing the way and the horse and mule falling into ravines before they reached the miserable shack on their return journey. On 21 September Isabella wrote; 'We never reached Estes Park.'

Estes Park was an irregular narrow valley high in the Rockies. It was totally unlike any English conception of a 'Park', being full of beavers, mountain lions and grizzly bears. After solitary incursions by Indians, the Mountain Men trapped for pelts and one of these, Joel Estes, gave the area his name. An Irish nobleman, the Earl of Dunraven, crossed the Divide on a hunting expedition and decided to build a great estate and game preserve but Colorado people had the area thrown open for settlement and homesteaders filed on some of the land. In the 1880s there was a mining boom, but the mining business never thrived and most of the claims were later abandoned. Dunraven bought up a great many claims in and around Estes Park but never rounded out his great estate. The whole of the magnificent area later became part of the Rocky Mountains National Park.

Isabella was still determined to reach Estes Park; the air was 'one of the finest in North America' and was considered ideal for consumptives and asthma-sufferers, the cure lasting for three or four months. For Isabella, with all her disaffections, it might prove to be the panacea for all her ills. At the St Vrain hotel, in the little town of Longmount, she enlisted the sympathy of her landlord who asked if she could 'rough it' and added that it was a shame for her not to see Estes Park, 'the most beautiful scenery in Colorado'. With two young men, described by the landlord as 'innocent' she set out on a hired horse, a creature of beauty, with quivering nostrils and restless ears and eyes.

Through the magnificent St Vrain Canyon they cantered, losing their way time and time again before they entered the Rocky Mountains and ascended to feel their way along great ridges before the trail broadened into a long gulch with swathes of grass bordered by pines. After two days of riding on a horse with which she had become 'firm friends', she saw Estes Park lying below her. Almost deliriously, she wrote to Hennie on 28 September 'Estes Park!!!' With her two men companions, S. S. Downer and Platt Rogers (a future mayor of Denver) she was to ascend Long's Peak, ascended five years before for the first time.

By late afternoon they had ridden into Muggins Gulch, Isabella keen-eyed for a sight of 'Mountain Jim', the 'four-flusher' and once-famous scout of the plains, now a trapper and man of the wilderness. 'When he's sober Jim's a perfect gentleman; but when he's had liquor he's the most awful ruffian in Colorado.' At the entrance to the Park, among the scrub, was a rude black log cabin, the mud roof covered with beaver and furs laid out to dry; a hobbled mare grazed and a collie dog barked; in the golden light of the setting sun, amid colossal wonders of purple peaks and rocks crested with pines, Isabella met 'Mountain Jim' and forgot 'both his reputation and appearance, for his manner was that of a chivalrous gentleman, his accent refined, and his language easy and elegant'. She wrote to Hennie in a letter dated 28 September;

Roused by the growling of his dog, his owner came out, a broad, thickset man, about the middle height, with an old cap on his head, and wearing a grey hunting suit much the worse for wear (almost falling to pieces in fact), a digger's scarf knotted round his waist, a knife in his belt, and a 'bosom friend', a revolver sticking out of the breast pocket of his coat; his feet, which were very small, were bare, except for some dilapidated moccasins made of horse hide. The marvel was how his clothes hung together, and on him. The scarf round his waist must have had something to do with it. His face was remarkable. He is a man about forty-five, and must have been strikingly handsome. He had large grey-blue eyes, deeply set, with well-marked eyebrows, a handsome aquiline nose, and a very handsome mouth. His face was smooth shaven except for a dense mustache imperial. Tawny hair, in thin uncared-for curls, fell from under his hunter's cap and over his collar. One eye was entirely gone, and the loss made one side of the face repulsive, while the other might have been modeled in marble. 'Desperado' was written in large letters all over him.

They entered into conversation, 'Mountain Jim' explaining the loss of his eye, due to an encounter with a grizzly bear. 'You are not an American. I know from your voice that you are a countrywoman of mine. I hope you will allow me the pleasure of calling on you.' The pleasure was granted: she and Jim, with the two young men, were to ascend Long's Peak in the Rockies, one of the most rugged parts of the Continental Divide.

In the meantime, Isabella found a comfortable little cabin in the Estes Park settlement, where summer visitors came. Griffith Evans, a Welshman from Llanberis, and his partner Edwards owned a ranch of one thousand head of cattle. Griff had made his cabin homely, with rocking-chairs, a stone fireplace full of logs, a couch, and skins and Indian trophies hanging on the walls. Isabella was thoroughly at home; the bracing Colorado air revived her spirits and the 'joviality' of the little settlement, with its neat cabins surrounded by corrals for cattle, captivated her. The prospect of a climb up Long's Peak was worth all the hardship of the long ride to Estes Park. Griff Evans was kind, thoughtful, and jovial and the fact that he drank a little too much did not trouble Isabella unduly, for the wild scenery, mountain air, and the presence of 'Rocky Mountain Jim' had brought a new urgency into her life.

Jim Nugent, known as 'Rocky Mountain Jim' or 'Mountain Jim' was an Irishman born in Canada. He was a man of considerable natural ability who had left his native land for reasons of expediency and taken service with the United States Government as a frontier scout in the days of westward expansion. He became one of the most famous Indian scouts of the plains, with many daring deeds on records, some of them 'bloody'. At a later period of his life he joined a gang of border ruffians in Kansas but when Isabella knew him he was living as a trapper in a hut at Estes Park, 'it looked like the den of a wild beast', according to George Kingsley. He was well-read, intelligent and chivalrous to women; but he drank, was extremely super-stitious, and would be a 'nuisance' with pistols when his dark moods overtook him. Peaceably disposed citizens were wont to regard him as a relic of the lawless frontier days which were fast becoming woven into the history of the State of Colorado.

Jim called on Isabella as he had promised and, with the two young men as travelling companions, they set off early in October on the ride to Long's Peak, by way of Fish Creek and the start of the trail. They carried the minimum of equipment and food for three days; Isabella was loaded up for she carried three pairs of blankets and a quilt and a pair of Evans' boots which she had borrowed hung on the horn of the Mexican saddle. With a light heart and eyes bright, at the prospect of riding out into still wilder country, Isabella left behind the little cabin, saying her good-byes to the Evans' family and Griff, 'the hospitable, careless, reckless, jolly, social, convivial, peppery, good-natured' Welshman, who liked most folk but loathed Jim Nugent.

Long's Peak had first been seen by Colonel Stephen H. Long in 1820. Frederick H. Chapin, in his book *Mountaineering in Colorado*, published in 1889, described the ascent to the summit and drew attention to the hundred people or so who attempted the climb each year, many of them getting no further than the 'Key-Hole', due to their lack of training and inability to stand the rarified atmosphere. It dwarfed all the surrounding mountains and blocked up one end of Estes Park. 'Here, under its shadow', Isabella wrote, 'one learns how naturally nature worship, and the propitiation of the forces of nature, arose in minds which had no better light.' The ride 'was one series of glories and surprises, of "park" and glade, of lake and stream, of mountains on mountains, culminating in the rent pinnacles of Long's Peak, which looked yet grander and ghastlier as we crossed an attendant mountain 11,000 feet high'.

With Long's Peak towering nearly 3,000 feet above them, they made camp; Jim made a great fire, they ate strips of beef with the smell of pine smoke on them, and Isabella settled down to sleep, with Jim's dog 'Ring' lying warm and snug against her back. 'Treat Jim as a gentleman and you'll find him one', Isabella had been told and she found this to be true for he was very agreeable and kind. On her 'luxurious bed' of pine-needles, with the hoots of owls and the terrifying sound of wolves in her ears, Isabella felt released, happy, and deliciously intrigued.

Before the sun rose they were saddled and off across the plains, and by seven they had passed into the 'Lava Beds' (which were afterwards discovered by geologists and surveyors to be of glacial origin) and had negotiated the 'Notch' to find themselves on a knife-edge. The whole ascent had been one of sheer terror for Isabella; 'had I known that the ascent was a real mountaineering feat I should not have felt the slightest ambition to perform it'. Isabella suffered greatly, for her feet slipped on the bare rocks and Jim had to drag her up 'like a bale of goods'. She suffered from giddiness and pain from bruised ankles and it was only with Jim's patience and understanding that she eventually reached the summit. The view was breath-taking, with the wide sweep of the peaks, the green plains and the Thompson river snaking south, on a bosom of snow. They carved their names in a crevice and decided to descend as one of the young men suffered from lung trouble. Jim took a safer route than the one coming up; even here there was much physical hardship for Isabella for she had falls into crevasses and once hung by her frock, which Jim severed with a hunting knife. Boulders of 'enormous' size impeded their path and accentuated the steepness of the terrifying descent.

We were driven lower down the mountains than he had intended by impassable tracts of ice, and the descent was tremendous ... sometimes I drew myself upon hands and knees, sometimes crawled, sometimes 'Jim' pulled me up by my arms or a lariat, and sometimes I stood on his shoulders, or he made steps for me of his feet and hands, but at six we stood on the 'Notch' in the splendor of the sinking sun all color deepening, all peaks glorifying, all shadows purpling, all peril past.

All physical peril may have been past, but there remained a deeper peril into which Isabella was in danger of falling. At 'Jim's Grove Camp', she bedded down for the night in a soft green bower, but sleep eluded her; the great fire, the moonlight, the 'beloved stars of my far-off homes, The Plough, and the Pole Star and "Orion's studded belt"', shining in the clear night, entranced her; the nearness of Jim, upon whose broad shoulders she had placed her blistering feet in the long descent from the summit, disturbed her mind and spirit. There was undoubtedly a *rapport* between them; it had sprung up in the early stages of the ride, when he had driven his small Arab mare alongside and in a courtly manner conversed with her for three hours. The 'desperado' of Muggins Gulch, the strange, melancholy, moody, kind and savage man, the legendary figure of frontier skirmishes hiding away in his dark, cluttered cabin, hugging to himself all the secrets of past dissipation and sins of womanizing and crimes, now talked with her at the Camp Site and unburdened himself as he had seldom done before. There had been a great sorrow in his youth, one which had started him on a life of crime. 'His voice trembled and tears rolled down his cheek.' We can imagine Henrietta ruminating over the bizarre incident as she read Isabella's latest letter in the quiet primness of the Tobermory cottage. 'For five minutes', she wrote, 'at the camping ground his manner was such that I thought this possible. I put it away as egregious vanity, unpardonable in a woman of forty.'

If there had been any incident which had touched off Isabella's vanity or induced her to imagine the possibility of further friendship with Jim it was soon half-forgotten. There was no doubt, however, that an attraction of some kind existed between them; Platt Rogers himself had remarked; 'Jim took quite a fancy to her and she took quite a fancy to Jim.'

She gloried in Estes Park, living out of doors and riding on a Mexican saddle dressed in her thread-bare Hawaiian dress of full Turkish trousers reaching to the ankles. She scrubbed out her cabin her 'cheery mountain home' and took time out to write a long explanation of Estes Park, the two ranchmen and their families, and her own mode of life. She lived off the fat of the land, 'we all ate like hunters', and depleted her income by eight dollars a week. She also rode out with Mr Nugent, he on his great horse and she on her wooden saddle, considering him 'splendid company, with a sort of breezy mountain recklessness in everything, he passes remarkably acute judgments on men and events, on women also'. There was hardly a newspaper which did not contain some reference to him and his past exploits and Isabella considered his conversation to be 'brilliant, and full of the light and fitfulness of genius'. Isabella was clearly bewitched, but regarded his life 'as a ruined and wasted one, and one asks what good can the future have in store for one who has for so long chosen evil'.

Evans had gone to Denver but returned by the middle of October, bringing with him a young man who played and sang and had a repertoire of anthems, strathspeys and funeral marches, enlivening the evenings for the three campers in Black Canyon by playing 'Yankee Doodle' and 'Rule Britannia' on his mouth organ. She passed Sundays in Bible reading in the lonely cabin by the lake and wrote long letters to Hennie. It was all very pleasant, comfortable and 'safe', but Isabella began to think of departing to see more of Colorado; the feckless, slovenly camping family who had come up to see the 'Park' during the summer had begun to grate and their lawlessness and demoralization, while interesting, had no part in Isabella's strict up-bringing with its strong moral code and high ideals.

She had written to Hennie;

One of the most painful things in the Western States and Territories, is the extinction of childhood. I have never seen any children, only debased imitations of men and women, cankered by greed and selfishness, and asserting and gaining complete independence of their parents at ten years old. The atmosphere in which they are brought up is one of greed, godlessness, and frequently of profanity. Consequently these sweet things seem like flowers in a desert.

Bored with the greed and gossip among the log cabins, and possibly with the absence of Jim at Denver, Isabella thought of taking a trip and instructed Evans to bring her back a suitable horse when he returned from Denver. No horse arrived, however, for he had appropriated her $100 note as he was hard-up; he did promise to re-imburse the money and gave her as interest a good horse and saddle for her proposed 600 mile journey. The money was, incidentally, repaid down to the last cent. In the meantime, Isabella went on a cattle drive, where she drove cattle all day and forded the Big Thompson river about twenty times. She earned high praise from Evans and on 12 October wrote; 'I am still here', for Evans had called through her door before daylight; 'Miss Bird, I say we've got to drive cattle fifteen miles, I wish you'd lend a hand; there's not enough of us; I'll give you a good horse.' The drive was at a height of 7,500 feet with 2,000 head of half-wild Texan cattle being driven from the Snowy Range to be branded in the 'Park'. Snowbound for three days she could well ask, 'Shall I ever get away?' Evans offered her six dollars a week if she would stay while Mrs Evans was away for the winter in Denver but Isabella did not fancy playing 'hired girl', and on 20 October she left on a bay Indian pony named 'Birdie' with the musical French Canadian. 'Birdie' was, 'a little beauty, with legs of iron, fast, enduring, gentle, and wise; and with luggage for some weeks, including a black silk dress, behind my saddle. I am tolerably independent.'

On the way out she was waylaid at Muggins Gulch by Jim; he leant on her horse and said; 'I'm so happy to have met you, so very happy. God bless you.' Mr Power (her fellow traveller) 'remarked what a thorough gentleman he is and how very much he likes me, both of which things are true'. With her carpet bag strapped on to Birdie and her skirts adjusted for side-saddle riding, she rode into Denver; 'I looked down where the great braggart city lay spread, brown and treeless, upon a brown and treeless plain which seemed to nourish nothing but wormwood and Spanish bayonet . . . I saw a great sand storm, which in a few minutes covered the city, blotting it out of sight with a dense brown cloud.'

No one man was responsible for Denver. Louis Vasquez, a fur trader, built a post in 1832 and in September 1858 a party from Kansas were drawn to the area on reports of a gold find. By the end of 1858 there were some twenty cabins and on 24 June, 1870, the first transcontinental train puffed into the station, following the telegraph line, which remained of poor service due to buffalo herds rubbing down the poles and Indians stripping away the wires. The year of the great silver camps around 1880 saw a phenomenal growth of population and bonanza kings and cattle barons built their brick and sandstone mansions and Italian villas. When Isabella rode into Denver in 1872, it was a city of 'Peltry shops', where the sportsman and the emigrant could be rigged out at fifty different stores. People came from the east to try the 'camp cure' and start for the mountains; invalids who could not bear the rough life of the west filled the town's boarding houses, and Indians added their colour to the streets. Women were few and far between; Isabella saw 'but five in a day', but there were plenty of men in every rig; hunters and trappers in buckskins; teamsters in leather suits; horsemen in fur coats and buffalo-hide boots; Broadway dandies in yellow kid gloves – and rich Englishmen, sporting tourists, 'supercilious-looking'. Alexander K. McClure, writing in 1869, observed that 'those who come here overflowing with knowledge, and the grace to dispense it in a patronising way . . . generally go wooling and come shorn; but those who come as gentlemen . . . meet with gentlemen and receive the treatment due'. Isabella had been enchanted with Estes Park, and had perhaps entertained romantic notions of Jim Nugent, but she met no 'gentlemen' in Denver.

After only two calls in town, she pushed on to Colorado Springs, staying at ranch houses, paying her way and meeting cattle barons and millionaires. Iliff, of South Platte, who owned nine ranches and 35,000 cattle and was known as the 'Cattle King', gave her hospitality and Miss P. gave her a pair of men's socks before she set out for the long ascent of the Arkansas Divide. She made the perilous ascent, with everything covered in a 'glittering shroud of snow', with Birdie sagaciously refusing to cross a broken bridge. On the third day out from Denver she passed places with names like Horse-shoe Gulch, Handcart Gulch and Bitter Foot Mountain, riding in solitary silence through a blanket of snow, with no cabins for miles around. From Manitou she travelled by a passable road into Colorado Springs, which had been 'highly recommended' by Rose Kingsley.

The founders of Colorado Springs developed the town along quite different lines to those of Denver. It was planned as a community to attract people of social standing and 'good moral character and strict temperance habits'. Saloons and gambling houses were to be confined to Colorado City – Colorado Springs was laid out with broad thoroughfares and cross streets with Indian, Spanish and French names. A short-lived speak-easy of the day had a revolving contrivance known as a 'Spiritual Wheel' upon which a customer placed a two-bit piece and received a glass of liquor from a hidden potman. Pike's Peak was already a national landmark and tubercular sanatoria had been established in the dry, invigorating air. First named Fountain Colony, on its position on Fountain Creek, Colorado Springs thrived, twenty acres of land being donated for Colorado College. Isabella, as always, had to get out and about. She visited the famous 'Garden of the Gods', 'In which', she remarked, 'were I a divinity, I certainly should not choose to dwell.' She was not impressed. So she saddled up Birdie, and rode westwards across the Ute Pass, where only a few years before, Indians had helped themselves to white scalps, across the Continental Divide at Brecken-bridge Pass and down into Denver, which she reached on 8 November. She was disillusioned with many of the 'parks' and gulches and longed for a sight of Estes. She had seen many magnificent parts of the Rockies and had met a lot of curious folk. There were rough and ready settlers and campers, where 'the almighty dollar is the true divinity'; English 'high-toners' with deep contempt for the native American ('I cannot think why Englishmen put on these broad mouthing tones and give so many personal details') and true backwoodsmen like Comanche Bill, 'a notorious des-perado', who had lost his family in an Indian raid, but whose manner to her was 'respectful and frank'. But it was Estes Park which tore at her spirit, especially now that the Denver Banks could not cash her notes, due to a financial crisis. Her old longing to live 'free', unencumbered by de-pression and frustration drove her to seek out Estes; on 20 November, after a mile-long ride in darkness, she and Birdie rode 'tediously down M'Ginn's Gulch', only to find Evans's cabin empty and the stores very low. The two young men who were roughing it in the absence of Edwards and his family welcomed her and soon Jim himself appeared with one of his horses loaded down with valuable furs. There was not another woman with-in twenty-five miles, but they all got along famously, although there were no mattresses (a large bag filled with hay served for Isabella). No towels or table-cloths graced the hut. After a fierce gale, the parlour was two inches deep in mud from the leaking roof. Isabella dusted the 'parlour' with a buffalo tail and spent her days in cooking and washing. 'Jim came in yesterday in a silent mood, and sat looking vacantly into the fire. The young men said that this mood was the usual precursor of "an ugly fit".'

The next eight days were recounted to Hennie in the vein of a novelette, 'I must attempt to put down the trifling events of each day just as they occur.' To Isabella and Jim, they must have been far from 'trifling'. Two middle-aged people, of different backgrounds, living in a close, rough, little community, one woman amongst three men, one of whom had 'black fits', drawn together with a strange *rapport* born of the savagery and loneliness of the wilderness.

On the second day they went riding to see the beaver dams on the Black Canyon. 'His mood was dark as the sky overhead. He went off at a gallop, and then throwing his mare on her haunches close to me, said, "You're the first man or woman who's treated me like a human being for many years."' He bared his soul to her. 'Then came a terrible revelation that as soon as I had gone away he had discovered he was attached to me and it was killing him. "It began on Long's Peak", he said. I was terrified. It made me shake all over and even cry. He is a man whom any woman might love, but who no sane woman would marry. Nor did he ask me to marry him, he knew enough for that . . . Again he stopped his horse; "Now you see a man who has made a devil of himself! Lost! Lost! Lost! I believe in God. I've given him no choice but to put me with the devil and his angels. I'm afraid to die. You've stirred the better nature in me too late . . . Don't speak to me of repentance and reformation. I can't reform." My heart dissolved with pity for him and his dark lost self-ruined life. He is so lovable and fascinating yet so terrible. I told him I could not speak to him, I was so nervous, and he said if I could not speak to him he would not see me again. He would go and camp out on the Snowy Range till I was gone.'

Her letter to Hennie, with its quaint Victorian melodramatic phraseology, would probably be read and mulled over in the tea-parties of Tobermory, and a wondering Hennie, so busy with mundane do-gooding amongst her cottagers, would inevitably glance up at the 'murky skies' (Isabella's own description) and try to picture those glorious sunsets and majestic peaks of the far country where her sister had found a dark and terrible affinity with a man of violence and dark secrets. Isabella gave him a note written in her spidery hand. 'There can be nothing between us but constraint.'

She busied herself with household chores and delved into the state of her apparel; some of her clothes had been torn up for dish-cloths and she was 'reduced to a single change'. 'I have a solitary pocket handkerchief and one pair of stockings, such a mass of darns that hardly a trace of the original wool remains. Owing to my inability to get money in Denver I am almost without shoes, have nothing but a pair of slippers and some "arctics". For outer garments – well, I have a trained black silk dress, with a black silk polonaise! and nothing else but my old flannel riding suit, which is quite threadbare and requires much frequent mending that I am sometimes obliged to "dress" for supper, and patch and darn it during the evening. You will laugh, but it is singular that one can face the bitter winds with the mercury at zero, and below it, in exactly the same clothing which I wore in the tropics.' The days of bitter winds and snow continued; Jim became ill with an old arrow wound in his lung and Isabella wrote to Hennie in a mood of remorse; 'He looked so ill and wretched going to his dark, lonely lair, and I felt I had stabbed him and had not made sufficient allowance for him.' On 9 December, 1873, she rode Jim's Arab mare as far as the Greeley Stage on the Big Thompson; he escorted her on his mule, their arrival at the St Louis Stage Station causing not a little excitement. On the stage Isabella found an old friend, an Englishman, something of a dandy. When Isabella introduced him to Jim 'he put out a small hand cased in a perfectly-fitting lemon-coloured kid glove'. As the trapper stood there in his grotesque rags and odds and ends of apparel, his gentlemanliness of deportment brought into relief the innate vulgarity of a rich *parvenue*. 'Mr Fodder prattled so amusingly as we drove away that I never realized that my Rocky Mountain life was at an end, not even when I saw "Mountain Jim", with his golden hair yellow in the sunshine, slowly leading the beautiful mare over the snowy Plains back to Estes Park, equipped with the saddle on which I had ridden 800 miles. A drive of several hours over the Plains brought us to Greeley, and a few hours later, in the far blue distance, the Rocky Mountains, and all that they enclose, went down below the prairie sea.'

In June 1874, 'Mountain Jim' was shot by Griff Evans from the porch of his ranch-house after a quarrel. It was gossiped that Jim had been paying attention to Griff's daughter, Jinny, and that he had been conniving with the Earl of Dunraven, one of those 'sporting' members of the English aristocracy, those 'johnny-come-latelies' who came with their sporting guns and their pathetic drawls to buy up large tracts of land and to take Estes Park from the squatters. The whole affair of the shooting was wrapped in mystery, and from 1873 to as late as 1967, occupied the pages of erudite Western Journals whose writers had been intrigued by the legendary figure of 'Mountain Jim'. There is no doubt that some kind of a romance had sprung up between Jim and Isabella Bird and that his death at the hands of Griff Evans was not fully established; the *Pueblo Daily Chieftain* of 1874 refers to the shooting in a heading; 'Rocky Mountain Jim said he was ordered shot by Earl of Dunraven'. George Henry Kingsley, in his *Notes on Sport and Travel*, writes of the shooting and of the 'most fearful yellings and howlings that were ever heard out of Bedlam or the "Zoo" coming from the canyon below'. 'Now, though I by no means loved the Mountainous One (as we sometimes playfully called him on account of the extraordinary altitude of his lies), considering him a humbug and a scroundrel, my medical instinct told me, of course, to go and do the best that I could for him.' Jim was taken into the log-hut and there Dr Kingsley found all the bullets ('blue whistlers; large, round shot') had gone through, except one; in the hospital at Denver Jim quickly recovered, but the bullet which Dr Kingsley insisted had penetrated the brain, still remained. The story went that Griff and the Earl of Dunraven were in the vicinity of the log-hut; Griff dozing in his bed by the open door and the Englishman seated on the doorstep, when Jim came along leading his pony and sheltering behind the wheels of the timber machine. He tried 'to draw a bead' on the seated Earl of Dunraven, who shouted to Griff 'Jim's on the shoot!' Jim's mad fits were well known and, for the most part, anticipated. Jim was taken down to Denver where he lived for three months with two halves of a bullet in his brain; as the Doctor expected, one day he tumbled 'head over heels like a well-killed rabbit' and died. In the *Roundup Denver Westerners* of 1967, an account is given of the Estes Park Elk Festival held with re-enactment of the killing of Rocky Mountain Jim Nugent.

The impossible love had borne no fruit. Isabella was in Switzerland at the time of the shooting and in her letters she describes his return to her in spirit form, presenting himself in her hotel room in trapper's garb and bowing low with much charm; they had discussed spiritualism whilst on Long's Peak.

Isabella returned to Edinburgh, spending part of each summer in Mull, doing social work and attending to the publication of her book *Six Months in the Sandwich Islands*. The abortive affair with Jim Nugent was considerably reduced in size now that the invigorating air of the Rockies had given way to the damp pall of Tobermory; 'Don't let anybody think that I was in love with Mountain Jim . . . but it was pity and yearning to save him that I felt'; Isabella's passion had gone down 'below the prairie sea'.

In 1878 Isabella was in Edinburgh with Henrietta at their home in Atholl Crescent and it was here that Dr Bishop, the family physician, paid frequent visits. It was his earnest wish that Isabella should marry him, but Miss Bird could not face 'being an invalid wife'. As her old troubles of sickness and spinal trouble, coupled with lassitude, had re-appeared, she planned a trip to the Orient and in the late spring of 1878 she reached Japan after a circuitous route via San Francisco and Salt Lake City. The Japanese were progressing fast; the name of the ancient capital, Yeddo, had been changed to Tokyo and by the end of the 1850s three of their ports had been opened to foreign trade.

She obtained a guide-interpreter, a youth named Ito and together they set off, Isabella dressed in a habit of 'dust-coloured striped tweed', a 'light bowl-shaped hat of plaited bamboo' and high boots. Sir Harry Parkes, Resident Minister in Japan, had given her a passport, which she carried in a bag around her waist. An india-rubber bath, travelling bed, folding chair, an air pillow, a large map of Japan and a few volumes of *The Proceedings of the English-Asiatic Society* and some brandy, 'in case of need', completed her travelling kit. Perched on an unruly mare, she set off in search of the medieval Japan. They saw the famous temples at Nikko and then turned northward through forests with few paths into a wet, hilly land. It was now that travelling became almost insufferable for the inns were crowded and noisy and Isabella lost sleep through lack of privacy for she was tormented by travellers who came to peer at her little room with its flea-ridden netting 'jugglers, musicians, blind shampooers, and singing girls, all pushed the screens aside'.

She was continually in a state of wet chill and her hands and feet were bitten by hornet-ants and gadflies. Village women, 'lugging on their backs gristly babies whose shorn heads are frizzling in the sun and wobbling about as though they must drop off' crowded all night in the courtyards to stare at the 'foreigner' and followed her to the village boundaries. But all these annoyances were as nothing compared with the Japanese horses. 'I have now ridden, or rather sat, upon seventy-six horses, all horrible', she wrote to Hennie, 'They all stumble. The loins of some are higher than their shoulders, so that one slips forward and the backbones of all are ridgy.' Straw shoes were tied on the horse's feet and within a mile or so they would become thin and the horse would stumble. The first American Consul had introduced the horse-shoe in 1856 but the remote parts of Japan still continued to use straw-shoes for years afterwards. Although Isabella Bird was an accomplished horsewoman, she found no joy in riding the mares and the 'vicious stallions' and, on the ride out from Nikko, she was thrown over the beast's head. How she must have longed for her dear Birdie!

Towards the end of July they crossed over to Hokkaido, the home of the Ainu, the Japanese aborigine. They crossed over in an old paddle boat and spent fourteen hours on deck covered with several blankets while squally rain poured down and the steamer shipped several heavy seas. They reached Hakodate and the view pleased Isabella 'from its breezy Northern look'. She went to the Church Mission House and stayed with a Mr and Mrs Dening, writing to Hennie; 'How musical the clamour of the northern ocean is! How inspiring the shrieking and howling of the boisterous wind!' 'You cannot imagine the delight of being in a room with a door that will lock, to be in a bed instead of on a stretcher, of finding twenty-three letters containing good news, and of being able to read them in warmth and quietness under the roof of an English home!'

Hokkaido ('the Northern Sea Circuit') was a wild land, where 'a taste for algae, crustaceae and marine oddities are essential to happiness'. So wrote the editor of *The Japan Mail* five years before Isabella Bird's visit – and little had changed since. But from 1869 various schemes for development had been inaugurated and the capital, Sapporo, had been laid out in imitation of Washington, with avenues and rectangles and columns and a flag. There was even a Botanical Gardens of sorts. The winters were long and bitter and fishing the chief industry; indeed, there was such a supply that Yezo smelled of fish permanently.

But it was the Ainu that Isabella had come all this way to see. The Ainu were a docile, dirty, primitive, hirsute people, of aboriginal origin who had been pushed up into the far north by the Japanese and had been left to their own devices, bereft of interest and education. They lived on the banks of rivers or in high huts on swampy land and their lethargy in this damp land led the vigorous Japanese to despise them. The forest was the home of the first tribe they visited; Ito was not in favour of the visit for he 'whimpered very much. You would have thought that he was going to the stake.' But the Ainu chief received her courteously and she stayed in the thatched hut on a seat at the fire's head 'as the fleas on the floor beneath were legion'. His mother of eighty years, watched her sternly for two days. The evening meal was shared by several Ainu men, Isabella watched the culinary proceedings as sea-slugs, horse cooked in bear grease and other unmentionable delicacies were thrown into the communal pot. Through an interpreter, Isabella asked them questions about their way of life, 'I said that no one who looked into their faces could think that they ever told lies. They were very much pleased, and waved their hands and stroked their beards repeatedly.' Isabella went on to visit other settlements, speaking to the Ainu of their beliefs and religion and worship of the bear. But it was time to return to the mainland of Japan. Ito had now completed his tour of duty with her, 'Are you sorry it's the last morning?' he asked; 'I am.' It was autumn when she reached the south a few weeks later and visited Kyoto, the ancient capital, with its Buddhist shrines and temples and streets of open shops where exquisite silks and brocades were for sale along with vases, teapots and angular bronze cranes. Buddhism she could not understand, although she had tried; spiritual introspection and the attainment of Nirvana through continual re-birth on the wheel of life was alien to her nature and belief. She left Japan that winter and wrote to her publisher; 'I am not fascinated with Japan. It is deeply *interesting* and tempts one to make it a serious study.' But Isabella Bird did not linger there long enough for a serious study. She embarked on the steamer *Rainbow* for Malacca and the 'Golden Chersonese'.

The name 'Chersonese' was taken from Ptolemy and Milton and really denotes the whole of the Malay Peninsula, now part of Malaysia. But 'Golden' it certainly was for it was such a contrast to the damp, clammy and primitive land of the Ainu and provided such absorbing and fascinating details of wonderful and exotic life lived amongst strange and fascinating people, at a time when the whole political picture was changing. Isabella went on to Perak and at Kuala Kangsa was escorted for her first tramp through the jungle by William Maxwell, Assistant Resident of Perak and experienced her first elephant ride. It was the most ludicrous one of her life. She was dropped into a basket on the side of the beast and wrote 'This mode of riding is not comfortable. One sits facing forwards with the feet dangling over the edge of the basket. This edge soon produces a sharp ache or cramp, and when one tries to get relief by leaning back on anything, the awkward, rolling motion is so painful, that one reverts to the former position until it again becomes intolerable.'

At the Residency at Kuala Kangsa she became a guest of Hugh Low, the Resident who was at that time away, and sat down to a well-appointed table in the company of a large ape, a small one, and a retriever, which a Malay lad tied to her chair. The manners of the ape left much to be desired. 'I felt; shall I ever enjoy a dinner party as much again?' She liked Kuala Kangsa; the men paid her compliments and admired her as a traveller and she was not at all troubled at the absence of women at Perak. 'There is not a European woman within a twelve-hour journey of Kuala Kangsa and it is a happy thing.'

Nevertheless, she packed her little valise and canvas roll and the various knick-knacks she had purchased, rode through the jungle paths and caught the steamer from Penang, sailing out in 'glorious sunshine'. 'My tropic dream is fading and the "Golden Chersonese" is already a memory.' At Cairo she caught a fever and at Sinai she camped on the slopes for four nights, arriving back in Tobermory very weak from pleurodynia. Hennie, 'My dearest Pet' and 'My ownest', nursed her, undoubtedly glad to have her back in Mull and Dr John Bishop, their medical adviser, called frequently. He was ten years Isabella's junior and had first proposed to her in 1877, but she refused him, saying that she was 'scarcely a marrying woman'. He was a much-admired and respected man and plainly Isabella liked him; 'He has acted nobly and sweetly to me, never saying one word about his own suffering'; his health was not of the best. In October 1879 Isabella's

[245]

book *A Lady's Life in the Rocky Mountains* appeared; a *Times* reviewer commented that Miss Bird 'donned masculine habiliments for her greater convenience'. As the wide-frilled trousers were merely for the greater comfort of riding astride, Isbella was furious and explained that travellers were 'privileged to do the most improper things with perfect propriety'.

Hennie became ill. 'Hennie has been very poorly from a chill caught at church – in bed eight days, and I have been anxious about her.' Hennie wrote to a Mrs Macdiarmid; 'I long very much for a single week of stillness and pure air, but such longings must be stifled for some time to come ... "*She*" is toiling to finish her book.' The book was *Unbeaten tracks in Japan*, but the publication was delayed. Henrietta went to Mull after a week of suffering in their winter quarters at No. 19, Coates Crescent, Edinburgh, whilst Isabella returned to the city from trips to London and Birdsall, where she met Miss Gordon Cumming, fresh from her own treks abroad. When Isabella arrived at the cottage in Tobermory, she found Hennie too weak to speak or to open her eyes, and on 26 May Dr Bishop, the family physician wrote to Mr Murray, Isabella's publisher; 'Miss Isabella Bird desires me to tell you that she is here watching her sister, who is dangerously ill with typhoid fever, of which this is the thirty-sixth day ... I am to say that she has had many difficulties and hardships in travelling, as you know, but never anything equal to this, apart from the anxiety. This has arisen from the remoteness and isolation of the island at this season, the smallness of the house, the madness of an old and valued servant, the breakdown (from typhoid) of the volunteer substitute, and from the abject panic amongst the natives, who fly The Cottage as a pest house.' Cooked food was sent in, and the poor sorrowed, but Hennie 'the blessed one' died in early June. She was buried in Dean Cemetery in Edinburgh, where her father and mother had been interred; Miss Isabella Bird wrote to Mrs Macdiarmid in July; 'She loved you so dearly. In going over her papers, I found every note and letter you had ever written her tied up in packets by years ... I seem as if I must return to Tobermory to the scenes and people she loved, and spend some weeks in reading her precious papers. I seem hardly to care what becomes of me, and yet I pray God to make me follow her helpful, loving footsteps.' Isabella did not follow her footsteps, for she married Dr John Bishop on 8 March, 1881; the considerate, gentle, unassuming and loyal physician had finally won her hand in marriage.

There were no guests at the church and no honeymoon for the fifty-year old Isabella and soon life at Tobermory, despite John Bishop's 'reverential tenderness' began to pall. The tea-parties and church festivals, the visiting and the comforting of the poor and needy in the closely-knit community were no substitute for the free life that Isabella loved in the strange and wild places of the earth. Men of the calibre of Jim Nugent were few and far between, and the joviality and informality of life at Estes Park was ill-suited to the daily routine of the little two-bedroomed cottage.

At a publisher's party given for Isabella another traveller, Miss North, recorded her impressions of her, 'a very solid and substantial little person, short but broad, very decided and measured in her way of talking, rather as if she were reciting from one of her books'. The marriage lasted only for five years; John Bishop was struck down with erysipelas and passed away after a painful illness, devotedly cared for and nursed by Isabella. She now entered on a period of self-abnegation. She became interested in Medical Missions and took a course of nursing at St Mary's, Paddington including among her plans the use of her house in London's Maida Vale as an invalid home. She took counsel as to the possibility of becoming a Baptist missionary and was duly immersed, along with eighteen others, on 23 February, 1888. More in sorrow than in anger she wrote to her friend, Mrs Blackie; 'The Church of my fathers has cast me out by means of inanities, puerilities, music, and squabblings, and I go regularly to a Presbyterian church, where there is earnest praying, vigorous preaching, and an air of reality.' But the house in Maida Vale brought her only 'carking cares' and the guests were a fatigue to her, as her health failed to improve. Back at Tobermory she read books about the country between China and north India, sewed an outfit of Jaeger flannel and gave lectures to the local Y.W.C.A. at Glasgow. On 15 February, 1889, Isabella Bird Bishop set foot on the deck of the *Kerbela* and was 'delighted with the ship, its officers, crew, and passengers'. Prostrate with sorrow at the loss of Hennie and her husband, she may have been, wreathed around with remorse and self-pity she undoubtedly was, but the old search for the inaccessible still remained.

The 'country which lies between China and N. India' was now her goal and from India, where the *Kerbela* had taken her, to seek out the Medical Missions and obtain a site for the building of a Memorial Hospital to Dr Bishop. She planned an ascent to the plateaux of Lesser Tibet. On 22 June she arrived by house-boat at Ganderbal and thus entered Leh. She was glad to escape from Kashmir, for it was now mid-June and the city was 'in season'. 'There is an English hubbub most monstrous and the wretched coolies are beaten and cheated and lawn tennis, polo and horse racing, which have been played out below, invade the most secluded valleys, and the country is over-run by tourists and sportsmen from the plains.' She had a Cabul tent, a kettle, copper pot, and frying pan, clothing, sketching materials and wadded quilts for bedding. Her only stores were tea, Edwards' desiccated soup and 'a little saccharin'. Her attendants, Hassan Khan, a *seis*, and Mando, a Kashmiri lad, completed the company. In addition, there was the horse 'Gyalpo', a spirited silver-grey Arab steed, not to be forgotten, 'for he left the marks of his heels or teeth on every one'. 'He walked five miles an hour jumped like a deer, climbed like a yak, was strong and steady in perilous fords, tireless, hardy, hungry, frolicked along ledges of precipices and over crevassed glaciers, was absolutely fearless, and his slender legs and the use he made of them were the marvel of all.' Isabella 'contrived to get on with him'. At Shergol, the first village of Tibetan Buddhists, the human interest began. She found the Kashmiris false and suspicious; the Tibetans truthful and trusting. Isabella spent two months on the journey into western Tibet and on her return to Edinburgh, she gave a lecture to the London Members of the Royal Scottish Geographical Society.

On 11 August 1889, Isabella wrote to Lady Middleton from Leh; 'I have now been nearly two months in Western Tibet; it is most interesting, and in some respects wonderful, but living at an altitude varying from 11,000 to 17,000 feet had not improved my health. I feel very weak.' She descended to the Punjab through Lahul, or British Tibet, taking four weeks on the journey. Interest had vanished for her with the appearance of 'A creature in a nondescript dress, speaking Hindustani volubly. On a band across the breast were the British crown and the words "Commissioner's *chaprassie*, Kula District"! I never felt so extinguished. Liberty seemed lost, and the romance of the desert to have died out in one moment.'

In Simla, she completed the work which had brought her to India; a site had been chosen for the Henrietta Bird Hospital and she ascertained that good progress had been made on her hospital at Srinagar. There was nothing to keep her in the sub-continent and Kashmir; the summer season was over and the 'Englishness' of the place bored her. She contemplated returning to England, her dream of visiting Persia and the ancient Christian communities of the Armenians and the Nestorians of Kurdistan slowly fading into oblivion. All this changed with the advent of Major Herbert Sawyer of the Intelligence Branch of the Quartermaster's Department of the Indian Army, whom she had met at a lunch at the Residency and who had impressed her with his good looks and military bearing. He was tall, thirty-eight years of age, 'distracted' by the recent loss of his wife. 'I cannot spend much sympathy on him because the more distracted men are [in contrast to faithful womankind is the implication] the sooner they re-marry.' A wise observation.

Herbert Sawyer came on the scene at just the right time for himself and for Isabella Bird. For her, although she would have preferred to have travelled alone, an escort was necessary in the wild country through which they would have to pass to proceed to Tehran and, for him, the company of a nondescript middle-aged woman riding on a mule provided the perfect 'cover' which would enable him to carry out his reconnoitring activities, unknown to the Persian authorities.

This was the age of the 'Great Game', the contestants being Britain and Russia, competing for the prize of Central Asia and India. During the nineteenth century, the struggle between the great empires of Britain and Russia had involved Persia and threatened her isolationist spirit. Russia's advances in Turkestan and Transcaspia and her imperialistic designs on Central Asia had contributed to the *Pénétration Pacifique* by rivers, railways and trade. Lord Curzon's view was that the Russian policy was one of expansionism and hostility and that her annexation of Bokhara and Samarkand would inevitably lead to the snatching of Persia. The biggest prize was India. 'Without India', wrote Curzon, 'the British Empire would not exist. The possession of India is the inalienable badge of sovereignty in the eastern hemisphere.' Curzon's theme was the strengthening of Persia; the 'over-ripe pear' must remain on the tree until adequate lines of communication, such as roads, railways, and navigable rivers, had provided transport for trade and military needs. The Karun river had been an issue as early as 1871, for it provided a water route into south-western Iran and the opening up to vessels of all nations in 1888 provided a route through Khuzestan with its mineral wealth.

Major Herbert Sawyer, surveyor and military engineer, had his instructions to survey the land on the north-east of the Zagros range and assess its potential for mining and land development. He entered into Isabella's life at just the right time and gave her the filip she needed and the same electric shock that Jim Nugent had provided. He was her kind of gentleman, commanding and, to her consternation, given to bullying. 'I had given up the idea of travelling in Persia, and was preparing to leave India for England, when an officer, with whom I was then unacquainted, and who was about to proceed to Tehran on business, kindly offered me his escort', she added in a footnote to her book *Journeys in Persia and Kurdistan*. With her 'escort', whom she always wrote about as 'M', a man-of-all-work whom she called 'Hadji', three mules, a saddle mule for herself, a revolver, a brazier, two mule *yekdans* or leather trunks, and her usual folding bed and chair, she started out from Baghdad on 21 January and arrived in Tehran on 26 February, 1890.

It was a journey of nightmare proportions. 'It is expected that the journey will be a very severe one', she wrote, and added in her footnote; 'The journey turned out one of extreme hardship and difficulty, and had it not been for his kindness and efficient help I do not think that I should have accomplished it.' At Kirmanshah in Persia they made a long halt and Isabella wrote some of her own dagger-sharp observations; 'I have learned two things: one I have been learning for nine months past, the utter error of Canon Taylor's estimate of Islam. I think it the most blighting, withering, degrading influence of any of the false creeds. This is a ruined, played-out country, perishing for want of people, of water, of fuel, and above all for want of security, crushed by the most grinding exactions to which there is no limit but the total ruin of those on whom they press, without a middle class and without hope.'

After riding for six hours in rain and wet snow they came to the village of Kasr-i-Shirin and crossed low hills in deep mud to a caravanserai. 'It was simply loathsome, with its stench, its foulness, and its mire, and was already crowded and noisy with men and beasts. There was a great court-yard with arched recesses all round, too abominable to be occupied, too exposed and ruinous, even had they been cleaned, to give shelter from the driving sleet. The floor was deep with the manure of ages and piled with bales and boxes. In the side recesses, which are about the height of a mule's back, the muleteers camped with their fires and their goods, and laid the provender for their beasts in the front. These places are the mangers of the eastern caravanserai, or *khan*, or inn. Such must have been the inn at Bethlehem and surely the first step to the humiliation of "the death of the cross" must have been the birth in the manger, amidst the crowd and horrors of such a stable. The odour was overpowering and the noise stunning, and when our wet, mud-covered baggage animals came in, adding to the din, there was hardly room to move, far less for the roll in which all mules indulge when the loads are taken off; and the crush resulted in a fight, and one mule got his fore-feet upon my "manger" and threatened to share it with me. It was an awful place to come to after a six hours march in rain and snow.'

On the road to Kirmanshah she found some relief in the appalling journey for they were now passing through a region 'steeped in history' where dwelt the 'Davidites', the Ali-Ilahis, followers of David of Israel. With their Jewish names and veneration for David, they had been named as historical descendants of the 'lost tribes', with many synagogues in the Zagros mountains. 'The Ali-Ilahis believe in 1001 incarnations of the God-head in a series; among them Benjamin, Moses, Elias, David, Jesus Christ, Ali and Salman his tutor, the Imam Houssein and the Haftan (or seven bodies), the chief spiritual guides in the early ages of Islam.' However, Islam had no appeal for Isabella Bird; she preferred the practical Christianity of the Medical Missions which she considered 'the outcome of the living teachings of our faith'.

Between Kermanshah and Kum the weather was some of the worst she had ever encountered; the Rockies on Birdie were a joysome pilgrimage compared with the nine hours at a crawling pace in savage weather and a 'demon wind' which blew from the Pamirs. 'The six woollen layers of my mask, my three pairs of gloves, my sheepskin coat, fur cloak, and mackintosh piled on over a swaddling mass of woollen clothing, were as nothing before that awful blast. It is not a question of comfort or discomfort, or of suffering more or less severe, but of life or death, as the corpses a few miles ahead of us show. I am certain that if it had lasted another half-hour I too should have perished. The torture of my limbs down to my feet, of my temples and cheek-bones, the anguish and uselessness of my hands, from which the reins had dropped, were of small consequence compared with a chill which crept round my heart, threatening a cessation of work.' Added to all their physical discomfort was the danger of frost-bite, necessitating a great deal of extra clothing. 'In addition to double woollen underclothing I put on a pair of thick Chitral socks over two pairs of woollen stockings, and over these a pair of long, loose Afghan boots, made of sheepskin with the fur inside. Over my riding dress which is of flannel lined with heavy homespun, I had a long homespun jacket, an Afghan sheepskin coat, a heavy fur cloak over my knees, and a stout "regulation" waterproof to keep out the wind. Add to this a cork helmet, a fisherman's hood, a "six-ply" mask, two pairs of woollen gloves with mittens and double gauntlets, and the difficulty of mounting and dismounting for a person thus *swaddled* may be imagined! The Persians are all in cotton clothes.'

On the last 7,000 foot mountain pass the baggage straps broke many times and the heavy loads rolled down into deep snow crevasses; Isabella was in constant pain owing to spinal trouble and had lost twenty-two pounds in weight. Their final worry was to arrive at Tehran before the closing of the city gates, due to the lateness of the hour, but they slipped through and saw the lighted windows of the British Legation and carriages arriving for a dinner party. 'Arriving from the mud of the Kavir and the slush of the streets, after riding ten hours in ceaseless rain on a worn-out horse; caked with mud from head to foot, dripping, exhausted, nearly blind from fatigue, fresh from mud hovels and the congenial barbarism of the desert, and with the rags and travel-stains of a winter journey of forty-six days upon me, light and festivities were overwhelming.' Isabella was taken up to her room where a great coal fire burned, and slept till four o'clock the next morning, the only garment removed being the mackintosh cloak 'weighted with mud'.

She would have preferred to have travelled alone, without Major Sawyer as escort; she had not been impressed by his behaviour in the local bazaars in Baghdad 'holding a handkerchief to his nose and looking utterly *blasé* and disgusted at everything', but she admitted, with her ingrained sense of honesty, that she could never have made the journey without him and was thankful that he was there when her poor mule went down with cold 'M – kindly put my saddle on a powerful Kermanshah Arab. I soon found that my intense fatigue on this journey had been caused by riding mules, which have no elasticity of movement.' On the last few miles to the British Legation he constantly called out in the darkness, 'Are you surviving?'

She departed from Tehran with a Persian cook 'with sleepy eyes and a portion of a nose', and an educated young Brahmin, Mirza Yusuf, whom she found 'faithful, truthful, and trustworthy'. She met Dervishes on the road and at Julfa stayed at the Church Mission House. Julfa, the Armenian suburb of Isfahan, afforded her a haven of rest for several weeks. In the meaner streets of the city she had been hooted and spat upon, for in her reversion to European dress the rabble of men and boys regarded her as a 'Nazarene'. But it was a haven from the 'howling bigots of Isfahan'. At a palace down by the river she attended the yearly picnic of the Armenian Congregation; there were 260 people and all the women, save three, came dressed in red. Major Sawyer also gave a picnic at the top of a mountain where the eight Europeans were entertained. In spite of their differences, Isabella wrote well of him;

Major Sawyer is making an immense sensation in this minute community, which vegetates in superlative stagnation. His splendid appearance, force of character, wit, brutal frankness, ability, and kind-heartedness make a great breeze, and I hear that his sayings and doings are the one topic. He has shown a great deal of good feeling in some very difficult circumstances. I have only seen him once here for a few minutes to talk with; but we are very good comrades, and I hope and believe that in the wonderful journey before us nothing will happen worse than a little friction, which will not affect the good-comradeship.

This was Mary Bird country, where Mary Bird, a cousin of Isabella's father, had lived and worked from the time she had reached Persia in May, 1891. She had returned to England for a much-needed rest, but left again in 1899 for five more years in the country of her adoption. She worked in Liverpool for a time, but once again returned to Persia. She died on 16 August 1914, 'one of the greatest missionaries of her generation'.

From Julfa Isabella contemplated a journey to the Bakhtiari country, inhabited by the Lurs, a nomadic tribe. She took the usual mules, servants, a horse named 'Screw', and presents for the 'savages' in the form of 100 thimbles, small china buttons for children's caps, 1000 needles, Russian thread, double-bladed knives, and strong scissors. 'I am sorry to leave Julfa and these kind-hearted friends, but the prospect of the unknown has its charm.' It always 'had its charms' for Isabella and on 30 April the expedition to the Bakhtiari country began, with Isabella smarting under the terms of a very strict agreement which limited her short excursions to the outer ring of sentries. With her went a Miss Bruce and a Mr Douglas as escort. There had been objections to her trip at Tehran, but they had been overcome by Sir Henry Drummond Wolff. Safe conduct had been guaranteed and arrangements made for her comfort by the Sultan himself. After three marches, Miss Bruce and Mr Douglas left her on the frontier.

It had been impressed on her at Tehran that the Lurs were 'savages', but that they had the mark of 'true civilization' for they were clothed – and clothed in Manchester cotton! She spent four months among the Bakhtiari and found them to be a pleasant people, among whom she could move with perfect safety if their customs were observed. No man of the Bakhtiari tribe ever disabused her privacy and lifted the curtain of her tent; outside the Bakhtiari country proper, however, people were suspicious and their party was twice fired on by irate tribesmen. There were also Bakhtiari thieves, who robbed her of all her money, leaving her penniless, but Bakhtiari justice meted out summary justice and the money was repaid by the local *cadi* and the decision as to whether the thief should have his right hand or his left hand cut off was referred to Isabella! She was in great demand by crowds of sick people, bringing children afflicted with ophthalmia and scabies and adults suffering miserably from headaches and dyspepsia. Charms and love portions were plaintively requested and her Burroughs and Wellcome Medicine Chest was in constant use round the clock. Isabella's chief interest was an ethnological one. Polygamy was the custom of the country, but the women were unveiled and had a great deal of freedom; during the vicious inter-tribal warfare, women were always safe. They believed in a Supreme Being and an Intercessor, a future life, and a final day of judgement and the great virtues were charity to the poor and chastity. Cowardice was a sin and women were not admitted to immortality. It was all tremendously interesting, but after two months Isabella decided that 'savage life did not bear a near view. Its total lack of privacy, its rough brutality, its dirt, its undisguised greed, its unconcealed jealousies and hatred, its falsehood and its pure selfishness and treachery are all painful on a close inspection.' She now believed that distance lent enchantment to the savage life and that the life of the Bakhtiari was no exception. There was also tension between her and Major Sawyer, who entertained very imperialistic views. His manner to the great chiefs whom he should have been placating, evidently distressed Isabella and she sincerely considered that, if this mission had been successful, a great deal of that success was due to her own friendliness, sympathy and tireless energy in the field of medicine amongst the Khans and the Bakhtiari people.

On 10 August she faced the unknown alone, for Major Sawyer's mission ended at Burujird; each of them was doubtless relieved to be rid of the other, although they wished each other 'good-bye' as comrades who had shared innumerable hardships. She dismissed all thoughts of returning to Julfa and decided to make her way through western Persia to Urmi and finally to Trebizond on the Black Sea. She had just completed a wild journey of 1,500 miles on saddle-mule, knew very little about the Armenian question and was apprehensive about future relations with the people themselves. Her march to Urmi began on 15 September; she faced a journey of 309 miles with five mules, a *charvadar* in charge who was a bullying Turk, and a young Armenian to look after the commissariat. The journey lay through Kurdistan and the gorge of the river Karun to the Ilyat camps where there was plenty of food, although the milk of the sheep, cows and goats was all mixed 'with dirty hands into dirty copper pots', thus turning the milk into a sour mass 'like whipped cream in appearance', but entirely inedible to a European. She rested at Urmi for a week, entertained by the missionaries of Anglican and American churches, then replenished her stores for her next long march through Turkish Kurdistan. In spite of difficulties, Isabella liked the life of simplicity 'free from purposeless bothers' – she was doubtless thinking of Sawyer's 'boot and saddle' syndrome. From Urmi she pushed on, staying the first night at the house of the Nestorian Pastor; the country was infested by Kurds who attacked villages and sometimes murdered the Nestorians and desecrated their churches. In the villages of the plain of

Gawar she lodged with the Christian Nestorians and learned something of their history, and in an underground stable she was visited by priests and deacons who pleaded with her to send them teachers from England. 'Beseech for a teacher to come and sit among us and lighten our darkness before we pass away as the morning shadows . . . our people are as sheep lost upon the mountains.' Mrs Bishop's attitude towards Christian missions was now one of unflinching loyalty. She gave them her unswerving support, and wrote;

Several of the Asiatic faiths, and notably Buddhism, started with noble conceptions and a morality far in advance of their age. But the good has been mainly lost out of them in their passage down the centuries, and Buddhism in China is now much on a level with the idolatries of barbarous nations . . . there is no resurrection power in any of them.

She was impressed with the fidelity of the Nestorian Christians to their church and the tenacity and courage with which they clung to their faith, in spite of Kurdish maltreatment. 'Apostasy', she wrote, 'would be immediate emancipation from terror and ruin, but it is nearly unknown. Their churches are like catacombs. Few things can be more pathetic than a congregation standing in the dark and dismal nave, kissing the common wooden cross, and passing from hand to hand the kiss of peace, while the priest, in dress like their own, with girdle and stole of the poorest material, moves among the ancient liturgies in front of the dusty sanctuary, leading the worshippers in prayers and chants which have come down from the earliest ages of Christianity – from the triumphant church of the East to the persecuted remnant of to-day.'

There were lighter moments, a relief from the intense sorrow of the Nestorian Christians and the sad tales of the persecuted Armenians. She had enjoyed the Bakhtiari country, where she had found the Kurds 'manly, frank, hospitable'. They had besieged Mirza Yusuf, her young Armenian 'caterer', with all kinds of questions regarding the 'foreign woman'; 'Why didn't her eyebrows meet in the middle?' 'How old was she?' 'Why didn't she dye her hair?' With Sawyer, they had been even more personal; 'How many wives did he have?' Across the mountain passes of the Ilyats the sheep and goats blocked up the way for hours at a stretch and in the harems the women gazed with awe at the 'foreign lady'. 'The ladies took off my hat, untwisted my hair, felt my hands, and shrieked when they found that my gloves came off; laughed immoderately at my Bakhtiari shoes, which, it seems, are only worn by men; put their rings on my fingers, put my hat on their own heads, asked if I could give them better hair dyes than their own, and cosmetics to make their skins fair; paid the usual compliments, told me to regard everything as *pishkash*, asked for medicines and charms and regretted that I would not sleep in their house, because, as they said, they "never went anywhere or saw anything".'

She started on the final leg of her journey to Trebizond on 2 December, and reached it on 12 December, after four months of gruelling travel. The last of the icy descents from the mountains brought her to forests, orchards, and waterfalls, after a ride of 2,500 miles through Persia, Kurdistan, and Armenia. The 'bleak mountains and poverty-stricken plateaux ravaged by the Kurd' were left far behind. She returned home via the Orient Express and Paris and found herself in London on 26 December at 6 a.m. Back home in Edinburgh, after a short visit to Mull where she stayed only three days, her life centred around her writing and her lectures. She wrote six hours a day, preparing her book *Journeys in Persia*; her views on the Armenian question were widely sought by people in all walks of life and Mr Gladstone himself met her at a dinner and questioned her closely. Although her life was more pedestrian in Edinburgh and London than it had been whilst riding with an escort of wild Kurds, there were several pleasant and rewarding instances in her daily routine. The Royal Geographical Society in London conferred upon her the honour of Fellowship, the first woman to be given this distinction. At a meeting of the Society on 5 February, 1917, the President, J. Scott Keltie, reading from his paper on 'Thirty years work of the Royal Geographical Society' said; 'Nor must we forget the name of the first lady who ever gave a paper at an ordinary meeting of the Society, Mrs. Bishop, who was never well except when she was enduring the hardships of travel in remote parts of Asia.' She was also invited to dinner in May, 1897 by the Geographical Club; with her usual self-effacement she 'hoped that things will go on just as usual, and that the innovation will not entail any trouble to anybody'. On the title-page of her book *The Yangtze Valley and Beyond*, she placed the initials F.R.G.S. after her name, thereby acknowledging the accolade with pride.

Besides the pleasant social engagements, she found time to take up photography and later became quite an expert. 'I am almost ashamed to say', she wrote in a letter to a friend who had originally suggested her procurement of a camera, 'that photography has become a complete craze. I like it better than any pursuit I ever undertook, and if I should ever have time to give to the *technique* of the art, I hope I improve *considerably*.' She also received instruction in the use of the prismatic compass and, according to Mr John Coles, 'was able to make good use of it'.

By the year 1893 Isabella Bird Bishop was suffering from an inefficient action of the heart and overwhelming fatigue. In an article in *The Edinburgh Medical Journal* written after her death, an eminent physician of the day wrote; 'To the lay mind (i.e. the mind untrained in physiological science) Mrs. Bishop was indeed, if not a mass of physical contradictions, yet very much of a paradox. It was difficult to comprehend how a woman who in the quiet of her home life seemed so fragile, sensitive, and dependent could possibly submit to, or even survive, the experiences of her multitudinous travels. The invalid at home and the Samson abroad do not form a very usual combination, yet in her case these two ran in tandem for many years. Mrs. Bishop was indeed one of those subjects who are dependent to the last degree upon their environment to bring out their possibilities. It is not a question of dual personality, it is the varied response of a single personality under varied conditions.'

In her 4,000 foot climb to the crater of Kilauea in company with Mr Green; in the storm-and-wind-laden ride on Birdie's back to Denver; in the deceptively idyllic villages of Northern Japan; in the appalling experiences of Persia and Kurdistan, Isabella experienced life under many 'varied conditions'. By the end of 1890, she was ready to experience them again for she contemplated a journey to China and Japan with a view to visiting Korea. There were many reasons which had prompted her to undertake the intense physical activity to which she had grown accustomed; an increasing sense of responsibility towards those less fortunate than herself; a growing awareness of the importance of the Christian Missions in remote parts of the globe; a genuine desire to come to terms with her own selfishness by taking on her shoulders the burdens of humanity throughout the world. The persecution of the Armenians and Syrian Christians had shocked and distressed her; the ill-treatment of Christian peasants and the cruelties to which they had been subjected by the Kurds aroused in her a militant spirit which almost involved her in politics.

Sixty-three years of age and physically weak and in bad shape, suffering from lung trouble and rheumatic gout, she boarded the steamer *Mongolia* in January 1894 for Yokohama. In her book on Korea she writes that the journey was 'part of a plan of study of the leading characteristics of the Mongolian races'. That may have been so, but the Isabella who was 'very much of a paradox' was once again quite ready to desert the drawing rooms and church meetings and the dull, prosaic, cluttered-up life for more 'varied conditions'.

She reached Chemulpo on 1 March and placed her feet for the first time on the soil of Korea; there were to be three other visits between 1894 and 1897, but Korea made little impact. 'Korea took less hold on me than any country I ever travelled in. It is monotonous in every way, and the Koreans seem the dregs of a race, indolent, cunning, limp, unmanly.' When she arrived in March 1894, the Chinese still held sway over an ancient dynasty dating back to 1392 whose monarch presided over an old-fashioned Oriental kingdom struggling to keep its image in a corrupt court full of medieval flummery. 'A royal figurehead enveloped in the mysteries of the palace and the harem', as George Curzon put it. The chief object of Isabella's visit to Russian Manchuria was to see for herself the conditions of those Koreans whom the Russians had taken under their wing and who were now being banished back to Korea; an estimated number of 20,000 in Seoul alone. She saw the settlements and the striking view from the Chinese frontier and spent a week on the Ussuri Railway, the eastern branch of the Trans-Siberian railway. She was particularly interested in the position of Korean women. 'The seclusion of women was introduced five centuries ago by the present dynasty, in a time of great social corruption, for the protection of the family, and had probably been continued, not, as a Korean frankly told Mr. Heber Jones, because men distrust their wives, but because they distrust each other, and with good reason, for the immorality of the cities and of the upper classes almost exceeds belief. Thus all young women, and all older women except those of the lowest class, are secluded within the inner courts of the houses by a custom which has more than the force of law. To go out suitably concealed at night, or on occasions when it is necessary to travel or to make a visit, in a rigidly-closed chair, are the only "outings" of a Korean woman of the middle and upper classes, and the low-class woman only goes out for purposes of work. Daughters have been put to death by fathers, wives by their husbands, and women have even committed suicide, according to Dallett, when strange men, whether by accident or design, have even touched their hands.' Although Isabella deplored the low status of women, she noted in her book *Korea and her Neighbours*, 'I am far from saying that the women fret and groan under this system, or crave for the freedom which Europeans enjoy. Seclusion is the custom of centuries.'

In a chair with six bearers she travelled to the city of Seoul, passing through gates of elegant and whimsical names; gate of High Ceremony, gate of Bright Amiability and so on.

One of the 'sights' of Seoul is the stream or drain or watercourse, a wide, walled, open conduit, along which a dark-coloured festering stream slowly drags its malodorous length, among manure and refuse heaps which cover up most of what was once its shingly bed. There, tired of crowds masculine solely, one may be refreshed by the sight of women of the poorest class, some ladling into pails, the compound which passes for water, and others washing clothes in fetid pools which passes for a stream. All wear one costume, which is peculiar to the capital, a green silk coat – a man's coat with the 'neck' put over the head and clutched below the eyes, and long wide sleeves falling from the ears. It is as well that the Korean woman is concealed, for she is not a houri. Washing is her manifest destiny so long as her lord wears white. She washes in his foul river, in the pond of the Mulberry Palace, in every wet ditch, and outside the walls in the few streams which exist. Clothes are partially unpicked, boiled with ley three times, rolled into hard bundles, and pounded with heavy sticks on stones. After being dried they are beaten with wooden sticks on cylinders, till they attain a polish resembling dull satin. The women are slaves to the laundry, and the only sound which breaks the stillness of a Seoul night is the regular beat of their laundry sticks.

Isabella tried to obtain a trustworthy servant and interpreter who would accompany her into the interior of the country, but the only English-speaking young man she could find was highly indignant when informed that he would have to strictly limit his baggage, although he had stipulated that he could not do with anything less than nine suits. It was pointed out to him by an incredulous Isabella that a foreigner would take only two. 'Yes', he replied, 'but foreigners are so dirty in their habits.' Isabella remained in Seoul and saw the *Kur-Dong* 'one of the most remarkable spectacles I ever saw'. The occasion was the visit of the King in state to sacrifice in an ancestral temple; he passed through two streets, gazed at in awe by thousands, a monarch in a secluded palace, whose subjects dared not pronounce his name. The huge spectacle, with horses, grandees in splendid costumes, with hats decorated with red velvet and peacocks' feathers, and throat-lashes of amber beads cost an estimated $25,000. From Seoul Isabella journeyed to Diamond Mountains up the river Han in company with a Mr Miller, of the Boys' Boarding School attached to one of the numerous Missions in Seoul. It was a ripe time for Christian Missions of all denominations for a spiritual gap had been left by the disestablishment of Buddhism three centuries ago and the introduction of Daemonism or Shamanism coupled with the dread of 'bodiless beings created by Korean fancy'. For five weeks Isabella floated on the sampan with two Chinese servants and Mr Miller, 'taking geographical notes, river measurements, collecting plants, and photographing all the lush sights in this "sportsman's paradise".' In the Diamond Mountains they spent the night at the monastery of Chang-an-Sa where hundreds of

Buddhist priests dwelt in serene contemplation and where the traveller, the blind and the sick could be sure of rest in dormitories and infirmaries. The monks were hospitable and benevolent. 'I am compelled to admit that they exercise a certain fascination and that I prefer to remember their virtues rather than their faults', she notes.

Returning from the Diamond Mountains Isabella found herself caught up in the imminent Sino-Japanese war and boarded a little Japanese steamer to Chefoo on the Chinese coast. As she had left her passport, money and clothes in Seoul it was imperative that the British Consulate be contacted, which she did with reluctance, 'It is one of my travelling rules never to be a source of embarrassment to British Officials', she explained. There were several visits after Chefoo; with her summer clothes, made up by the Consul's wife, and a further supply of bank credit, she went to Mukden in Manchuria and experienced boat life in a 'pea boat' battling in the worst tempest for years whilst her bed and belongings were swamped with bilge-water. From Mukden she returned to Korea, not before she had visited the Korean settlements in Siberia which, after all, had been the reason for her journey to Korea. She went to China and travelled by houseboat to Hang-chow and Shao Hsing where she stayed with the Rev. W. G. Walshe. He recorded her visit and wrote an illuminating account of her way of life. 'She usually rode in a sedan chair on her expeditions, and, though generally very much exhausted when the close of the day came, she appeared to be tireless so long as anything of interest remained to claim her attention.' His note that 'she generally adopted a costume which was designed to fulfil the Chinese canons of good taste', throws an illuminating sidelight on Isabella's propriety and code of ethics. Early in 1895 she was in Hong Kong, lecturing on Tibet and Korea and finding time to visit the Missions, some of them now far inland. To her friend Miss Cullen she wrote, 'My interests have been solely among missions since I left Hong Kong. I liked and admired the English Presbyterians at Swatow and Wuking far more than any body of men and women that I have seen. In the Fukien Province a great deal of work is being done, but the most spiritual part by the fifty missionaries of the C.M.S. The China Inland Missionaries as a rule are delightful, but they tell me they are not meeting with marked success.' She was not impressed with the Manchurian missionaries and thought that the Roman Catholic men and women were an example to others for they remained at their posts 'at Mukden and elsewhere'.

As she was ill with sciatica she went to Tokyo for quiet and for the baths but returned once again to Korea as she had heard rumours of the assassination of the Queen. But her interest was in the social changes which were coming about since the Japanese invasion; it had been decreed that the Korean top-knot should go and 'this set the country aflame' wrote Isabella. The top-knot was a symbol of manhood; the hair was pulled up on the crown of the head twisted and arranged with strings, then put under a tall black gauze hat. 'There is no other single article of male equipment that I am aware of which plays so important a part or is regarded with such reverence or is clung to so tenaciously as the Korean top-knot', wrote Isabella.

But top-knots or no, the mission of the traveller was to travel. Isabella would have agreed wholeheartedly with the sermon preached on 19 April, the day after Livingstone's death, in Westminster Abbey where the speaker in his oration said; 'The humblest wayfarer in the far East or the farther South has it in his power, by fairness, by kindness, by justice, to leave behind him his stamp on those who in him, perhaps for the first and the last time, have the chance of knowing what is meant by a European, by an Englishman, a Christian.'

Isabella was now sixty-four and contemplating a journey to the Chinese mainland. The map of China spread temptingly in front of her; she had visited Hong Kong and Canton, 'the most wonderful and picturesque city on earth' and had been as far south as Swatow but oriental cosmopolitanism she had not, so far, encountered. She left Seoul at Christmas time on board the *Genkai Maru* for Shanghai, and was welcomed at the British Consulate by Mr Lowndes Bullock. The great Treaty Port did not interest Isabella and she had no desire to enter into the life of sport, entertainments and cosmopolitan decadence by which many of the Europeans lived. The Japanese, Russians and Germans were taking Chinese trade away from the British and 'spheres of influence' was considered by Isabella to be 'a most unfortunate term'. On 10 January, 1896 she left the Shanghai Consulate on the *Poyang* for a 1,000 mile journey up the Yangtze, calling at treaty ports on the way until Ichang was reached and here Isabella hired her first native boat. The Yangtze Kiang, with a length estimated at 3,602 miles, is known as the Yangtze but every section in the upper river has its local name. It is 'the river of golden sand' as it enters China on its way to the sea and the Minkiang after it joins with the Min. In the course of its journey it passes through gorges, circumnavigates whirlpools and cuts its way to the east through Szechwan by means of rapids.

Isabella's boat was a flat-bottomed houseboat, with projecting rudder, towed by sixteen bo   gorges. Before leaving Ichang

Isabella had asked a foreign resident how travellers passed their time on the voyage upstream. 'Surely it must be a monotonous one?' He replied, 'People have enough to do looking after their lives.' The method of ascent was a gruelling and extremely difficult one; trackers hauled the boats up the cataracts.

The huge coil of plaited bamboo, frequently a quarter of a mile long, is landed after being passed over the mast-head, a man on board paying out or hauling in as is required. The trackers make a peculiar movement; their steps are very short, and with each, swing the arms and body forward, stooping so low to their work that their hands nearly touch the ground, and at a distance they look like quadrupeds.

Over slippery boulders the trackers went, on precipices where there was hardly a foothold, climbing upwards on each other's shoulders, paying out the plaited bamboo as they went and performing 'the hardiest and riskiest work I have ever seen done in any country, inhumanly hard, week after week, from dawn to sunset', Isabella wrote. There were many disasters and boats and people were often lost. Mr Parker, who went up the Yangtze some years before Isabella, wrote about such disasters from the native pilot's point of view. Witness was born to the fact 'which has been disputed in certain quarters, that the villagers at the Ch'ing or Hsin T'an Rapid were in the habit of purposely obstructing the river, in order to reap a harvest, whether as pilots or coolies, from the disasters befalling merchant-junks at that place'.

Before each cataract, every boat had to queue.

Miserable nights they were. It was as bad as being in a rough sea, for we were in the swell of the cataract and within the sound of its swish and roar. The boat rolled and pitched; the great rudder creaked and banged; we thumped our neighbours and they thumped us; there were unholy sounds of tom-toms, the weather relapsed, the wind howled, and above all the angry yells of the boat baby were heard. The splash of a 'sea' came in at my open window and deluged my camp bed and it was very cold.

The Chinese New Year added zest to the long journey; great feasts of sal pork were served up and opium smoking was the delectable delight n the stern of the *Poyang*, turning it into a 'downright opium den with fourteen ragged men curled up on their quilts with their opium pipes beside them, in the height of sensuous felicity'. Isabella had plenty to occupy her and her photography blossomed, 'each print was a joy and a triumph', in spite of difficulties such as the washing out of 'hypo' and the hanging out of printing-frames.

Wan was the end of the journey for Isabella and now she left the boat and travelled in Chinese dress in an open chair. Her journey was to take her 900 miles into Szechwan within sight of Tibet and her nights were to be spent in those salubrious wayside inns which she had learned are the lot of the traveller. She writes of one of them, which was typical,

The walls were black and slimy with dirt and damp of many years; the paper with which the rafters had once been covered was hanging from them in tatters, and when the candle was lit beetles, 'slaters', cockroaches and other abominable things crawled on the walls and dropped from the rafters, one pink, fleshy thing dropping upon, and putting out, the candle!

But she had a good rest of five months of nights of solid sleep with a ration of only half-a-candle to write her *Journal* by, until darkness closed in, surrounding her 'by a world of busy and predatory life'. The Spring-time countryside with its rice-terraces, bean blossoms and groves of bamboo, 'a creation of exquisite grace, light and delicate with its stem as straight as an arrow', enchanted her; there was nothing to mar the bustling sylvan scenes until she reached the city of Liang-shan Hsien where she encountered an anti-foreign crowd.

Men began to pour into the roadway from every quarter, hooting, and some ran ahead – always a bad sign. I proposed to walk, but the chair-men said it was not safe. The open chair, however, was equally an abomination. The crowd became dense and noisy; there was much hooting and yelling. I recognised many cries of *'Yang kwei-tze'* (foreign devil) and 'Child eater'! swelling into a roar; the narrow street became almost impassable; my chair was struck repeatedly with sticks mud, and unsavoury missiles were thrown with excellent aim; a well-dressed man, bolder or more cowardly than the rest, hit me a smart whack across the chest, which left a weal; others from behind hit me across the shoulders; the howling was infernal; it was an angry Chinese mob. There was nothing for it but to sit up stolidly, and not to appear hurt, frightened or annoyed, though I was all three.

It must have been a frightening experience for Isabella Bird Bishop, used to travelling alone and always a little piqued at the presence of escorts. She pushed on, sleeping in out-of-the-way villages, where people were not so hostile, and reducing her food to two meals a day. Living conditions were rougher than she had ever known. At Paoning-fu she was again in the midst of her great missionary love, the China Inland Mission, whose missionaries took great pains not to offend Chinese susceptibilities by offending Chinese customs. Dr Cassels of the Anglican clergy wrote;

I was very much struck with Mrs. Bishop's bravery in travelling in an open chair. She came right across from Wan-Hsien on the Yantze to my station, a ten day's journey, without other escort than that of a Chinese servant, who knew just a little English ... I took her to see one or two houses, and she most kindly and generously sent me later on a cheque for £100 towards founding a hospital as the Henrietta Bird Hospital. It was shortly afterwards opened, and is now in the charge of Dr. William Shackleton.

She planned to travel three hundred miles northwards from Wan-Hsien which would bring her among many of the Tibetan and aboriginal tribes. 'I had no intention of being a Chinese traveller, but have drifted into it.'

On 12 April she turned northward again and came into the Man-tze country through forests and thick carpets of flowers and ferns through clear mountain air but her return plan was frustrated by the refusal of the Man-tze authorities to supply provisions and she was compelled to return to Chengtu. On 20 May she left Chengtu on a voyage of 2,000 miles in a flat-bottomed *wupan* and by the end of June had reached Shanghai. To Mrs Bullock she wrote; 'Missionaries on going home are often called "returned empties", and I feel myself one.'

She had completed her last great encirclement and had travelled 8,000 miles in China, very often under appalling conditions and sometimes in very real physical danger. She would return home with a new perspective on China and the Chinese; the opium trade shocked her but she considered the Chinese to be 'practically one of the freest and most democratic people on earth'. The Christian Missions had a great part to play and she was still of the opinion that medical missions were the most effective spearheads for the spreading of Christianity. At Seoul, under Bishop Corfe, a hospital was built and, under Bishop Cassels, one at Paoning-fu and another one at Chow-fu and an orphanage for twenty-five earthquake victims at Tokyo, under Bishop Bickersteth. All these were memorials to her sister Hennie and to her husband and parents, built, fortunately, at a time when the price of silver was low.

From Shanghai to Japan, to try the sulphur baths at Yumoto and from there back to Seoul, where she sent out a New Year's card with a Persian proverb;

> The Spent Arrow
> The Spoken Word
> The Lost Opportunity
> 'Three things that never return.'

On the last day of January, 1897, she left from Chemulpo for home and took rooms in Hill Street in London. She was fully occupied; she lectured, addressed the 'Bible Lands Mission', and on the same day at 7 o'clock dined by invitation of the Geographical Club, giving a lecture afterwards; 200 of her photographs were exhibited. She also spent some time working in the Library of the Royal Geographical Society where, as a Fellow, she was privileged to go. She was much concerned with Missionary work and deeply conscious of adverse Chinese criticism regarding the lady missionaries sent out to China; there were hindrances to their work due to lack of knowledge of Chinese etiquette and Isabella felt that it was *de rigueur* for them to wear Chinese dress and follow the example of the lady missionaries of the China Inland Mission.

With lecturing and social visiting and the writing of her book; *The Yangtze Valley and Beyond* her time was fully occupied in spite of her increasing ill-health. Tobermory no longer interested her and the little cottage, so beloved of Hennie, was no longer a 'home' and in March she began packing her possessions for dispatch to England. To her biographer, Anna M. Stoddart, she confided;

Tobermory is certainly four years worse. Drink is ravaging it. Several young men are at this time dying of it, and many of the older men have come to wreck with it since I was last here. The Temperance Society and the Band of Hope are both defunct. And this after it has been worked for and wept for and prayed for with strong crying and tears out of mind.

There were accidents to her person as there always had been. On a walk to the lighthouse at Tobermory she slipped and fell saving herself from a long drop down the cliff face by seizing hold of a tree. Then she crushed her thumb in the door of a railway carriage on one of her lecture tours. After all this to-ing and fro-ing Isabella proposed to go to Morocco for 'a rest'. The steamer reached Tangier on New Year's Day, the officers and passengers cheered her as, due to rough seas, she was lowered in a coal basket into the boat. With camel, mule, donkey and horse, she reached Marakesh in six days, 'Marakesh is awful; an African city of 80,000 people, the most crowded, noisiest, vilest, filthiest, busiest city I have seen in the world.' She was received by the Sultan, and with a Mr Summers as fellow traveller, set out on an expedition to the Atlas, riding 'astride on a superb horse in full blue trousers and a short full skirt, with great brass spurs belonging to the generalissimo of the Moorish army, and riding down places awful even to think of, where a rolling stone or a slip would mean destruction. In these wild mountains we are among tribes which Rome failed to conquer'. On the way back to Tangier, they were pursued by a party of armed and mounted Arabs and had to really ride for their lives.

Back home in England her health deteriorated, although she fully intended to go once again to China but the old symptoms of heart disease returned and she moved to nursing homes and to the homes of friends, dropping thankfully into the arms of devoted women. Her intellect was as bright and brilliant as always and from a nursing home she was gently removed to rooms at Bruntsfield Terrace in Edinburgh; 'I am not going to be a cipher any longer', she said. Her appetite was keen and her sense of humour undiminished. Agnes Grainger Stewart, in *Some Recollections of Isabella Bishop* written in November 1904, writes;

Over her weakness and weariness one saw the daily triumph of interest in life. 'Please, young ladies', said her maid one morning to some girls who were staying with her, as they sat at breakfast, 'Mrs. Bishop would like to know what you were laughing at', and to the emissary who carried what I have no doubt was a very sorry joke as answer, she said, 'It sounded so delicious, and I felt so far away, that I had to ring the bell and find out.' The people who ring bells in order to share in other people's merriment may not be many, but they enjoy more jokes than the rest of the world.

'The born traveller' died on 7 October 1904 in Edinburgh, surrounded by flowers, friends and potted palms, embarking on a journey more beautiful than any she had ever known.

For Reader's Notes

For Reader's Notes

For Reader's Notes

For Reader's Notes

For Reader's Notes

For Reader's Notes